The Real Menstrual Cycle

The Real Menstrual Cycle

Doreen Asso,
Department of Psychology,
University of London Goldsmiths' College

JOHN WILEY & SONS,
Chichester · New York · Brisbane · Toronto · Singapore

Copyright © 1983 by John Wiley & Sons Ltd.

Library of Congress Cataloging in Publication Data:

Asso, Doreen.
  The real menstrual cycle.

  Includes indexes.
  1. Menstruation. 2. Menopause. I. Title. [DNLM:
1. Menstruation. WP 540 A849r]
QP263.A77 1983   612'.662   83–5890

ISBN 0 471 90043 5
ISBN 0 471 90175 X (pbk.)

British Library Cataloguing in Publication Data:

Asso Doreen
  The real menstrual cycle.
  1. Menstruation
  I. Title
  612'.662   QP263

ISBN 0 471 90043 5
ISBN 0 471 90175 X (pbk)

Phototypeset by Input Typesetting Ltd., London SW19 8DR
and printed by The Pitman Press, Bath, Avon

To
Clive Gabriel

Acknowledgements

In any book which presents a considerable amount of evidence in a wide area the indebtedness to a large number of research workers is obvious. The aim has been to include all work which appears to be of value in forming a comprehensive view of the menstrual cycle. Any errors of omission in this respect are unintended.

I thank Celia Bird, Wendy Hudlass and everyone at Wiley for their generous interest and help, and for their efficiency. Gloria Shayler prepared the illustrations with great competence. Edna Pellett undertook the typing of all stages of the book with flexibility, humour and skill, and I am particularly grateful to her.

Contents

Introduction

In Western society, patterns of child-bearing have been revolutionized and a woman's reproductive cycle is unused for most of the time. Having children is still a momentous and fundamental human experience; but, biologically, it now occupies only a small part of the reproductive years. The reproductive years themselves, in an expected lifetime of around 70, constitute about half of the normal lifespan; small families are usual and many women remain childless altogether. Within the last one or two generations we have seen a change of emphasis from the idea of the woman as child-bearer and home-maker to a broader view of those important activities as two of many facets of a long and varied life.

In spite of this redundancy the menstrual cycle goes on, with all its manifestations, from girlhood to middle age. Every month, for the 30–40 years between puberty and the menopause, the scene is set for the development of the ovum and preparation of the womb for its reception after fertilization. If there is no pregnancy the ovum and the specially-prepared lining of the womb are discarded and the whole process begins again. Throughout the cycle, there are changes not only in hormonal levels and in the reproductive organs, but also in many bodily systems, in mood and in behaviour. The natural design is continually implemented with its pattern of rhythms and drifts and swings.

This background of a complete cycle of marked and continual change within a month in many different systems of the body is peculiar to women. Certain aspects of functioning in men are cyclical but the changes are considerably less marked, less comprehensive and on different time scales. This book will suggest some of the ways in which the internal environment of women differs from that of men.

The prevailing view of the menstrual cycle is distorted in its almost exclusive emphasis on the four or five days of the premenstrual phase. Clinicians have understandably been concerned mainly with premenstrual distress. Clinical research also tends to focus on the investigation of symptoms rather than on health and happiness. Until relatively recently many writers in both the specialized and the lay press emphasized the inevitability, for several days each month, of symptoms which, they said or implied, impair the competence and reliability of women. Now the pendulum has swung and many writers suggest that premenstrual symptoms are somehow not real; they believe that if women experience and report distress in the few days before menstruation it is only because of pressure from society to do so. Images are conjured up of distraught (and very gullible) women, either victims of their own biology or of social pressures, taboo, and prejudice. The next stage will doubtless see the emergence of a more balanced approach with a full acceptance of the biological realities as a basis for improved adaptations to the cycle.

With the focusing of attention on the four to five days before the onset of bleeding the essential characteristics of the cycle have been lost to sight. There is no general recognition that every month the cycle turns through a myriad of changes which for most of the time create in women an entirely positive physical and psychological climate. The many advantages which the menstrual cycle confers are barely mentioned and the positive aspects of living with a marked rhythm of change remain unexploited. Discussion of the cycle has been in a medical context rather than one of normal existence.

If the reproductive cycle is considered in its broad biological context the changes are entirely comprehensible and reveal a very different picture than is usually presented. In the first half of the cycle, from menstruation onwards, there is a time of progressive emotional relaxation and of release of tension. This merges, while a new ovum is ripening in the ovaries, into rising alertness, self-confidence, and a sense of well-being. Around ovulation there is a peak of responsiveness, assertiveness, and receptivity, all encouraging consummation and conception. Afterwards, when the womb is being made ready for the embedding of a fertilized ovum there is a more narcissistic, passive, and contented phase; a time of consolidation, and preparation. If fertilization does not take place and hormonal levels no longer maintain the womb in a state of readiness, there is another, often dramatic, upsurge of heightened awareness and of aroused feelings, but now invested with the negative tones of aggressiveness, hostility, tension, and anxiety. This phase brings the end of one cycle and, simultanteously, the beginning of the next. A view of the whole cycle which encompasses continual change in feelings, mood, and behaviour, as well as in hormonal levels and in the reproductive organs is not merely a common sense or intuitive one. It has, as we shall see, considerable empirical support.

The innate, biological nature of the process is obvious. There are also other important influences which are acquired during a lifetime of learning and experience. For example, it has been suggested that the original purpose of the deterioration in mood towards the end of the cycle was to repel the male when the activity of orgasm might jeopardize the survival of a fertilized ovum. The highly evolved behaviour of the present day is quite contrary to this and the time around menstruation is one of high sexual arousal and sexual activity. We are dealing with the oldest of cycles, overlaid with millenia of individual and social development and experience. A more up-to-date and more balanced approach to this highly influential cycle will improve the well-being of one half of the population directly and that of the other half indirectly.

The aim of this book is to present the available information on the various changes of the whole cycle, not just the time around menstruation, and to discuss the possible causes of those changes. It will suggest ways in which the reproductive cycle influences to a greater or lesser degree the feelings and behaviour of women. We shall also see that it is an important determinant of the ways in which behaviour and symptoms are acquired and maintained and that the extent to which all of this is so will depend partly on the knowledge that each woman has of herself and partly on the way in which she is able to use that knowledge.

The first step towards a more constructive approach will be to overcome the ambivalent feelings that most of us have about menstruation. On the one hand it suggests reproductive ability and femininity and on the other it is often seen as something that is base, dirty, and a sign of the less pleasant aspects of being a woman. Both of these seemingly paradoxical views are in fact realistic. Menstruation is indeed an enduring symbol of femininity and motherhood; equally it presents difficulties of hygiene and personal management as well as profound and often sudden changes in bodily processes and in mood.

It is worth going beyond the generalizations to take a closer look at what actually happens throughout the cycle.

CHAPTER I

The background: biological cycles

Rhythms and cycles are characteristic of the whole of existence and yet there has only recently been any general awareness of them. Like Molière's character who was amazed to find he had been speaking prose all his life, we realize with surprise the extent to which regular periodic variations are present in every aspect of life, from the most obscure physiological functions to highly skilled activities.

The present discussion of some of the characteristics of biological cycles will have the limited aim of providing a context for an understanding of the menstrual cycle. Many detailed accounts of biological rhythms are available, for example Brady, 1979; Conroy and Mills, 1970; Minors and Waterhouse, 1981; Saunders, 1977; Ward, 1972.

The most popular view of biological rhythms, known as biorhythm theory (Gittelson, 1979) originated in an idea of Fliess (1909) of female cells giving rise to a 28-day emotional cycle and male cells causing a 23-day physical cycle. A 33-day intellectual rhythm was added several years later (see Thommen, 1973). In this theory it is claimed that human behaviour is influenced in predictable ways by these three cycles, emotional, physical, and intellectual. The important practical implication is that, armed with relevant information about their own cycles, people can exert a larger measure of control over their lives.

Although this general principle of seeking better adaptations to influential cycles is excellent, there is no good evidence that three rhythms, as now presented in biorhythm theory, can be accurately defined for any individual. Nor is there any rigorous demonstration of any systematic effect of three such rhythms on events, and in fact evidence to the contrary is accumulating (Ahlgren, 1974; Kripke, Yelverton, and Kripke, 1979; McConnell, 1978; Shaffer, Schmidt, Zlotowitz, and Fisher, 1978; Wolcott, McMeekin, Burgin, and Yanowitch, 1977; Wood, Krider, and Fezer, 1979).

The real situation is much more complex and it is clear that such a simple model does not reflect the number of different rhythms, their interactions, and their various effects. The range is huge, from the repetitive firing of single nerve fibres to the one great developmental cycle from conception to

1

death experienced once by each individual but perpetually recurring in the species (Conroy and Mills, 1970). Within each individual, and in nature, cycles are constantly interacting to produce more or less subtle influences on every aspect of existence. Timing of separate events is an inherent feature of biological systems and is crucial in the adaptation of any organism to the external world. Each individual has to have a physiological timetable and this timetabling is at the heart of all rhythms. Rhythms are produced by oscillations, the frequency of which will of course be determined by the time required for the completion of the whole cycle. The menstrual cycle is an example of relatively long-period oscillations as it involves the rather slow processes of cell maturation and tissue growth.

Some descriptive detail of the functioning of cycles is emerging. The question of where their ultimate control resides is not yet settled.

THE ORIGINS OF CYCLES

The majority view is that all biological cycles are endogenous. That is, that rhythmic activity is built in as an essential feature and is not dependent for its existence on any periodic events in the environment. Although extraneous factors may influence the rhythms to a greater or lesser extent, these factors cannot create rhythmicity (Brady, 1979). Others believe that external factors can cause rhythms, not just entrain them. A case has been put, notably by F. A. Brown, that there is no evidence that individuals have fully independent timing systems. The belief is that all organisms are ultimately under the influence, for their timing, of what Brown has called subtle geophysical synchronizers such as barometric pressure, electromagnetic fields, and cosmic rays, (see for example Brown, 1980). There is certainly no evidence to show that such forces are not operating on individual cycles but firm evidence for this ultimate exogenous control is difficult to obtain. Although it is known that organisms can perceive these subtle geophysical stimuli the unanswered question is whether their rhythms are determined by them (Brady, 1979).

Whether or not geophysical forces are the sole arbiters of all biological rhythms, the menstrual cycle provides one example of the ways in which these forces may be operating. Cutler (1980) cites findings which suggest that the lunar cycle of 29.5 days may be a basic time unit for human biological cycles (Menaker and Menaker, 1959; Miles, Raynal, and Wilson, 1977; Wever, 1974). For the menstrual cycle, although conventionally a nominal 28-day cycle is adopted, in fact the mean and median durations are 29.5 days. This raises the question of a possible relationship between the phases of the moon and the menstrual cycle. Cutler suggests that if there is any association between the lunar and menstrual cycles (which has not yet been fully demonstrated) it may be through the effect of the moon phases on electromagnetic fields whose rhythm in turn may be reflected in phase-locking of the menstrual cycle. It seems certain that any lunar effect would have to be of an indirect kind. In the study by Cutler (above), which showed some association between the lunar phase and onset of menstruation, the women lived in cities and any direct systematic photic effect of moonlight was precluded. Also, more generally, Brown and Park (1967) have suggested that lunar changes continue to have indirect influence, through geophysical effects, on organisms placed in a laboratory under constant light conditions. Finally, in humans removed from the light/dark cycle but exposed to naturally occurring electromagnetic fields there is entrainment of the circadian rhythm to close on the lunar day of 24.87 hours (Wever, 1974). So that what might appear to be a direct relationship between the lunar and menstrual cycles is probably a reflection of the association of both of them with other forces. Neither does there appear to be a case for the strongly-held belief of a direct relationship between the moon and any cyclical aspects of abnormal behaviour, many of which are often in turn related in fact or by hearsay to the menstrual cycle. Campbell and Beets (1978) reviewed studies of psychiatric hospital admissions, suicides, and murders, and found no association between these events and lunar phases.

Whatever the ultimate origins of biological cycles they can usefully be seen on a continuum of the extent to which they are subject to external influences. It is important to make this distinction between origins and the actual work-ings of the cycles. Cycles of some functions, for example heart-rate and respiratory functions, although they may be intrinsically generated are strongly dominated by other timing mechanisms. Other cycles are only slightly modified to synchronize with external events. Many circadian rhythms for instance have an inherent timing which is very close to 24 hours. If left to themselves without light/dark influences they range in duration from 24.7 to 26.0 hours, with different cycles and different individuals varying within that range, both in cycle duration and in the pattern of the curves, see for example Wever (1979). In normal circumstances they are slightly re-set to synchronize with the light/dark cycle by some event, usually sunrise or sunset or both (Brady, 1979). Temperature is an important example of a cycle with an inherent rhythm which is only slightly modified by external forces in the interests of over-all synchrony. There are also systematic variations in temperature with the menstrual cycle and this will be mentioned again.

MODE OF OPERATION OF BIOLOGICAL RHYTHMS

The detailed mechanisms of the biological rhythms have not been clarified. It is assumed that in very broad terms oscillation is determined by the device familiar in physiology of a control circuit operating on the principle of feedback, and there is some evidence for this assumption (Oatley and Goodwin, 1971). The oscillators which are presumed to drive the rhythms are often described as physiological clocks but no clock mechanism has ever been observed directly and the neural processes which would constitute the clocks are not fully understood. The results of animal work suggest the importance of the hypothalamus, especially the suprachiasmatic nucleus, in providing over-all control (Kawamura and Ibuka, 1978). It is presumed that this structure is responsible for synchronizing the oscillations in various cells or cell groups of the body. The inference is that there is rhythmicity built into all cells, which are synchronized by neural circuits (Holloway, 1977). Recent findings with rats suggest that circuitry which can generate a circadian rhythm of firing rate of single cells is contained in the suprachiasmatic nucleus (Green and Gillette, 1982). For a full discussion of the mechanisms of circadian rhythms, see Minors and Waterhouse, 1981.

All of this still leaves unanswered the question, already raised, of whether the ultimate control of rhythms is outside of the organism. Brown, as already mentioned, would have it that it is not a question of individual clocks each carrying out their own timing but that each 'organism has biological clock works with remarkably similar properties throughout all plants and animals, beautifully adapted for maximal usefulness to the organism and dependent for their timing upon continuing response to the subtle geophysical environment'.

What is certain is that the cycles have at some stage to be started by an internal, physiological event. Also there is reason to suppose that different biological cycles have widely different trigger mechanisms. For example the menstrual cycle, unlike many others, is not determined directly by a central rhythm but by the ovary itself which has its own inherent rhythmicity. This ovulatory cycle can be seen as endogenously driven, but subject to exogenous influences which can alter the basic rhythm via the hormones (Cutler and Garcia, 1980). Although the ovarian rhythm, and hence the timing of the key event of ovulation, may be affected by various factors, once it has happened the events leading to menstruation will proceed. This means that the post-ovulatory phase, from ovulation to onset of bleeding, is normally constant (with some individual variability with age) and independent of the length of the whole cycle. Hence any variations in cycle length normally occur in the phase from menstruation to ovulation (Cutler and Garcia, 1980; Presser, 1974; Vollman, 1977).

In the absence of the key event of ovulation there may be bleeding which is superficially indistinguishable from the menstrual bleeding of a normal cycle (Garcia and Rosenfeld, 1977). The clinical implications of anovulatory cycles, with or without amenorrhea, are complex and are outside the scope of this book (see for example Speroff, 1977). At one level, failure to ovulate reflects a disturbance in the inherent rhythm of the ovary, the most immediate cause presumably being hormonal. The ultimate causes are probably not all known but anovulatory cycles are certainly closely associated for example with the first few and last few years of reproductive life when hormonal levels are less stable, and are also associated with extremes of body weight and with various other events.

As regards the hormonal mechanisms of ovarian rhythmicity, oestrogen appears to be quite fundamental. Speroff (1977) has pointed out that changing levels of oestrogen are critical in determining the levels of the other hormones which change through the cycle. One of the routes by which extraneous events can exert their influence on the ovarian rhythm is exemplified in an account by Speroff of women who gain a great deal of weight and become anovulatory. It is now known that in general androstenedione is converted to oestrogen in peripheral tissue and that the per cent conversion increases with weight. Speroff suggests that as an individual gains weight she produces more and more oestrogen and hence may never achieve a low enough level of oestrogen to allow, by negative feedback, a rise in follicle stimulating hormone (FSH) which leads to ovulation. The ultimate reasons for the overeating and weight gain may of course be psychological, physiological, or a combination of those.

Calkins (1981) has discussed the timing mechanisms involved in the ending of the life cycle, death. He points out that although various factors have resulted in a dramatic increase, for the average person, in the lifespan, the upper limit for the human species remains unchanged around 100 years. All species appear to have a maximal lifespan which any member may reach if their life is not interrupted by disease or accident. Calkins links this with the fact that the age of menopause also remains essentially unchanged, in spite of changing social conditions. Facts like these have led to a point of view that there must be some timing mechanism which is able to switch on or off various sets of genes. These genes could code for activation of self-destruction mechanisms, or there might be deactivation of genes coding for self-maintenance functions (Romero, 1978). There is some evidence of the importance of neuroendocrine processes in the operation of the timing mechanism. There is, for example, progressive failure of the dopaminergic system with age (McGeer and McGeer, 1978). Also there is a possibility that the timing mechanism of the menopause, and perhaps of death, can be influenced by pharmacological manipulation of neurotransmitter function. Female rats differ from humans in that the ovaries continue to secrete significant amounts of steroids well after the end of the reproductive cycle. It is nevertheless of interest that systematic treatment with the catecholamine precursor L-dopa, or direct application of L-dopa in the medial preoptic area of the brain, reinstates vaginal cycling in aged rats. As regards the life cycle, in several experiments with animals the lifespan has been significantly prolonged by administration of dopamine agonists (Clemens, Fuller, and Owen, 1978).

INFLUENCE, ENTRAINMENT AND SYNCHRONIZATION

Regardless of the origins of rhythmicity and regardless of the particular mode of operation, each cycle will to a greater or lesser extent be affected by more or less obvious forces, by other cycles, as well as by social and individual factors. The implications of this complexity are only gradually becoming clear. In the biological sciences the discovery is slowly being made that the response to any stimulus will vary with the phase of many relevant cycles.

6

These variations have rarely in the past been taken into account. The effects of the menstrual cycle, for instance, are rarely controlled for. Bell, Christie, and Venables (1975) have reported the results of a survey of representative psychophysiological studies from 1964 to 1970: 54.5% of studies used only male subjects; only 7% used all females. Of these, only 1.6% controlled for the menstrual cycle. A survey by Schultz (1969) of four volumes of the *Journal of Experimental Psychology* showed that whereas 22.3% of experiments used all male subjects, only 6% used all females, and no information was given about any control for the menstrual cycle. Satinder and Mastronardi (1974) have also pointed out that even studies which claim to investigate sex differences in behaviour during women's reproductive years have not taken into account the stage of the menstrual cycle in their female subjects. Another example is of the many investigations in which temperature is a variable and in which no account has been taken of time of day. So that in studies of human behaviour there has been a strong bias towards male subjects and there has been almost no recognition of possible cyclical influences on subjects. There are now signs of growing awareness of these shortcomings. Future investigations will also have to take into account the considerable interactions of different cycles. The effects of the menstrual cycle will clearly vary at different times of day, that is, at various points in the circadian cycle. For example, the circadian cycles in urine flow (Conroy and Mills, 1970) and in arousal (Akerstedt, 1979) can give rise to systematic fluctuations in fluid retention and mood, which also vary with the menstrual cycle. In addition, the hormones which are the basis of the menstrual variations have marked diurnal variations (Shaw, 1978). The interactive effects of circadian rhythms and the menstrual cycle have, remarkably, not yet been investigated. There are signs that these interactions are quite crucial in obtaining accurate observations of menstrual variations (see for example, a discussion of prolactin levels in Steiner and Carroll, 1977). If these interactive effects are taken into account, the quality of information will be greatly improved; it will, for instance, doubtless throw some light on the frequent reports of the labile nature of the premenstrual symptoms.

Entrainment is an important principle in the oscillations of most biological rhythms. This was probably first observed by Huygens in the eighteenth century (see Minorsky, 1962), and his observations provide a simple analogy for visualizing entrainment. He noticed that two clocks hung on the same thin board and running at different speeds came to be synchronized. Apparently the ticking of the clocks was transmitted through the board. This interaction, though weak, was enough to synchronize the clocks. This entrainment is characteristic of the oscillators which produce biological rhythms. There is entrainment or synchronization of the cycles of different human beings with each other. Within the individual there is linking of different cycles, and entrainment of rhythms by various environmental and social factors (*Zeitgeber*). Human beings can become synchronized with each other in various ways. The most obvious way is through the intermediary of the

24-hour light/dark cycle. People have many cycles in common because those cycles are all either generated or regulated by the variations in light and darkness and by the social factors connected with them.

The menstrual cycle of several women can in some circumstances tend to convergence. So far there are only a few properly established cases of menstrual synchrony, following close social interaction. McClintock (1971) found some synchronization of onset dates of menstruation in women in a college dormitory. Another study also found synchrony in room-mates and close friends (Quadagno, Shubeita, Deck, and Francoeur, 1981). Graham and McGrew (1980) reported synchronization, but also found that this was only true of closest friends. Close friendship compounds at least two variables, of physical proximity and of affiliation, and more research is needed to distinguish these two possible contributions. Suggestions as to how menstrual cycles become synchronized are still speculative, but interesting. One possible mechanism is by way of pheromones, which are chemical substances secreted to the exterior by an individual and received by a second individual. This releases in the second individual a specific reaction, for example, a definite behaviour or a developmental process (Karlson and Luscher, 1959). The concept of internal chemical messengers is familiar in our understanding of the endocrine system. External messengers are also presumed to regulate and influence mammalian behaviour. These substances, now known as pheromones, were originally called ecto-hormones and may be the evolutionary precursors of hormones (Wilson, 1975). It is known that humans can detect chemical substances produced by the human body; it is also known that detection thresholds can vary with hormone levels. There is no clear evidence yet that these chemical substances act as pheromones and it is not known whether they control behaviour in a manner similar to that known, for example, in insects (Rogel, 1978). Nevertheless there are signs of similar processes in humans. In one small study, perspiration was taken from one donor woman and rubbed on the upper lip of a group of five women. Six control subjects were rubbed with plain alcohol. The group which received the perspiration showed a shift towards the donor's monthly cycle; the control group showed no shift in menstrual timing, see Figure 1 (Russell, Switz, and Thompson, 1980). The pheromone explanation would assume that the chemical substances are detected olfactorily or transmitted through the skin and that they release a reaction in the endocrine and reproductive systems. The details of the reaction are unknown but the effect would be to induce a change in rhythm. There is at present insufficient evidence to draw firm conclusions about the role of chemical communication in menstrual convergence, but it may certainly play some part. Other possible mechanisms of synchronization (which should be seen in the context of the views regarding origins of cycles already discussed) are such things as fluctuations in atmospheric pressure or variations in the intensity of cosmic radiation.

Within any individual, linking together of rhythms is characteristic and has the biologically adaptive purpose of putting order into a large number of

8

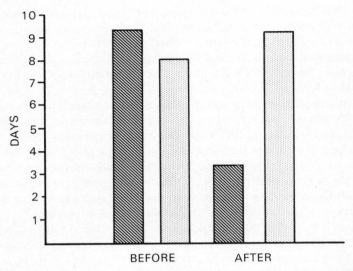

Figure 1. The mean number of days difference between the donor's menstrual cycle and the subjects' menstrual cycles, before and after treatment. The hatched bar represents the experimental group (received odour from donor), the dotted bar represents the control group (received plain alcohol only). Redrawn, by permission of Ankho International Inc., from M. J. Russell, Switz, and Thompson (1980). Olfactory influences on the human menstrual cycle. *Pharmacology, Biochemistry and Behaviour*, **13**, 737–738

processes and hence of achieving smoother operation. This linking does not alter the essential nature of the individual rhythms though it may alter the manifestations of the cycles, as in the example given of the influences of the circadian variations on the menstrual cycle. It is often said that ovulation tends to occur at the same time in the 24-hour cycle for each woman. Certainly there is much evidence from work on mammals that events within the ovarian cycle occur at a specific time of day (Campbell and Turek, 1981). The menstrual cycle remains nevertheless an entirely autonomous process which requires for its inception the specific physiological trigger from the ovary. The rhythm of the ovary can simply become re-set to coincide with a point in the circadian cycle. This is not surprising in view of the marked circadian variation in hormones which have releasing effects at crucial points in the cycle. Prolactin levels, for example, show a diurnal rhythm which is dependent on the 24-hour sleep/wake cycle (Cutler and Garcia, 1980). Important examples of linking of cycles in an individual are some of the circadian rhythms. They are highly influenced both by other circadian rhythms directly and through habits associated with them. For instance the curve of heart-rate, blood-clotting, and respiratory variations through the 24 hours will depend largely on habits of activity during the day (though also, to an important extent, on temperature). Likewise the pattern of most of the circadian variations in endocrine functions appears to be determined by habit, posture, and so on. These hormone levels in turn act as transmitter mechanisms to synchronize rhythms in various cells and organs of the body. An example of how cycles which are clearly endogenous adapt their activities to other cycles, presumably in the interests of optimal functioning, is given by Oatley and Goodwin (1971). Cells which are growing and dividing in, for example, skin, smooth muscle, and gastric mucosa have a striking convergence of division times, either in the neighbourhood of 24 hours or of multiples of 24 hours. Since the internal world of the organism which constitutes their environment has adapted to a basic 24-hour periodicity they have likewise adapted to it. Rhythms at different levels of organization, from the cellular to the higher centres in the brain, frequently influence each other in this way, as regards onset. The timing of the complete process remains an inherent feature of the cycle. There is no detailed knowledge of the mechanisms by which endogenous rhythms are synchronized with each other and with external events, though it must be achieved by some sort of clocking in of the internal oscillator to the other rhythm or to the external condition. Apart from the wider question of how the driving oscillators themselves work, Brady (1979) points out that an understanding of the mechanisms of entrainment entails information on how the occurrence of the influencing *Zeitgeber* is detected, then how it gets coupled to the driving oscillator to achieve a change in phase. It may be that the synchronizing signal is transmitted by hormones to various parts of the body. It seems unlikely that there is something like one physiological clock with comprehensive control but rather that there are many oscillators which can become linked with other internal events, often themselves responding to the light/dark cycle, and more directly to external events. Rhythms also communicate with each other by some form of weak coupling, as in the Huygens observation.

Some insight into the intricacies of the interactions of rhythmic variations is provided by the example of temperature. It is one of many cyclical functions which, in women, are subject to two major rhythmic influences. In addition to its normal circadian rhythm (rising slowly from a minimum in the early hours of the morning to an early evening peak and then a rather faster decline back to the morning minimum) it also varies systematically with the menstrual cycle. So that to be superimposed on the 24-hour curve are the different temperature levels which are found in the first and second half of the menstrual cycle. That is, from the beginning of the cycle a decline in temperature up to ovulation and a rise thereafter, being lowest at midcycle and highest in the few days before menstruation. This typical biphasic temperature curve is generated by the physiological activity of the ovary and hence is controlled from a different source than is the circadian temperature rhythm. No monthly variation is observed in girls before menarche or in women after menopause or after bilateral removal of the ovaries or in men. It is unaffected by hysterectomy leaving the ovaries intact (Vollman, 1977).

The propensity of some cycles to become synchronized or desynchronized depends on many factors such as the origins of the cycle and, in humans, individual differences. The menstrual cycle is fairly resistant, though by no means immune, to influence, in most individuals. For instance, the only reports of menstrual synchrony are of special situations in which the women were living in close proximity to each other. Even then, there are marked individual differences. In the chemical odour study, for example (cited above) one of the five subjects changed from a 16-day difference from the donor's onset date of menstruation to no difference; whereas another subject went from a 14-day difference to a 4-day one but in the 5 months of the experiment had reverted finally to a 14-day difference. In general, for whatever reasons, in most women only rather extreme conditions bring about marked change in the menstrual cycle but, in a minority of women, chronic irregularity is the rule. Investigations have shown that the majority of women have fairly regular cycles most of the time (Chapter 2). There are doubtless many factors which account for the individual differences. One possible source of variation is suggested by the findings of a study by Dewan, Menkin, and Rock (1980). They studied the role of light as a synchronizing agent influencing the menstrual cycle and found in a controlled study that exposure to artificial light at night tended to regularize the cycles of eight out of eleven women with irregular cycles. That is, an unusual amount of exposure to light helped to establish a more regular pattern. In general it appears that light has significant endocrine effects via melatonin and it would therefore not be surprising to find that individual differences in sensitivity to light have some effect on menstrual regularity. There is a further discussion (below) of individual differences in other cycles and all of these have to be borne in mind when considering the effects of extraneous influences.

Not all of the changes in rhythm which are brought about by other influences are always repeated or systematic. Neither are they always adaptive, and sometimes they are maladaptive. They may simply happen as a result of events at the time. The possible sources of influence are legion, from other internal states, including pathological ones, to various social and psychological influences. There is constant reciprocal influence between the whole network of cycles and other events. Some further examples will suggest the complexities of the interactions which form the background to any attempt at a fuller understanding of the nature of cycles:

1. Beard growth in men is an index of levels of testosterone; a rise in level of testosterone is associated with sexual activity (Bancroft, 1978; Kraemer, Becker, Brodie, Doering, Moos, and Hamburg, 1976). It is therefore not surprising that rate of beard growth appears to be associated with sexual activity (Anonymous, 1970). Insofar as sexual activity is determined by environmental factors, any observed fluctuations in beard growth and in testosterone levels are partly determined by the same environmental factors. There is the further complication that, as we might expect, there is evidence which suggests that men respond to the cycles of the women with whom they live (Henderson, 1976). Certainly, to the extent that environmental factors will play a part in producing variations in men of

patterns in sexual activity, hormone levels, mood changes and so on, the
menstrual cycle of women partners is a central part of that environment.
2. There are many examples of events which are influenced by circadian
rhythms, by the 24-hour light/dark cycle and by habits arising from it:
   (a) The number of deaths, including post-operative deaths, peaks in the
   early hours of the morning, presumably as a function of the circadian
   variation in physiological functions (Conroy and Mills, 1970).
   (b) The onset of labour, defined as spontaneous initiation of painful
   contractions and/or rupture of foetal membranes, takes place significantly more often around 1 a.m. than at any other time (Smolensky,
   Halberg, and Sargent, 1972). Normal births are 30% more common
   around 4 a.m. than during the day (Brady, 1979; Conroy and Mills,
   1970). This is in contrast with stillbirths and births associated with
   neonatal mortality which reach a peak around mid-morning, as do
   induced births (Kaiser and Halberg, 1962; Smolensky, Halberg, and
   Sargent, 1972). (See Figure 2.) The correspondence between the
   distribution of natural labour onset and normal births with the light/
   dark cycle is assumed to be somewhat related to posture, which is a

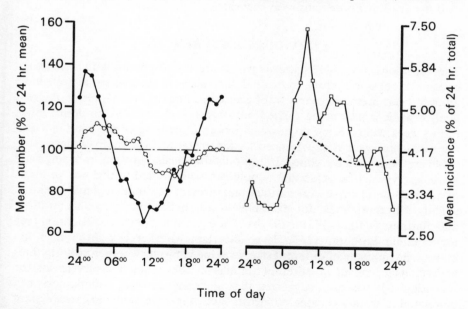

Figure 2. Mean circadian changes in human labour and birth.
● Hourly frequency of initiation of spontaneous labour based on 207,918 labours.
○ Hourly frequency of parturition based on 2,082,453 natural births.
□ Hourly frequency of parturition based on 30,493 induced births.
▲ Average incidence of 12,081 stillbirths summarized for 3-hour spans.
Redrawn, by permission of Igaku Shoin Ltd, from Smolensky, Halberg, and Sargent
(1972). Chronobiology of the life sequence, in Ito, Ogata, and Yoshimura (eds.),
Advances in climatic physiology

function of the 24-hour sleep/waking pattern, though hormonal influences on the maintenance of the foetus and initiation of parturition may also be involved. The pattern of stillbirths and induced births possibly reflects obstetric practice; but there is also a little evidence of problems associated with delivery at 'unusual' times (Minors and Waterhouse, 1981).

(c) Also thought to be related to posture is onset of menstruation which occurs more frequently in the morning than in the evening (Malek, Gleich, and Maly, 1962).

(d) There are variations in response to drugs and these are a reflection of circadian rhythms in physiological processes (Brady, 1979; Bunning, 1973).

3. The menstrual cycle as we shall see not only has far-reaching psychological, behavioural, and bodily effects but is also itself influenced by various factors, such as food deprivation, the seasons, travel, stress, and emotional upheaval. As already mentioned, the conditions have to be rather extreme, and all individuals do not react in the same way. Often there are reciprocal effects between these factors and the cycle and it is difficult to attribute causation accurately.

INDIVIDUAL DIFFERENCES

The variations in cyclical patterns which are found among individuals have become a focus of interest. Individual differences in the menstrual cycle have already been mentioned and will be discussed again in Chapter 4. A great deal of work is also being carried out on other cycles, and no doubt much of this work will be found to have an important bearing on the ways in which the menstrual cycle is experienced. A few instances will be given here.

Several studies have concentrated on differences between 'morning' and 'evening' types. It appears that people can be classified in this way in terms of their 24-hour curves on various measures. They tend to have peaks at slightly different times, for example on adrenaline output, concentration, and alertness (Patkai, 1971a, 1971b). These results require confirmation (see for example Froberg, 1977). It is uncertain whether any differences are merely the outcome of different sleep/waking habits or whether both rhythms and habits originate in different timings in the endogenous cycles of the individuals. It has been suggested that morning-ness and evening-ness may be related to certain personality factors such as introversion and extraversion, but this is probably an oversimplified view and has certainly not yet been satisfactorily demonstrated (Horne and Ostberg, 1977). By the same token, there are suggestions of a relationship between individual differences in sleep patterns and personality characteristics (Cohen, 1979).

Sex differences in various circadian rhythms have been suggested though there is still much more exploration of this source of variation to be carried out. Males and females appear for instance to have rather different diurnal curves for temperature and for some performance tests (Christie and McBrearty, 1979).

Some but not all individuals produce rhythmic patterns in the symptoms of certain illnesses such as epilepsy, schizophrenia, manic-depressive illness, and thyroid deficiency. It seems very likely that these cycles of symptoms are related in some way to normal biological rhythms but the exact relationship is uncertain. The short ones may be based originally on the 24-hour light/dark cycle, others seem to centre on an intermediate period of around 14 days. Some of the rhythms appear to be roughly based on a 30-day cycle. It has been suggested that this cycle, of 30 days on average but with a wide range, is a common cycle which both men and women possess but which has tended to become submerged in the process of evolution. Though hidden for the most part it remains potentially important and can occasionally show itself under certain conditions such as illness. If this primitive cycle does exist, its relationship with other cycles is not known. The human reproductive cycle is thought to have become independent of this universal monthly cycle in the course of evolution (Richter, 1968). More recently, advances in chronobiological techniques raise the possibility of early detection of diseases in men and women by systematic monitoring of rhythms (Smolensky, 1980).

There can be no doubt of the pervasive influence of cycles and of the practical implications of this influence. There is increasing acceptance of the importance of biological timing throughout human existence. The study of rhythms and cycles has now become more widespread, in various scientific disciplines. In general, there are great advantages in recognizing rhythms and co-operating with them. With increasing awareness of their influence the possibility of better adaptations will open up.

SUMMARY

Biological cycles have profound and complex effects on the whole of life. Whatever the ultimate origin of all the rhythms, they are constantly interacting with each other and with social factors and environmental events. As an important part of this network of relationships, the menstrual cycle has to be studied with due regard both to all the influences upon it, and to the far-reaching effects which it has.

Different biological cycles have different mechanisms. The menstrual cycle is determined by the inherent rhythmicity of the ovary. The key event is ovulation which can be affected by various factors but which, once it has occurred, determines the events of the next cycle. Oestrogen seems to be fundamental to the ovarian rhythm. It is believed that timing mechanisms control various genes which are coded for self-maintenance and for self-destruction. These timing devices would maintain the constancy of both the maximal lifespan and the age of menopause both of which persist in spite of social and environmental change.

Synchronization of different cycles within an individual, and of the cycles of different individuals, is an important characteristic of biological organization. Further demonstration is needed of the possibility that ovulation may become linked to the 24-hour cycle,and that menstruation onset tends to converge in women living in close proximity. Clarification of the intricacies of the mechanisms of synchronization will be of theoretical and practical interest. Cycles differ in their propensity to become synchronized, or desynchronized. There are also individual differences in this propensity. The regularity of the menstrual cycle is maintained in most women in all but exceptional circumstances. In a minority of women irregularity is the rule. The individual differences may be partly a reflection of variations in sensitivity to the effects of other cycles, such as light. Individual differences in other rhythms, particularly the circadian cycle, can be expected to influence the ways in which the menstrual cycle is experienced.

The importance, and the advantages, of taking account of the effects of cycles has not in the past been sufficiently recognized. This is true in research, in clinical applications, and in general adaptations to life.

interpreted as such. There have been admirable attempts to solve the problems of analysing menstrual bleeding patterns (see for example Rodriguez, Faundes-Latham, and Atkinson, 1976). The general problems of recording menstrual data are discussed in the World Health Organization report (1981b) already mentioned. The studies depend on the co-operation of competent volunteers over a long period of time. For various reasons there is a constant loss of participants, frequently resulting in biased samples. The information comes in very slowly since significant variations in any woman are often only apparent over many months or years. There is a lack of comparability between studies. For example, many have used reports based on memory, which are considerably less accurate than those based on record-keeping (see for example Presser, 1974).

Menopause, defined as the last menstrual period, marks the end of the reproductive years. The mean age of menopause in Western societies is about 50 years and the median age is about 51 (Brand and Lehert, 1978; McKinlay, Jefferys, and Thompson, 1972). The figures are approximate, given the difficulties in establishing the precise age of menopause in large groups of women. It is often said that those women who started menstruating early have a late menopause, so that early starters are thought to have a longer reproductive life. Recent studies suggest that this is not the case (Ernster and Petrakis, 1981; McKinlay, Jefferys, and Thompson, 1972). This kind of uncertainty about the facts is inevitable when there are such enormous methodological difficulties, some of which have already been mentioned. In addition, most studies of age have been retrospective and have relied on women recalling accurately the details of the timing of their menarche and of their menopause. One study (Frommer, 1964) found a tendency to round off to 5-year intervals in recalling the date of menopause. It may be that the beginning of menstruation is better remembered. Damon and Bajima (1974) had access to data from a longitudinal growth study started in 1922 in which ages at menarche of 143 women had been recorded. They found that the women's memory of their age of first menstruation showed a mean error of only 0.2 years after 39 years. It is unlikely that there would be a highly consistent relationship between age of menarche and age of menopause because there are so many factors which affect the reproductive history in the course of 35 to 40 years. Details of how such factors as numbers of childbirths and miscarriages, diet, smoking, diseases, and stress affect the ages of menarche and menopause are unknown. They will only emerge as a result of large-scale prospective studies of the same women over the whole reproductive lifespan. Some studies are already in train and will eventually provide much more detailed and reliable information than has been possible in the past. Another point which has yet to be confirmed is whether the age of menopause is increasing in each generation. This has been difficult to establish, since women's life expectancy a century ago, in Western societies, was about 48 years and has only reached the seventies in about the last 30 years. Now that most women are living for many years after the menopause, and that rather more reliable records are available, accurate comparisons of the menopausal ages of successive generations are being carried out. For the moment there are many conflicting findings on this subject, but there is no good evidence to confirm suggestions that there has been a significant raising of the age of menopause, in the last century anyway (McKinlay, Jefferys, and Thompson, 1972). At least one author is of the opinion that the mean age has not changed since the sixth century A.D. (Utian, 1980). More details of all aspects of the menopause are given in Chapter 6.

There is growing interest in the temporal characteristics and in their effects on other aspects of the cycle. The development of new techniques of analysis are leading to more accurate statements about the relationships between timing of the cycle and other variables (see for example Rogel, 1980; Smolensky, 1980).

EVENTS WHICH DEFINE THE CYCLE: CHANGES IN HORMONAL LEVELS AND IN THE REPRODUCTIVE ORGANS

Viewed in the general context of biological rhythms, the menstrual cycle can be seen dispassionately as a series of related events designed to favour receptivity, consummation, conception, and reproduction. For these purposes the design is good, with an appropriate pattern of hormonal and bodily changes, as well as variations in mood and behaviour.

The cycle can be described in terms of two types of event:
1. The events which define the cycle: these are the changes in hormone levels and in the reproductive organs. These changes are the most fundamental and the most invariable and they normally occur in all women throughout the reproductive years, with individual variations in the timing, and with the occurrence of some cycles in which ovulation, and the usual neuroendocrine events, do not occur.
2. Changes which are consistently associated with the menstrual cycle: although very widespread, their incidence varies in different women and in each woman at different times.

The events in (1) are discussed in this chapter. Those in (2) are described in the next two chapters. Throughout the book, the usual convention is adopted of a 28-day cycle, with the day of onset of bleeding called Day 1.

The basic facts about the cyclical changes in hormonal levels and in the reproductive organs are well known and appear in all textbooks. The aim of this account is to provide the background to subsequent discussion of the other changes associated with the menstrual cycle, and of their underlying mechanisms.

The neuroendocrine mechanisms which control the reproductive cycle are by no means completely understood, though considerable progress has been made in recent years. Most interest has centred on the ovarian hormones oestrogen and progesterone, and on their influence on the release of follicle stimulating hormone (FSH) and luteinizing hormone (LH) from the pituitary.

21

The levels of these hormones through the cycle are shown in Figure 4. The figure also shows a conventional way of dividing up and naming the different phases of the cycle, as follows:
Menstrual phase—Days 1 to 5
Follicular phase—Days 6 to 12
Ovulatory phase—Days 13 to 15
Luteal phase—Days 16 to 23
Premenstrual phase—Days 24 to 28

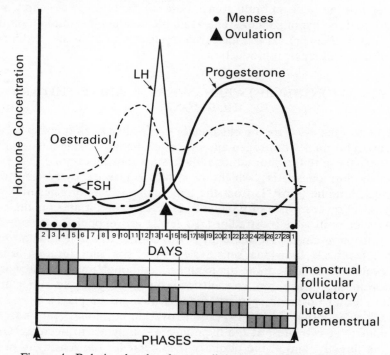

Figure 4. Relative levels of oestradiol, progesterone, FSH, and LH throughout the menstrual cycle. Adapted from Shaw (1978). Neuroendocrinology of the menstrual cycle in humans. *Clinics in Endocrinology and Metabolism*, **7**, 531–559 and reproduced by permission of W. B. Saunders Co.

The term 'paramenstruum' (introduced by Dalton) will be used to refer to the combination of the premenstrual and the menstrual phases.

Cyclical levels of hormones other than those shown in the figure are less well established, but are beginning to receive more attention. The role of these other hormones is clearly of interest in understanding the psychological and behavioural changes of the menstrual cycle.

For simplicity, in this discussion the several oestrogen compounds will usually be referred to as oestrogen or oestrogens. Most studies have in fact measured oestradiol-17β, which is the main oestrogenic product of the ovary and is the predominant oestrogen during the reproductive years. The other compounds are oestrone which comes from androstenedione which is produced by the adrenal cortex and metabolized into oestrone in the fat and skin; and oestriol, a very weak oestrogen which is anabolized mostly during pregnancy. These statements about oestrogens are rather oversimplified (see, for example, Fishman and Martucci, 1980). Of the progestational hormones, progesterone is usually the only one measured, though in very occasional studies 17 α-hydroxyprogesterone is also included.

As regards the relevant brain areas, these will be referred to simply as the pituitary and the hypothalamus. The available detailed information on these areas, and of their part in the menstrual cycle is set out in any textbook of the neurophysiology of reproduction.

RELATIONSHIP BETWEEN OVARIAN AND PITUITARY HORMONES

The events of the cycle are the outcome of the feedback relationship between the ovarian hormones oestrogen and progesterone on the one hand, and, on the other, the pituitary hormones follicle stimulating hormone (FSH) and luteinizing hormones (LH), which are in turn controlled by gonadotrophin releasing hormone (GnRH) from the hypothalmus. There is negative feedback control by oestrogen of FSH and LH release, and it appears that small increases in oestrogen (oestradiol-17ß) levels are enough to suppress the gonadrotrophin release. Absolute levels are not the sole determinants of the negative feedback. Individual sensitivity, rate of rise, and duration of increased levels will also determine the feedback. Although much of the work on gonadotrophin release has concentrated on oestrogen the other major ovarian steroid hormone, progesterone, is thought to play a part in the feedback relationship (Shaw, 1978). The ovarian hormones appear to exert their control at two sites; at the hypothalamus they act to decrease GnRH secretion directly, and at the pituitary they decrease the sensitivity of FSH and LH to GnRH (Shaw, 1978). There is also a positive feedback action of oestrogen, but the details of its operation in humans are not known. The pre-ovulatory rise in oestrogen, for example, is certainly the trigger for the mid-cycle gonadotrophin surge. It may achieve this by direct positive feedback (which can be achieved experimentally if certain minimum levels and duration of oestrogen are maintained); or by removal of negative feedback following a reduction in oestrogen levels (Shaw, 1978). Figure 4 shows how oestrogen starts to decline just prior to the FSH and LH peaks.

Recent evidence appears to provide a satisfactory explanation for the paradoxical positive and negative feedback effects of oestrogen on gonadotrophins at different times in the menstrual cycle. There is support for a model of LH synthesis and storage taking place in two pools, one concerned with release, one with storage (Yen and Lein, 1976). The 'primary' pool reflects pituitary sensitivity and is immediately releasable; the 'secondary' pool represents pituitary reserve, though it is hardly secondary in the sense that oestrogen in fact preferentially impedes sensitivity, to induce the augmentation of reserve. In these terms the pre-ovulatory LH surge would be accounted for by a positive feedback effect of the increased amount of oestrogen from the ovary in the late follicular phase. Under the influence of these elevated levels of oestrogen the sensitivity of the gonadotropes to GnRH reaches a point where GnRH exerts its full priming effect which has the result of transferring gonadotrophins from the secondary reserve pool to the primary releasable pool. This results in the massive LH ovulatory surge (see Figure 4). It is through this feedback action that the inherent rhythmicity of the ovary, already referred to, determines the timing of the menstrual cycle. The ovary is the oscillator.

Another mechanism to be aware of is a non-steroid substance, inhibin, which is present in follicular fluid (de Jong and Sharpe, 1976; Schwartz and Channing, 1977) and which may be another factor specifically in the control of pituitary secretion of gonadotrophins, particularly of FSH.

EVENTS IN EACH PHASE OF THE CYCLE

Beginning of the cycle

The negative feedback of oestrogen is, towards the end of one cycle, already initiating the events of the next one. Although it is useful to refer to the onset of bleeding as the simultaneous ending of one cycle and the beginning of the next (Day 1) the events of any two cycles overlap. FSH, which will ensure sustained growth of a group of follicles and hence prepare for the critical events of the new cycle, has already started to rise before menstruation (see Figure 4). This is probably simply an outcome of the negative feedback relationship between FSH and oestrogen. The premenstrual fall in oestrogen stimulates hypothalamic release of GnRH to the pituitary which then starts a rise in FSH, a rise which becomes more appreciable during menstruation when oestrogen reaches its lowest point.

Follicular phase

The FSH arrives at the ovaries and stimulates the growth of a group of follicles. These growing follicles in turn become an important source of oestrogen and the rising levels of oestrogen have their negative feedback effect on hypothalamus and pituitary, and FSH declines. The oestrogen rises sharply by Day 7, FSH levels remain low and only rise when oestrogen starts to decline before mid-cycle. The peak of oestrogen is towards the end of the follicular phase, when follicle size is maximal.

Pre-ovulation

All except one of the follicles succumb to the decline of FSH which has started with the rise in oestrogen. The precise mechanisms for the selection of a single follicle for ovulation are not known, though various factors have been postulated (Yen and Jaffe, 1978). The dominant follicle is known to be pre-selected from its cohort. Goodman, Nixon, Johnson, and Hodgen (1977) showed that removal of the dominant one does not result in the maturation of another, and that new follicles require the usual approximate time of 12.6 days to develop to an ovulable stage. Speroff (1977) has put forward one possible version of the mechanism by which normally only one follicle reaches ovulation, avoiding multiple ovulation. He suggests that it will be the largest follicle which will produce the most oestrogen. Locally, oestrogen promotes the uptake and binding of FSH and hence this follicle will best protect itself from the decline in FSH by taking more of it up. (In these terms, Speroff suggests that some fraternal twinning may simply represent the chance development of two follicles making similar amounts of oestrogen and taking up similar FSH.) The other follicles will make less oestrogen, will become more sensitive to the drop in FSH and will undergo atresia. Atresia is not, however, the end of all activity in the follicles. In the process of atresia, with the disappearance of tissue, stromal tissue forms and the follicles, instead of secreting principally oestrogen, now mainly secrete androgens (Speroff, 1977). This means that in the days prior to the mid-cycle gonadotrophin surge, the ovary is secreting small but significant amounts of androgens, mainly androstenedione which is 15% higher at mid-cycle than at any other time (Judd, 1976); also some testosterone and dehydroisoandosterone (Vande-Wiele, Bogumil, Dyrenfurth, Ferin, Jewelewicz, Warren, Rizkallah, and Mikhail, 1970). Levels of testosterone are higher in the ovulatory than in the follicular or luteal phases (Judd and Yen, 1973; Schreiner-Engel, Schiavi, Smith, and White, 1981). (See Figure 5). The role played by these hormones in the initiation or modification of the gonadotrophin surge is not known (Shaw, 1978). By Day 13 the follicles have brought about the oestrogen peak which usually precedes by one day the gonadotrophin mid-cycle surge (Shaw, 1978). To achieve the surge the oestrogen must not only reach a critical level, as yet unknown, but must also be maintained for several hours. The presumed mechanisms for the oestrogen-induced LH surge, outlined above, require detailed confirmation. There are indications that progesterone may also play a role in the regulation of the LH mid-cycle surge, but the positive feedback action of progesterone can only be induced on an oestrogen-primed pituitary. So that progesterone may serve to facilitate the oestrogen effect (Shaw, 1978).

Although both FSH and LH peak at mid-cycle, the role of FSH in the ovulatory process is not known. The mid-cycle surge of FSH does not always occur and sometimes does not coincide with the LH surge (though this is usually in abnormal cycles). The FSH surge may simply be due to a common

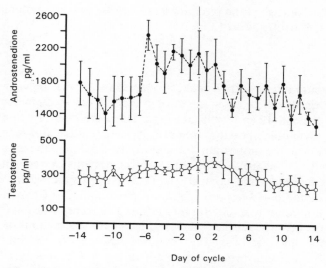

Figure 5. Mean values of androstenedione and testosterone in six women. The vertical bar represents one s.e. of the mean. 0 is ovulation day. For both hormones, levels in the middle third of the cycle were significantly higher than in the first or last thirds. Reproduced, by permission of The Endocrine Society, from Judd and Yen (1973). Serum androstenedione and testosterone levels during the menstrual cycle. *Journal of Clinical Endocrinology and Metabolism*, **36**, 475–481

releasing hormone inducing release of both gonadotrophins; or it may be that the combination of FSH and LH produces optimal functioning (Shaw, 1978). Clinically, it is possible to induce ovulation and pregnancy by drugs, simply by mimicking the LH surge and holding FSH constant (Speroff, 1977). The question of whether there are two different gonadotrophin-releasing hormones, one for FSH and one for LH, is not settled. Two separate releasing hormones have been postulated but have not been satisfactorily demonstrated (Cutler and Garcia, 1980; Shaw, 1978).

The rise in progesterone is a feature of the second half of the cycle. Nevertheless small quantities of this hormone are released by the follicles in the last few days of the follicular phase and progesterone appears to have both negative and positive feedback effects on the mid-cycle events. There is a very small but significant rise in progesterone which precedes the gonadotrophin surge and this is thought to play a facilitatory role in the surge by positive feedback action. It may also have a negative feedback influence, in the limitation of the LH surge to 24 hours. Both the negative and positive feedback action of progesterone depend upon the presence of oestrogen. The details of these effects of progesterone on the gonadotrophin mid-cycle peak are not known with certainty. It may be achieved by facilitating gonadotrophin release at the pituitary level, and/or at the hypothalamic level (Shaw, 1978; Speroff, 1977).

Ovulation

About 24 hours after the LH peak, around Day 15, the high levels of LH cause the largest follicle (now measuring about 2 cm in diameter) to burst and release the mature and fertilizable egg. There is a large rise in prostaglandins before ovulation, possibly induced by LH, (Cutler and Garcia, 1980) which appears to be important for physically expelling the egg (Speroff, 1977). Details of the role of various central nervous system and ovarian factors in the timing and control of the ovulatory process are emerging. These include the possible participation of melatonin, see Chapter 8, and of an ovarian hormone, relaxin (Burger, 1981). The transportation of the released ovum towards the uterus is achieved partly by contractions of the whole fallopian tube and partly by the rhythmic beating of the cilia within it. The contractions often produce the pain in the lower abdomen known as *Mittelschmerz* (see Chapter 3). Whereas male sperm have a post-ejaculation life of up to 2–3 days, the ovum has a maximal viability of 6 hours (Cutler and Garcia, 1980). If there is implantation of a fertilized ovum this is achieved by about Day 19.

Mention must be made of a mid-cycle rise in 17α-hydroxyprogesterone which starts at around the same time as the LH surge and which is hence presumably not instrumental in the surge and may be the first index of luteinization (Thorneycroft, Sribyatta, Tom, Nakamura, and Mishell, 1974). The rise and peak in this progestational hormone largely parallels the course of oestradiol, the main oestrogen at this time.

Around mid-cycle, on the day following the LH surge, the gradual increase which has been taking place in the karyopyknotic index of the vagina cells reaches a peak, though this is not very marked, and then steadily declines to the end of the cycle. Thickening of the vaginal epithelium takes place during the follicular phase (Moghissi, Syner, and Evans, 1972). Mid-cycle also sees the culmination of changes in the cervical mucus which have begun earlier in the cycle, presumably under the influence of oestrogen. The mucus is most abundant and clear before the LH surge and also there is the highest spinnbarkeit reading (this is a method of measuring the length of the mucus threads which at mid-cycle create channels through which spermatozoa can migrate). The peak of sperm penetrability occurs on the day of the LH surge, as does the maximal ferning. Ferning is a test of crystallization which derives from the fact that dried mid-cycle mucus, when viewed microscopically, forms a fern-like pattern; this ferning is determined by oestrogen stimulation and it disappears under the influence of progesterone. Cervical mucus proteins show a cyclical pattern. Albumin and globulins decrease two days before the LH surge and begin to rise thereafter. Mucins reach their height around mid-cycle and decrease thereafter (Moghissi, Syner, and Evans, 1972).

Luteal phase

The follicle vacated by the mature ovum collapses and is transformed into the corpus luteum by the LH. Not only does the luteinization of the follicle depend on LH but the maintenance of both the seven-day growth and the seven-day regression periods of the luteal phase (if no pregnancy takes place) depends on certain minimal levels of LH. The experimental evidence suggests that it is LH, rather than FSH, which is the principal factor in the production of the steroid hormones throughout the luteal phase (Cutler and Garcia, 1980); it is the luteal cells, probably the theca interna, which now provide both the prostegerone and also the oestrogen. During the first half of the cycle, the growing follicles are the principal source of oestrogen. The rise in basal body temperature in the second half of the cycle is temporally related to a central effect of progesterone. The unique role of progesterone in the preparation of the endometrium for pregnancy has been confirmed by experimental work showing a consistent relationship between endometrial histology and progesterone levels throughout the progesterone-producing days of the cycle (Rosenfeld and Garcia, 1976). The increase in progesterone secretion continues and completes a process which has begun early in the cycle when enough oestrogen is produced by the growing follicles to begin to stimulate the formation of a new endometrium. While the state of the endometrium relies on progesterone, it is probably oestrogen which is the crucial factor in the regression of the corpus luteum and the termination of the cycle, if no pregnancy occurs. It is thought that the luteal phase of development is brought to an end, and the regression phase is started, by an interactive mechanism of oestrogen with prostaglandins. It also appears to be the endometrium itself which provides prostaglandins. Some details of this process by which the endometrium produces a prostaglandin which in conjunction with oestrogen contributes to the regression of the corpus luteum, thus ending the luteal phase, and the whole cycle, are now emerging, but the information must still be considered provisional (Cutler and Garcia, 1980).

When an ovum is successfully fertilized the luteal regression is prevented by the secretion from the placenta of hCG (human chorionic gonadotrophin), predominantly into the maternal circulation, where it ultimately appears in the urine on about Day 10 of pregnancy. All the functions of hGC are not established, but it does maintain the otherwise transient existence of the corpus luteum, ensuring the production of ovarian progesterone until the placenta itself can secrete the progesterone which is essential for pregnancy. The transition to placental progesterone source occurs 6 to 8 weeks in gestation (Yen and Jaffe, 1978).

Premenstrual phase

In the absence of fertilization the luteal regression results in a sharp decline in oestrogen and progesterone for about four days from Day 24. These falling levels cause local change in the endometrium which lead to it being shed in the menstrual flow. The mechanisms of menstrual bleeding, apart from the ovarian steroid decline, are not known in every detail. The initiation of the vasospasm which precedes the breakdown and shedding of the endometrium is poorly understood though prostaglandins appear to be involved. Prostaglandins are found in high concentrations in the endometrium as menstruation approaches and are present in abundance in menstrual blood (Yen and Jaffe, 1978). Just as with the physical expulsion of the mature ovum at ovulation, prostaglandins are involved in the contractions of the uterus during the menstrual flow. They likewise play a role in the determination of volume and duration of bleeding. They are thus implicated in dysmenorrhea (see Chapter 3). Meanwhile, although gonadotrophin levels are low during the first part of the luteal phase, while the corpus luteum regresses, FSH begins gradually to rise, presumably from removal of negative feedback action as levels of oestrogen and progesterone decline. This FSH rise initiates the development of a new set of follicles, thus setting in train the events with which this review began, under the heading of the beginning of the cycle.

Various other areas of inquiry are important in the delineation of the mechanisms of the reproductive cycle and hence in a better understanding of the associated physical, psychological, and behavioural changes. Prolactin, for example, is involved in follicular maturation and in corpus luteum function, though its precise role is unknown. High levels of prolactin invariably produce anovulation and the women concerned have abnormalities of oestrogen feedback. This suggests that elevated prolactin levels act at the hypothalamic and pituitary levels. It seems probable that prolactin can modulate the secretion of ovarian steroids, and if this is confirmed it will greatly enhance our understanding of the regulation of the menstrual cycle (Shaw, 1978). Levels of prolactin during the cycle have in the past been a subject of disagreement, mainly because of wide individual differences, and frequent failure to take measurements throughout the 24-hour cycle. It appears that variability in levels is much greater during the luteal than during the follicular phase and that, at least in some women, levels are higher throughout the luteal and premenstural phase (Steiner and Carroll, 1977). Prolactin is also a factor in the breast changes which occur with the cycle. Clinically, compounds which reduce prolactin levels are very effective in alleviating breast symptoms (Brush, 1977). Again, the prolactin must interact with oestrogen levels. A study of breast sensitivity (measured by two-point discrimination and pain threshold tests) found a maximal sensitivity just after mid-cycle and again at menstruation. These sensitive phases coincided with low oestrogen levels and the first peak did not occur in a group of women using the contraceptive pill (Robinson and Short, 1979). The part played by the neurotransmitters is of particular interest in elucidating a comprehensive view of the menstrual cycle and its effects. It is probable that several neuro-transmitters are involved in the control of gonadotrophin release (Cutler and Garcia, 1980; Shaw, 1978). The implication of noradrenaline, adrenaline, serotonin, and dopamine, for example, in the menstrual cycle is well established (Cutler and Garcia, 1980; Shaw, 1978; Warren, Tedford, and Flynn, 1979).

SUMMARY

Investigation of the menstrual cycle, though widespread, has not been comprehensive. The temporal characteristics of the cycle are known in broad outline but many details are still to be confirmed. The age of menarche has been falling steadily, but not as dramatically as had been supposed. The upper age limit of menopause does not appear to have changed. The over-all patterns of length and regularity of cycle are related to age. Within those patterns, the cycle may be affected by various factors usually via delayed ovulation. Improvements in methodology are expected to produce more information about individual and cultural variations in the characteristics of the menstrual cycle.

The events which define the cycle, that is the changes in hormone levels and in the reproductive organs, are relatively well documented. The feedback relationship between ovarian and pituitary hormones is fundamental to these events. The cycle is initiated and maintained by the rhythmic activity of the ovaries which gives rise to the changing levels of pituitary and ovarian hormones. These fluctuations bring about the growth of follicles one of which matures and is released at ovulation. There are concomitant changes in the vagina and the cervix which also depend on variations in hormonal levels. After ovulation, the reciprocal relationship between ovarian and pituitary hormones likewise provides the basis for the production of the corpus luteum and the preparation of the womb for pregnancy, or alternatively the luteal regression which leads to the shedding of the endometrium in the menstrual flow. Various other neuroendocrine substances and processes are also involved throughout the reproductive cycle, and their elucidation will provide a more detailed picture than is at present available.

In the next two chapters is set out the available information on the various physical, psychological, and behavioural changes which are reliably associated with the menstrual cycle.

CHAPTER 3

Changes associated with the menstrual cycle: I

PROBLEMS OF METHODOLOGY AND INTERPRETATION

It is relatively simple to demonstrate that certain physiological, physical, mood, and behavioural measures vary at different points in the cycle. It is not so simple to show that these variations are specific to the menstrual cycle; that is, that the changes would not regularly occur in the same people independently of the cycle, nor in men, nor in non-menstruating women. If similar fluctuations are found in many or most people regardless of the menstrual cycle it is clearly both incorrect and not useful to attribute them to the cycle. This question is of more than academic interest, not only because a more effective approach will rely on accurate knowledge of all the antecedents of the changes of the cycle, but also because the menstrual cycle is a subject which attracts unsubstantiated statements. For historical, social, and political reasons, there is a tendency to present the menstrual cycle in more or less partisan or emotional ways. Views of the cycle are put forward with inadequate empirical support, often with a total disregard of the evidence, or with the backing of selected studies many of which are not acceptable on methodological grounds. There are considerable problems of methodology. None of the possible control groups of non-menstruating individuals are ideal. Most men live in close proximity to women and will be influenced by this fact, especially as regards changes of mood, variations in sexual behaviour, and so on. It is not impossible to find groups of men not regularly living with women but there are usually features of their lives which introduce other variables. Most groups of non-menstruating women, mainly those who are before puberty or after the menopause, will differ from other women, not only as regards menstruation but on other important variables, not the least being age. Young women who have had a hysterectomy provide valuable control groups and though, fortunately, they are only found in restricted numbers they have occasionally appeared in studies. The studies which include men or non-menstruating women for comparison, in spite of these reservations, provide very useful information and the results are given in this book.

Most studies simply compare the same or different women at several points in the cycle. This work provides comparisons between different phases of the cycle and is of practical and theoretical value. It does not directly guarantee that the same variations do not exist independently of the cycle. Nevertheless, when reliable observations of such changes are continually demonstrated in representative groups and when no comparable fluctuations are found in non-menstruating individuals it becomes increasingly likely that the changes are specific to the menstrual cycle. Demonstration of specificity does not of itself provide the aetiology of the changes. Variations which are specific to the cycle may be due to hormonal, psychological or social factors having their effect, singly or in combination, through a number of intervening variables.

The contraceptive pill seems to offer great potential for comparisons between naturally-menstruating women and groups of pill-users, who do not ovulate and in whom certain hormonal levels are more constant throughout the month. There are, however, difficulties of interpretation which are worth discussing because of the frequent choice of pill-users as comparison groups. No-one doubts the scale of the repercussions of the contraceptive pill. In our society where it was so widely adopted it has profoundly affected social attitudes and personal behaviour. The social and psychological climate surrounding the contraceptive pill has to be borne in mind in assessing its effects on the menstrual cycle. We are not interested here in all aspects, only in the ways in which it affects the menstrual changes, but reiteration of certain characteristics may be helpful in appraising the published work. The two categories of oral contraceptive, combination and sequential, differ considerably in the way in which they provide hormones. The combination pills provide both oestrogen and progestogen in each tablet for 21 consecutive days. The sequential pills (no longer prescribed for contraception in Britain) have oestrogen alone for about 15 days, followed by oestrogen combined with progestogen for about 5 days. The sequential pill is therefore considered to mimic the natural hormonal variations of the cycle more closely than does the combination pill. Although not now used clinically, studies of the effects of the sequential pill on cyclical changes are of considerable theoretical interest. Within the two categories there are pills with different amounts of each hormone. The hormones provided by the tablets are not the same as the natural ones. The various oestrogen compounds which circulate naturally cannot be used because they are not absorbed by oral administration. The artificial progestogens are far from similar to natural progesterone and in fact, in certain parts of the body, the synthetic progestogens can act like oestrogens and in general have some effects quite opposite to those of natural progesterone.

Apart from these considerations, there are several points to be taken into account in assessing reports of the contraceptive pill on menstrual changes. Pill-users are a selected group, either by preference or by suitability for that method of contraception and are therefore not representative of the whole population. The high dropout rate leaves pill groups which are even less representative. Many studies rightly use a placebo procedure, so that all the groups to be compared swallow a pill, in an attempt to control all variables other than hormonal levels. This procedure is not entirely credible to the takers since with mock pills being used other contraceptives have to be introduced at the same time. In this case, there is no real control in the pill group of non-hormonal factors such as fears about the safety of oral contraceptives; increase or decrease in conflicts and anxieties about sexual freedom and about pregnancy; a tendency to use the pill as a scapegoat for many different problems. The various contraceptive pills differ from each other pharmacologically and have different effects depending, among other things, on the existing balance between oestrogen and progesterone in the body and/or different amounts of sensitivity to the synthetic hormones. The published studies of the effects of the contraceptive pill on menstrual changes which are included in this chapter and the next do not always give details of the type of drug used. Where the information is available it is included.

These are broad questions of methodology. In addition there are particular problems of measuring certain changes and these will be discussed in the relevant sections. This chapter reports the findings of systemic changes; studies on psychological and behavioural changes are given in the next chapter. Any classification of these variations is arbitrary and it is a matter of convenience rather than a reflection of any fundamental distinctions. The aim has been to present all relatively recent results which appear to have attempted rigorous investigation, in spite of the methodological difficulties discussed above. Other reports are sometimes cited, with reservations. Brief conclusions from the findings appear after each item. The changes described are consistently associated with the menstrual cycle. Although widespread, their incidence varies in different women and in each woman at different times.

SYSTEMIC CHANGES

THE FIVE SENSES

Sight, hearing, smell, touch and taste all reach a peak of sensitivity at ovulation time (Barris, Dawson, and Theiss, 1980; Diamond, Diamond, and Mast, 1972; Doty, Huggins, Snyder, and Lowry, 1981; Good, Geary, and Engen, 1976; Henkin, 1974; Le Magnen, 1952; Mair, Bouffard, Engen, and Morton, 1978; Robinson and Short, 1977; Wong and Tong, 1974). A report of no cyclical olfactory variation (Amoore, Popplewell, and Whissell-Beuchy, 1975) has not been supported by subsequent studies (Doty, Huggins, Snyder, and Lowry, 1981). Apart from the mid-cycle peak in all sensory modalities, there is no unequivocal statement to be made about levels during the rest of the cycle. The over-all cyclical patterns seem to vary considerably among the different senses (Doty, Huggins, Snyder and Lowry, 1981). The ovulatory peak appears to reflect real changes in sensitivity and cannot be attributed to changes in judgemental factors (Barris, Dawson, and Theiss, 1980; Doty, Huggins, Snyder, and Lowry, 1981; Good, Geary and Engen, 1976; Wong and Tong, 1974). Judgemental factors have been considered particularly important in the premenstrual phase and this was investigated for vision by Ward, Stone, and Sandman, 1978. It was found that impaired visual detection premenstrually compared with the rest of the cycle was not related to lowered confidence ratings or to mood levels. The studies which included a comparison group of men found no cyclical variation in them (Barris, Dawson, and Theiss, 1980; Diamond, Diamond, and Mast, 1972; Doty, Huggins, Snyder, and Lowry, 1981). One of those studies, of visual sensitivity, (Diamond, Diamond, and Mast, 1972) also included a small group of four women on combination oral contraceptives who did not have the ovulatory increase. Another of the studies, of olfactory sensitivity, (Doty, Huggins, Snyder, and Lowry, 1981) did find cyclical variation in women on combined oral contraceptives, but there were only three of them and the data on one of those were not complete. The authors nevertheless suggest that their findings may indicate that ovarian hormones are not the sole factor determining the mid-cycle peak, which may persist with certain dosages of contraceptive drugs.

An investigation of tactile sensitivity of the breast during the cycle found a peak just after mid-cycle and again at menstruation, and this peak was absent in women taking combined oral contraceptives (Robinson and Short, 1977). Another study also found a peak in breast sensitivity after mid-cycle in the luteal phase (Hilgers, Daly, Prebil, and Hilgers, 1981). The same authors report that no differences were found in oestrogen and progesterone levels in women with or without breast tenderness. Many clinical studies report breast tenderness between ovulation and menstruation. Whatever the mechanisms of this, and although one of its manifestations is a sensory change of the skin, it doubtless has a different aetiology from the other sensory changes.

It is plausible to suppose that the sensory peak has the biological purpose of increasing the probability, at the time of ovulation, of coitus and hence of conception. The biological plan appears to be fairly refined. For instance, one study found that whereas tactile sensitivity in general rises at ovulation, response to cutaneous pain actually decreases at that time (Buzzelli, Voegelin, Procacci, and Bozza, 1968); there is another report of minimal responsiveness to electric shock at mid-cycle (Tedford, Warren, and Flynn, 1977; see 'Conditioning' below). This combination of heightened touch, and reduced pain, sensitivity would encourage receptivity. Also the mid-cycle heightened sensory response appears to be so specific to ovulation that there are, for example, certain odours to which ovulating women are in general more sensitive than are men or non-ovulating women. This is said to be true, for example, of exaltolide, which is a musky-smelling substance found in male urine (Koelega and Koster, 1974; Le Magnen, 1948).

Within any modality, cyclical variation is specific to certain stimuli. Olfactory sensitivity, for example, varies to a greater or lesser extent in response to different odorants (Mair, Bouffard, Engen, and Morton, 1978). There are differing amounts of variation in responses to different auditory tasks (Haggard and Gaston, 1978). These differing degress of susceptibility to variation with the cycle among stimuli are doubtless a reflection of both biological and non-sensory (mainly judgemental) factors. The non-sensory influences are now, in most studies, controlled for by the use of signal detection methods and the relative importance of sensory and non-sensory factors in responses to any particular stimulus can be known. No simple relationship has been found between the sensory variations and fluctuations in any one hormone level (Haggard and Gaston, 1978), so that any effect of hormones must be indirect or in combination with other variables. One report already mentioned (Doty, Huggins, Snyder, and Lowry, 1981) did find significant positive correlations between both LH levels and olfactory sensitivity and between oestrogen levels and olfactory sensitivity. Since, however, the three women taking the oral contraceptives in this study showed similar cyclical fluctuations in olfactory sensitivity to the non-pill women the authors concluded that an association between levels of gonadal hormones and olfactory sensitivity is not established. They suggest that if, for instance, oestrogens are involved it may be in a permissive role. The authors point out the complexities of the possible relationship between hormonal and neural factors in producing the cyclical changes in sensitivity. They also suggest that different mechanisms, and different relationships between them, are operating for the various sensory modalities. This would also explain why not all the cyclical changes are uniform as regards precise timings, magnitude and pattern through the cycle.

The mechanisms appear to reflect rather finely the particular biological purpose of the variations. In the case of odorants, for example, it has been suggested that peripheral mechanisms differentially select different odorants, depending on their volatility (Mair, Bouffard, Engen, and Morton, 1978); this would be in the interests of increasing the probability of reproduction. One report, in seeking to explain the greater sensitivity changes for exaltolide than for other compounds, points out that it is similar in odour and chemical structure to a mammalian sex-attractant called muscone. It may be that exaltolide imitates a human pheromone. In support of this possibility the authors point out that some sex steroids secreted by human sweat glands and in urine have musk-like odours, and are detectable by police dogs (Good, Geary, and Engen, 1976).

Confirmation is needed of many of the details of both the manifestations and the mechanisms of the biological determinants of the sensory changes with the cycle. They are doubtless complex and far-reaching. Beach (1975) has pointed out for example that physiological mechanisms such as hormones, instead of changing sensory thresholds, may affect perception and thus alter or even reverse preferences for particular forms of stimulation. In addition to hormonal influences there are powerful and complex psychological and social factors. These are not only constantly being shaped and re-shaped by the effects of hormones, but also themselves temporarily and permanently affect responses to hormones. Beach refers to the 'interactions and interdependencies among the endocrine system, the individual's environment, and his behaviour'. This applies to the sensory fluctuations, and to all the changes discussed in this book.

Conclusions

There is ample evidence of observable changes with the cycle in certain aspects of sensory sensitivity, in all modalities. These variations cannot be explained by non-sensory factors. The changes are limited to specific stimuli and to particular types of response in any sensory modality. Hormonal and neural mechanisms are involved in various ways in the variations, which are presumed to create optimal conditions for conception. Psychological and social factors doubtless also contribute to the sensory variations.

BODILY CHANGES

Fluid retention

Fluid retention increases during the premenstruum (De Marchi, 1976; Doty, Huggins, Snyder, and Lowry, 1981; Gruba and Rohrbaugh, 1975; Janowsky, Berens, and Davis, 1973; Silbergeld, Brast, and Noble, 1971; Voda, 1980; Wilcoxon, Schrader, and Sherif, 1976). This is one of the best-known and most often reported symptoms of the premenstrual phase. There is said to be an increase, a smaller one, around ovulation time (Reeves, Garvin, and McElin, 1971). Two studies (Doty, Huggins, Snyder, and Lowry, 1981; Wilcoxon, Schrader, and Sherif, 1976) also monitored a group of men and found no cyclical variations. As regards the effects of the contraceptive pill on these changes, reports differ, probably due to insufficient regard for differently constituted pills, different age groups, and so on. There are two findings of less fluid retention with the combination pill (Moos, 1969) and with a non-specified type of pill (Wilcoxon, Schrader, and Sherif, 1976); one report of no cyclical variation on combined pills (Doty, Huggins, Snyder, and Lowry, 1981) and one finding of increased retention with combination pills (Silbergeld, Brast, and Noble, 1971). In this last study, however, the drug used was Enovid, the earliest oral contraceptive to be licensed in the United States.

Fluid retention is thought to be related to progesterone withdrawal, and the possibility of an ultimately hormonal role is supported by the fact that there appears to be no cyclical variation in men and less or none in women on combined contraceptive pills. Dalton (1979) has claimed that progesterone relieves water retention. Many writers have suggested that the observed premenstrual fluid retention is related to the mood changes of that phase (see for example Bell, Christie, and Venables, 1975; Janowsky, Berens, and Davis, 1973; Voda, 1980), and more detailed demonstration of this suggestion would be welcome. Janowsky, Berens, and Davis (1973) have proposed a model of premenstrual symptoms, including fluid retention, being related to the renin–angiotensin–aldosterone system and this is mentioned again in the section on potassium and sodium levels. The exact mechanisms in the premenstrual retention of water are not yet clear. Voda (1980) found a significant correlation between progesterone and aldosterone, and no correlation between either of these and any other biochemical, physical, or subjective variable. There is a full discussion of fluid balance during the normal menstrual cycle and in premenstrual syndrome in Reid and Yen (1981).

Weight gain

There is a premenstrual weight increase in the order of 1 to 5 pounds, possibly more (Freedman, Ramcharan, Hoag and Goldfien, 1974; Janowsky, Berens and Davis, 1973; Smith, 1975). In the first study, weight was found to be at its lowest point around Day 21 of the cycle; this is not entirely in accord with studies of women staying on metabolic wards, where a luteal-phase *gain* was found (see Voda, 1980). Combination pill-users experience less weight gain, as well as less fluctuations with the cycle (Freedman, Ramcharan, Hoag, and Goldfien, 1974; Moos, 1969; Paige, 1971). Sequential pill-users showed a pattern of fluctuation similar to the non-users (Freedman, Ramcharan, Hoag, and Goldfien, 1974). The premenstrual weight gain is doubtless related to fluid retention though investigation of the influence of changing eating habits would be useful (see Voda, 1980). The detailed mechanisms of the observed increase in weight are not known.

Carbohydrate metabolism

Early reports found a lowered carbohydrate tolerance in the time around menstruation and, more specifically, a hypoglycaemic response to sugar tolerance tests premenstrually (Morton, Additon, Addison, Hunt, and Sullivan, 1953). Diabetic coma was found to be more frequent and insulin requirement increased around menstruation (Southam and Gonzaga, 1965).One later report, on glucose levels, found a steady rise through the cycle until the last 5 to 8 days when they began to decline. This was similar for combination-pill users. In women taking a sequential pill there was a drop around Day 20 (Freedman, Ramcharan, Hoag, and Goldfien, 1974). A partially-reported study found that food intake varies significantly with the cycle, the most marked effect being that protein ingestion is lowest premenstrually and at the beginning of menstruation (Abraham, Beumont, Argall, and Haywood 1981). Over-all food intake is said to be greater during the ten days after ovulation than the ten days before it (Dalvit, 1981). Increased premenstrual cravings for sweets have been reported (Smith and Sauder, 1969; Sutherland and Stewart, 1965). The first study found an association between craving for sweets and premenstrual depression and fluid retention. The authors believe this is a reflection of a common association with some other factor. Reid and Yen (1981) in a summary of the published work concluded that the limited evidence suggests that carbohydrate tolerance may be increased premenstrually and this may account for the craving for sweets experienced by some women at that time. They believe, though, that reactive hypoglycaemia would not explain other premenstrual symptoms.

There is thought to be a relationship between hormonal levels and carbohydrate metabolism but the results are not entirely consistent and need further demonstration (Reinke, Ansah, and Voigt, 1972). More generally, a systematic relationship between gonadal hormones and both ingestive behaviour and taste reactivity has been postulated (Weizenbaum, Benson, Solomon, and Brehony, 1980).

Alcohol metabolism

A report of several studies on alcohol metabolism in women found that they become more intoxicated (obtain a higher mean peak blood alcohol level) than men following a given dose of alcohol calculated on body weight (Jones and Jones, 1976). This was true of various alcohol doses. The authors suggest that this finding might be related to the difference in body water content in men and women. Men have a higher proportion of water to body weight (55% to 65%) than women (45% to 55%). Since alcohol is distributed throughout the body in proportion to the water content of the body tissues, the alcohol tends to be more diluted in the body of males than in females. The same authors report variations in alcohol metabolism through the menstrual cycle. The highest peak blood alcohol level, following a given dose of alcohol, was during the premenstrual phase. A group of men showed no cyclical variation, see Figure 6. The mean peak of the group of women was significantly higher than that of the men; the premenstrual peak was significantly higher than that during both the menstrual and intermenstrual times. Women taking oral contraceptives showed signs of a decreased rate of alcohol metabolism, as did women who were taking hormonal supplements after a hysterectomy. Belfer and Shader (1976) studied a group of alcoholic women, the majority of whom related their drinking to the menstrual cycle and, in particular, to the premenstrual phase. Within this group, there was no overt disturbance of menstrual functions; nor was there any correlation with severity of premenstrual symptoms. The general observation that alcohol may sometimes increase rather than reduce anxiety levels was shown in one

38

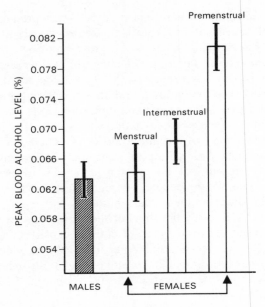

Figure 6. Mean (± s.e.) peak blood alcohol levels for males and for females tested at different times in the menstrual cycle. The premenstrual levels were significantly higher than the menstrual, intermenstrual and male levels. Redrawn, by permission of The New York Academy of Sciences, from Jones and Jones (1976). Alcohol effects in women during the menstrual cycle. *Annals of the New York Academy of Sciences*, **273**, 576–587

study to apply to women in the luteal phase of the cycle whereas the effect was not found in the follicular phase (Logue, Linnoila, Wallman, and Erwin, 1981).

It has been suggested that the cyclical variations in alcohol metabolism may be related to oestrogen levels (Jones and Jones, 1976) but this would need further demonstration.

Potassium and sodium levels

These appear to be higher in the last half of the cycle (Bell, Christie, and Venables, 1975). One study, which also found these higher levels in the last half, reported a drop premenstrually (Voda, 1980). These changes are interesting because they can be measured objectively and are known to be related in general to mood shifts, both in psychiatric and non-psychiatric groups of women (Bell, Christie, and Venables, 1975). There is also a report that negative feelings, weight and the potassium/sodium ratio vary together, with the cycle, all being elevated in the premenstrual phase (Janowsky, Berens, and Davis, 1973). The findings of this relationship led Janowsky to suggest that the premenstrual mood might be associated with activation of the renin-angiotensin-aldosterone system, but later studies have not supported this idea (see Steiner and Carroll, 1977). There are no reports on changes in potassium and sodium levels with the contraceptive pill.

The findings on potassium and sodium through the cycle need further clarification.

Gastrointestinal function

Transit time has been measured together with oestrogen and progesterone levels, through the menstrual cycle. A significant association was found; transit time was prolonged in the luteal phase, when progesterone levels were increased (Wald, Van Thiel, Hoechstetter, Gavaler, Egler, Verm, Scott, and Lester, 1981). The authors make no claim of a causal relationship but they point out that a similar association is found during pregnancy when progesterone levels are also raised. Further confirmation of these observations might lead to a better understanding of some of the reported discomfort in the phase leading up to menstruation.

Allergic reactions

There are early clinical reports of asthma and skin eruptions increasing in the premenstruum and, to a lesser extent, during menstruation (Dalton, 1964b; Southam and Gonzaga, 1965). A more recent study found that asthma worsened just prior to or at menstruation and that there was a significant reduction in peak expiratory flow rate at that time (Hanley, 1981). In a study which measured allergic response to histamine throughout the 24 hours, sensitivity rose from post-ovulation, throughout the luteal and premenstrual phase to a peak on Day 1 of the cycle, after which there was a sharp decline (Smolensky, Reinberg, Lee, and McGovern, 1974). This suggests that any clinical reports of increased incidence of asthma and skin eruptions during menstruation may reflect the continuing overt manifestations of the heightened premenstrual sensitivity. More generally, there are reports of increased rhinitis premenstrually (Dalton, 1979) and of some cyclical extragenital bleeding, especially in the nose (Dunn, 1972). Further investigation is needed of the observation that the mucous membranes of the nose and the uterus respond to the same hormonal stimuli. Skin disturbances and the degree of sensitivity to histamine were reduced in combination pill-users and no cyclical variations were found in them (Smolensky, Reinberg, Lee, and McGovern, 1974).

The data are suggestive of a hormonal basis to the observed changes in allergic responses with the cycle.

Dysmenorrhea

There is ample evidence that reported abdominal pain varies with the cycle and that it is at a maximum at menstruation (Doty, Huggins, Snyder, and Lowry, 1981; Garling and Roberts, 1980; Gruba and Rohrbraugh, 1975; Janowsky, Berens, and Davis, 1973; Silbergeld, Brast, and Noble, 1971; Webster, 1980; Wilcoxon, Schrader, and Sherif, 1976). The same fluctuations are not found in men (Doty, Huggins, Snyder and Lowry, 1981; Wilcoxon, Schrader and Sherif, 1976), non-menstruating (hysterectomized) women assessed on a group of physical symptoms which included abdominal pain (Beumont, Richards, and Gelder, 1975), or in users of contraceptive pills of various types (Culberg, 1972; Herzberg and Coppen, 1970; Moos, 1969; Silbergeld, Brast, and Noble, 1971; Wilcoxon, Schrader, and Sherif, 1976). Dysmenorrhea has been defined by Dalton (1964b) as pain during menstruation but she herself proposes two forms. One, spasmodic, starts on the first day of menstruation with spasms of pain in the pelvic region; the other, congestive, is manifest before menstruation as dull, aching pain, is part of the premenstrual syndrome and is relieved by the onset of menstruation. This view of two types of dysmenorrhea, spasmodic and congestive, and the corollary that any women in any one cycle will not suffer from both, since they are due to an opposite imbalance of the oestrogen/progesterone ratio, has gained wide credence. Some studies, however, have failed to find support for the distinction (see Webster, 1980). For discussion purposes, it seems preferable to distinguish dysmenorrhea (pain with menstruation) as one entity, and pain in the premenstrual phase as another, even though many of the studies cited above do not make this distinction.

As regards dysmenorrhea, observations are based on questionnaires which use many different words, such as cramps, pain, abdominal pain, abdominal discomfort. A general point worth noting is that a large number of studies have used the Menstrual Distress Questionnaire (Moos, 1969) and have given information about the pain scale of that questionnaire without providing a breakdown of the score on the constituent items. These items are muscle stiffness, headache, cramps, backache, fatigue, general aches, and pains. It is therefore difficult to be precise about cyclical variation and prevalence, but reports of pain during menstruation are very frequent.

The precise aetiology is unclear. Primary dysmenorrhea, that is, pain with menstruation with an absence of gross pathology, appears to be a result of hypercontractability of the uterus. This is due more to raised tonus and dysrhythmia of the contractions rather than to changes in the intensity of the contractions (Filler and Hall, 1970). As with all smooth muscle pain, uterine pain is often referred so that there is frequently a dull ache in the lower back and legs. This type of pain is in general thought to be liable to exacerbation by psychological factors, through an effect on muscular contraction and vasoconstriction (Nicassio, 1980). The role of hormonal mechanisms in the hypercontractability of the uterus is not clear. One recently reported study found no correlation between the symptoms of dysmenorrhea and the oestrogen/progesterone ratio (Webster, 1980); another found no relationship between the scores on the Menstrual Distress Questionnaire Pain Scale and any of the hormones measured—FSH, LH, oestrogens, progesterone, testosterone (Doty, Huggins, Snyder, and Lowry, 1981). Prostaglandins are known to be involved in the contractions of the uterus during the menstrual flow, and also in the determination of volume and duration of bleeding (see Chapter 8). It is thought that these prostaglandins are produced in the endometrium, where they are found in high concentrations as menstruation approaches (Yen and Jaffe, 1978). With more detailed demonstration of the role of prostaglandins in the menstrual cycle, the physiological factors in dysmenorrhea will probably be clarified. Dysmenorrhea is reportedly relieved by progestogen-dominated oral contraceptives (Culberg, 1972), but there is very little information about this.

Premenstrual pain

Pain in the premenstrual phase is reported, in the studies cited in the first paragraph above, but with lesser frequency than pain at menstruation. This premenstrual pain is also qualitatively different. It is described as a dull, aching pain in the lower abdomen. It is often accompanied by feelings of heaviness, fluid retention, aches and pains in other areas of the body, and various other so-called premenstrual symptoms. It is relieved by the onset of menstrual bleeding. As with dysmenorrhea, the precise aetiology is not clear. Dalton, as mentioned already, has suggested that women with a relative excess of oestrogen over progesterone are more likely to suffer from premenstrual pain (which she designates congestive dysmenorrhea). A study already referred to above (Webster, 1980) found that, in the premenstrual phase, the progesterone/oestrogen ratio was significantly correlated only with general achiness. The author points out that as there was also a significant positive correlation between progesterone level and general achiness this indicates that the ratio is 'probably representing its numerator'. Some clinical workers find that progesterone is effective in reducing premenstrual pain (Dalton, 1979). A controlled study of progesterone and placebo effects on premenstrual syndrome found that both placebo and progesterone at 200 mg.b.d. dosage reduced pain, but that placebo was a more effective treatment than 400 mg.b.d. of progesterone (Sampson, 1979). The available information does not firmly indicate the precise nature of the physiological mechanisms of premenstrual pain, nor of the psychological factors which probably also play their part.

Mid-cycle pain

This is also known as intermenstrual pain or *Mittelschmerz* and is associated with ovulation. Indeed it is one of the four presently available signs and symptoms of ovulation, the other three being the course of the basal body temperature, intermenstrual bleeding, and cervical mucorrhea (Vollman, 1977). It is an acute pain in the lower abdominal area which may be on the left side, the right side, in the middle or in combination. It is often associated with other, less specific, symptoms such as low backache and abdominal bloating. On average, the onset of intermenstrual pain precedes the rise of the basal body temperature by two days with a range of −9 to +2 days (Vollman, 1977). It may be observed in women throughout their reproductive life and is absent during pregnancy and amenorrhea. Detailed observations of mid-cycle pain have been made by Hilgers, Daly, Prebil, and Hilgers (1981). Right- and left-sided pain were noted in 12.5% of the cycles investigated, mid-line pain in 20.3%, and all three together in 32.8%. The same authors measured the mean oestradiol levels for Day 3 through Day 1 prior to the estimated time of ovulation and found no significant difference in women with and without abdominal pain. The precise cause of mid-cycle pain is unknown. Vollman (1977) suggests that it is due to hyperperistalsis in the uterine tube. An early study found swelling and accumulation of fluid in the tube (Doyle, 1951). Hilgers, Daly, Prebil, and Hilgers (1981) proposed that the pain may be the outcome of a combination of phsyiological events. Among these would be peritoneal irritation, caused at times by tubal peristalsis, tubal hyperaemia, pre-ovulatory follicular distension, and/or post-ovulatory collection of fluid.

Headache

There is not a great deal of information on headache separately from other pain. Headache seems to increase in the premenstrual phase (Dalton, 1964; Garling and Roberts, 1980; Kessel and Coppen, 1963; Nattero, 1982). One of these studies (Garling and Roberts, 1980) found a similar raised incidence during menstruation. The prevalence of headache is reported to be undiminished by the combination pill (Herzberg and Coppen, 1970; Silbergeld, Brast, and Noble, 1971). In a small group of men no cyclical variation was found on the Menstrual Distress Questionnaire Pain Scale, which includes headache (Doty, Huggins, Snyder, and Lowry, 1981). A study of migraine sufferers found that in only 14% of the 142 women surveyed was migraine related to the events of the menstrual cycle. Nevertheless, mean over-all oestrogen and progesterone levels were significantly higher in migraine patients than in non-sufferers for most of the cycle, with the most striking differences in progesterone levels in the luteal phase. No specific hormonal changes were associated with a migraine attack (Epstein, Hockaday, and Hockaday, 1975). In an investigation of specifically premenstrual migraine, Nattero (1982) found that both oestradiol and progesterone levels were significantly higher in migraine sufferers than in controls on Day 26 of the cycle. This author believes that headache of a migraine type is associated with the neurophysiological events of the premenstrual phase. The possible factors which contribute to any cyclical variation in headache cannot yet be stated with any certainty.

Other bodily changes

There are significant premenstrual and/or menstrual increases reported in various other bodily symptoms, notably, swelling of hands and feet, muscle stiffness, and backache (Beumont, Richards, and Gelder, 1975; Garling and Roberts, 1980; Moos, 1969; Paige, 1971). These increases in physical symptoms are reported to be reduced in women taking various types of contraceptive pill (Moos, 1969) and in combination pill-users (Paige, 1971; Silbergeld, Brast, and Noble, 1971). It is widely assumed that there is a physiological basis to these paramenstrual manifestations, and doubtless psychological factors also make their contribution.

Conclusions

In all the categories of bodily functions in this section significant changes with the cycle have been noted. Except for intermenstrual and menstrual pain, the changes are usually reported to be most marked in the premenstrual phase. Although physiological mechanisms are clearly implicated their detailed operation is not yet known. Psychological factors may also be expected to contribute to the changes but how this comes about is not clear.

CHANGES RELATED TO ILLNESS, ACCIDENT, AND DEATH

There is a very early report of three flying accidents in which the women pilots were menstruating at the time (Whitehead, 1934). It would be interesting to have confirmation of possible menstrually-related flying accidents and, if such a relationship does exist, whether it is simply a part of the reported paramenstrual proneness to accidents in general (see for example O'Connor, Shelley, and Stern, 1974) or whether accidents while flying, which involves highly complex behaviour, are even more likely.

Mothers take their children to the doctors more often in the premenstrual and menstrual phases (Dalton, 1966; Tuch, 1975). The fact that this is true of the menstrual period as well as premenstrually suggests that it may be rather more than just a reflection of the negative feelings of the mothers in the premenstrual phase. The increase in visits during menstruation, when there is a reported release of emotional tension and gradual relaxation, cannot be directly explained by negative mood. It may be that there are tangible physical reactions on the part of the children to their mother's premenstrual mood, and these reactions require treatment over a period which extends into the menstrual phase. Perhaps two factors are at work, that is, a direct effect of the mother's anxious and pessimistic behaviour premenstrually, and the actual appearance of symptoms in the children in response to the mother's premenstrual mood extending beyond that particular phase. Dalton, who first drew attention to the phenomenon (Dalton, 1966), concluded that not only were women, just before and during menstruation, unable to assess the severity of their children's symptoms but also that the children respond by feelings of ill health to the decrease in their mother's well-being. The later study, above (Tuch, 1975), has confirmed that the numbers of children brought to the doctor increases in the paramenstruum and that children brought in at that time were less ill and had been ill for a shorter period of time than those brought in intermenstrually. This author also suggests that both the mother's feelings and the proneness of the children to actually become ill then are salient factors. It is not known whether the contraceptive pill has any systematic effect on these changes in children's visits to the doctor.

Reactivity to stress may increase premenstrually but this needs confirmation. One study, using the objective method of measuring levels of cortisol, found a premenstrual increase. This cyclical variation did not take place in combination pill-users (Marinari, Leshner, and Doyle, 1976; see Figure 7).

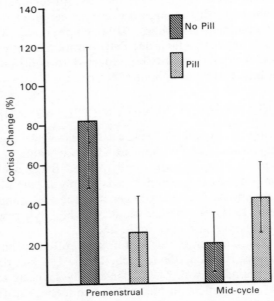

Figure 7. Means and standard errors of percentage cortisol change in a stressful test situation in women taking or not taking a contraceptive pill. Reproduced by permission of Pergamon Press, from Marinari, Leshner, and Doyle (1976). Menstrual cycle status and adrenocortical reactivity to psychological stress. *Psychoneuroendocrinology*, **1**, 213–218

In the same study, the women were asked to report their reactions to the experimentally-induced stress, and no cyclical variations were found in these reports. So that although most of the women were not subjectively aware of experiencing more stress premenstrually, the physiological measure of their stress level increased at that time. Another investigation (Wilcoxon, Schrader and Sherif, 1976) used a stress inventory which included stressful events related to life activities, rather than to experimental stress, and, with this kind of situation, premenstrual and menstrual increases in stress were reported by the women. In this study users of an unspecified contraceptive pill showed a premenstrual rise in stress but none during menstruation. A group of men reported no cyclical variation in stress. One study found no cyclical variation in physiological responsiveness to stress, i.e. in cortisol levels (Abplanalp, Livingston, Rose, and Sandwisch, 1977). Further studies of objectively and subjectively measured stress would provide a useful assessment of the extent to which this fluctuates with the cycle and the degree to which women are aware of the effects the cycle has upon them in this respect.

Various illnesses are reported to have a more frequent onset in the premenstrual phase than at any other time in the cycle (Southam and Gonzaga, 1965). They include hepatitis, influenza, and pneumonia. There are early reports of a cyclical pattern of acute attacks of various existing illnesses (see for example Richter, 1968). Frequently reported in early studies was a premenstrual increase in epileptic attacks (Laidlaw, 1956; Morell, 1959; Southam and Gonzaga, 1965). These findings are not borne out by a later study which indicates more seizures in the follicular phase and less throughout the second half of the cycle (Backstrom, 1977). In a study in 1976 Backstrom found a positive correlation between number of epileptic seizures and the mean oestrogen/progesterone ratios; he found a negative correlation with progesterone levels. There is a later report (Rosciszewska, 1980) of a four-year investigation of 69 women with epilepsy which found that 58% had increased seizures premenstrually and 9% during menstruation. This author believes that this increased incidence in the paramenstruum may be partly related to progesterone levels. Clearly, more information is needed on the pattern of epileptic attacks with the cycle. Sickness in industry, accidents, and acute hospital admissions all reach a peak just before menstruation (see O'Connor, Shelley, and Stern, 1974). More detailed studies are needed since, as was said in Chapter 1, periodic patterns in illness (not always monthly) are observed occasionally in men, and in women independently of the cycle.

As regards patterns of death with the cycle, some information is provided in an early study of post-mortem coroners' reports of the wombs of 102 women age 18 to 46 who died of various causes (MacKinnon, MacKinnon, and Thomson, 1959). The same study will be mentioned again in connection with suicide. Thirteen of the 102 deaths occurred in the first half of the cycle, 89 during the last half. Looking more closely at the different phases of the cycle, only 2 of the 102 deaths occurred during the time of the menstrual flow and very few deaths occurred mid-cycle. Of the 89 deaths in the last half of the cycle, 60 were during Days 17 to 23, and 29 were during the last 7 days before menstruation. So that the peak time for these deaths was the mid-luteal phase, followed by the premenstrual week. Obviously, the deaths dealt with in a coroner's mortuary are not representative of all deaths, since they receive suicides and accidental deaths, and only receive deaths from disease in exceptional circumstances. Of the 102 deaths in this study, for example, 50% were due to suicides and accidents whereas the figure for the whole population is about 5%. The interesting fact remains that nearly all of the deaths of women age 18 to 46 coming to the mortuary took place in the last half of the cycle. This kind of study, where post-mortem reports are available, are particularly valuable. It is worth noting that the higher incidence of accident rates, and in fact of suicide and crime, in the premenstrual phase are apparently still lower than the rates for men (Davidson, 1978).

There are no quantitative reports of the possible impact of the contraceptive pill on any cyclical patterns in illness and death.

There are reservations to be had about many of the findings in this section. Some of the items need to be confirmed by more rigorous methods. The persistent reports of variations in the incidence of illness, accident, and death with the cycle are nevertheless telling and cannot be ignored. The origins of the fluctuations are unknown. We can only make the trite assumption of a multiplicity of factors operating in various combinations for each of the changes. These factors would probably include, in addition to hormonal changes of the menstrual cycle, the influence of other biological cycles and many psychological and social factors.

Conclusions

The observations on illness, accidents, and death, although they require some detailed verification, suggest that there are certain fluctuations which are related to the menstrual cycle. The causal factors in these fluctuations have yet to be determined.

NERVOUS SYSTEM ACTIVITY

The close inter-relationship between the nervous and endocrine systems is constantly apparent. In view of the reciprocal influences of the two systems on each other it seems likely that nervous system activity is an important intermediary mechanism in the ways in which the hormonal changes of the cycle are experienced. This is discussed in Chapter 8. Most of the work on nervous system activity during the cycle has not specifically attempted to measure central and peripheral processes separately. The frequently different patterns in the activity of the central nervous system and the peripheral autonomic nervous system in general is well known (Claridge, 1967; Lacey, 1967; Martin, 1973). In addition, Thayer (1978) has presented evidence of a cortical/autonomic distinction in terms of self-awareness of activation. More specifically, independent variation in the two systems during the menstrual cycle has been suggested (Asso, 1978; Asso and Braier, 1982; Engel and Hildebrandt, 1974). The distinction will therefore be made in reviewing the published work. Since between them the central and autonomic nervous systems co-ordinate and control all information to and from the body as well as all internal adjustments, any changes with the cycle will have fundamental repercussions on the body and on behaviour and feelings. In spite of their importance, the quality and quantity of information on levels of activity in the central and autonomic nervous systems is limited. Although a great deal is known about their structure and the principles on which they operate, the exact measurement of changes in activity has proved difficult. The reliability of the various measures, and the relationships between them are not known with any certainty. There are nevertheless some indications of changes which appear to be related to the menstrual cycle, and these would merit more investigation.

Central nervous system activity

A variety of measures which are said to reflect levels of activity in the central nervous system have been used. Some studies have unfortunately compared only broad phases of the cycle, for instance the whole of the pre-ovulatory with the whole of the post-ovulatory time. In general, these reports indicate some lowering of central nervous system activity in the phase from after ovulation to menstruation (Grant and Pryse-Davies, 1968; Klaiber, Broverman, Vogel, and Kobayashi, 1974; Vogel, Broverman, and Klaiber, 1971). One report of findings which are not in agreement with the others was said by the authors to contain a possible artefact and they are carrying out further investigations to control for this factor (Creutzfeldt, Arnold, Becker, Langenstein, Tirsch, Wilhelm, and Wuttke, 1976). Studies of more finely defined phases show a decline in central nervous system activity in the premenstrual phase compared with the rest of the cycle (Asso and Braier, 1982; Belmaker, Murphy, Wyatt, and Loriaux, 1974; De Marchi and Tong, 1972; Engel and Hildebrandt, 1974; Kopell, Lunde, Clayton, and Moos, 1969). One study specified peak central nervous sensitivity at ovulation with low points premenstrually, at the beginning of menstruation, and at the mid-follicular time (Wong and Tong, 1974). One study, of sex differences, found cyclical variations in auditory after-effects which the authors take to be a measure of arousability, presumably of the central nervous system. In the group of women, highest arousability (lowest threshold) was at mid-cycle; the low point of arousability was at the premenstrual phase. In the group of men there was no cyclical variation and their consistent level of arousal was lower than that of women at any time in the cycle, though this difference did not reach statistical significance (Satinder and Mastronardi, 1974). There is a report of an investigation of kinaesthetic after-effect which is said to

48

reflect a central modulator mechanism which controls the subjective intensity
of incoming stimulation. It was found that the kinaesthetic after-effect reduction (damping down of stimulation) was greatest premenstrually, and at the
beginning of menstruation. There is no suggestion in the report of any cyclical
variation in the male comparison groups which were included (Baker, Kostin,
Mishara, and Parker, 1979). There is one report on habituation of skin
responses to successive auditory stimuli which is used by the authors as an
index of capacity to selectively inattend to stimuli and is related to central
nervous excitation. Arousal was high until ovulation after which it fell
sharply, only to rise again at the beginning of the next cycle (Friedman and
Meares, 1979; see Figure 8). An investigation of the cyclical course of an
index of brain activity, the contingent negative variation (CNV) is reported.
The highest mean amplitude of CNV (highest brain activation) was at mid-
cycle, the lowest point was around Day 22, with the next rise at the start of
menstruation. A group of men showed no variation and their constant level
was similar to the lowest women's values, around Day 22 (Abramovitz and
Dubrovsky, 1980). One study, (Parlee, 1980) had the purpose of clarifying

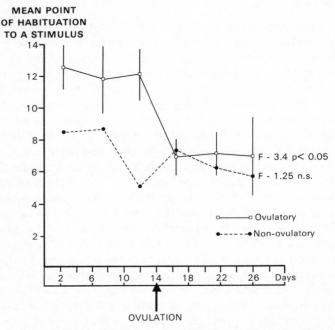

Figure 8. Change in mean point of habituation to a stimulus,
for ovulatory and for non-ovulatory (pill) cycles. Habituation
point varied significantly with phase of the cycle for ovulatory
cycles only. Reprinted with permission of the publisher, from
Friedman and Meares (1979). The menstrual cycle and habituation. *Psychosomatic Medicine*, **41**, 369–381. Copyright 1979
by The American Psychosomatic Society, Inc.

the nature of an activation and of a mood questionnaire, relating these to gross motor activity and seeing whether this is related to menstrual cycle phase. The activation questionnaire is said to distinguish between cortical and autonomic activity (Thayer, 1978). Parlee did not find the usually reported decline in central activation in the luteal and/or premenstrual phases. In fact the highest level was found premenstrually. Since this finding is rather unexpected the explanation may reside in the nature of the experiment and the group of subjects. The scores on the autonomic dimension in that study are mentioned in the next subsection below. There is very little information about the effects of the contraceptive pill on central nervous system activity. One of the studies above (Wong and Tong, 1974) found none of the cyclical variations with the combination pill. It seems likely, however, that this partly depends on the precise constituents of the drugs, particularly on the oestrogen/progestogen ratio (Grant and Pryse-Davies, 1968). The study, above, of Friedman and Meares (1979) found that the cyclical variations in skin response to auditory stimuli did not occur in women taking low-dose combination oral contraceptives.

The findings suggest that central nervous system activity may be lower in the premenstrual phase than at other times in the cycle, or this may be a tendency throughout the luteal and premenstrual phases. In view of the difficulties of measurement and of one or two inconsistent findings further information will be needed before definite conclusions can be drawn.

Autonomic nervous system activity

The autonomic nervous system is worth looking at in some detail because of its importance not only in emotion and feeling but also in the learning of behaviour and symptoms (this latter point is discussed again in the section on conditioning, and in Chapter 8). Appraisal of the work on the autonomic nervous system is complicated by the inherent difficulties of measurement. Because of the fragmentation of autonomic responses and of the wide variety of responses within and among individuals, the results have not been entirely clear-cut and have to be interpreted with reservations. Some studies using self-report measures of autonomic manifestations (Gruba and Rohrbraugh, 1975; Moos, Kopell, Melges, Yalom, Lunde, Clayton, and Hamburg, 1969) and some using other indices (Asso and Beech, 1975; Vila and Beech, 1977; Wineman, 1971) indicate increased activity in the premenstrual phase. Pulse rate is higher premenstrually, though the precise location of the rise depends somewhat on cycle length (Engel and Hilderbrandt, 1974). One study (Little and Zahn, 1974) using various different indices of autonomic activity, exemplifies the fragmentation of responses, with some being higher premenstrually and some not (e.g. skin conductance level rises from the mid-luteal time through the premenstrual phase; heart rate rises two to three days premenstrually and then drops sharply). Another study (Bell, Christie, and Venables, 1975) indicates increased autonomic activity in the post-ovulatory phase.

An intensive study of blood pressure in one subject found that both systolic and diastolic measures were higher from Day 22 (Williams, Levine, Teslow, and Halberg, 1980). A study already mentioned above (Asso and Braier, 1982) found evidence of raised autonomic activity premenstrually compared with intermenstrually. Another report mentioned (Parlee, 1980) found no significant variations with the cycle on a dimension of a self-report scale which is said to reflect autonomic activation (Thayer, 1978), though the premenstrual score was very slightly higher than at other points in the cycle. One study (Slade and Jenner, 1979) found no significant changes with the cycle in autonomic indices, either in seven normally-menstruating women or in seven women using the contraceptive pill, but the authors express some reservations about the results. A study of olfactory sensitivity which also measured, among other things, heart rate, found that this measure rose premenstrually but the rise did not reach statistical significance. There was no variation in heart rate in three men who acted as controls, nor in three women taking a contraceptive pill (Doty, Huggins, Snyder, and Lowry, 1981). In general, the main findings as regards the effect of the contraceptive pill on autonomic activation is of little or no variation in women taking a combination pill as opposed to no pill (Bell, Christie, and Venables, 1975).

Although there is some indication of a mid-luteal through premenstrual rise in autonomic activation the question of the extent of changes, and of which autonomic variables are involved, is still not settled. The difficulties of measurement are compounded by the fact that, even when physiological changes are not great, subjective feelings of high arousal may be present. This may partly explain why the findings on actual autonomic changes are not as entirely consistent as women's own reports, (Asso, 1978). It has been shown that in general there is only a weak relationship between a person's perception of autonomic responses and actual amount of autonomic discharge (Mandler, 1975). Past experience of events that have been the occasion for autonomic arousal can give rise again to perception of autonomic arousal (blushing, shaking, feelings of agitation, and so forth). Relatively small degrees of arousal may be perceived as more extreme, or may draw increasing attention, under some conditions. The premenstrual phase, for example, could evoke feelings and reponses which are not necessarily accompanied by all of the original physiological changes and which are the result of learned responses. This does not mean that there is not a continuing hormonal and physical basis to the changes but rather that, with time, a complex pattern of learning is overlaid upon them. If some of the mechanisms of this type of learning can be understood, within the context of the menstrual cycle, the practical implications might be considerable.

Conclusions

Conclusions about cyclical changes in central and autonomic nervous system activity are necessarily tentative at present. There are indications of different patterns in the central and in the autonomic nervous systems. Levels of central nervous system activity appear to be lower premenstrually than intermenstrually whereas autonomic activation is higher premenstrually than intermenstrually. The general assumption is that, where systematic changes are observed, these are related to the hormonal changes, and the basis of these assumptions will be given in Chapter 8. In turn, there are reasons to suppose that there is a functional relationship between nervous system activity and the subjective experience of the changes with the menstrual cycle. Some work has found agreement between objective measures of nervous system activity and subjective experience in general (Thayer, 1970) and with the cycle (Bell, Christie, and Venables, 1975; Belmaker, Murphy, Wyatt, and Loriaux, 1974; Janowsky, Berens, and Davis, 1973; Little and Zahn, 1974). One of the methods by which nervous system activity may become reflected in behaviour and feelings is conditioning, and this will now be mentioned briefly.

CONDITIONING

As a form of learning, conditioning is an important determinant of behaviour in general and of symptoms in particular. There are reports of a premenstrual increase in susceptibility to aversive conditioning (Asso and Beech, 1975; Vila and Beech, 1977, 1978). The last two reports studied only phobic patients. They indicate that in women taking a contraceptive pill there is an even greater susceptibility to acquiring skin responses (Vila and Beech, 1977) and similarly for heart-rate responses (Vila and Beech, 1978). The authors are aware that these findings are surprising since the usual effect of the combination pill is to reduce or eliminate many cyclical variations. Further results on conditioning and oral contraceptives would be useful. Sensitivity to shock was found to gradually increase from after ovulation rising to a peak after menstruation. No such variations were found in a control group of men or in a group of women taking combination pills (Tedford, Warren, and Flynn, 1977; see Figure 9). Koeske (1976, 1977) found enhanced sensitivity to strong stimulation premenstrually. Montgomery (1979) also reports a finding of heightened sensitivity and responsiveness premenstrually in ten women. A control group of ten men showed no cyclical variation, and also a consistently lower level of sensitivity. The findings of one study (Strauss, Schultheiss, and Cohen, 1983) do not agree with the other reports. Premenstrual levels of autonomic reactivity and of acquisition of conditioned responses were not significantly different from those in the four days immediately following menstrual flow. The choice of the post-menstrual days as a comparison point may at least partly explain these divergent results. It is possible that the most marked contrast is between the premenstrual and the mid-cycle phases, at least as regards sensitivity to aversive stimuli.

52

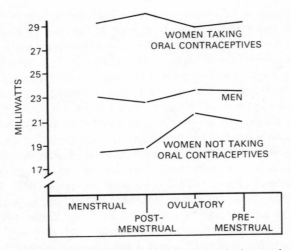

Figure 9. Average shock threshold in each menstrual phase. Variations with the cycle were significant only in the non-pill group, the maximum threshold being at ovulation. Reproduced by permission of The Psychonomic Society, from Tedford, Warren, and Flynn (1977). Alteration of shock aversion thresholds during the menstrual cycle. *Perception and Psychophysics*, **21**, 193–196

Conclusions

Most studies appear to suggest some cyclical variations in sensitivity to stimulation and in the likelihood of the formation of conditioned responses. This is doubtless partly a function of the changing levels of nervous system activity combined with various psychological and social factors.

SLEEPING AND DREAMING

There is not a great deal of work on sleep and the cycle; in most of the research on sleep and dreaming the subjects are men. Duration of sleep appears to be shortest at ovulation and longest premenstrually, at which time it is also more disturbed (Hartmann, 1966; Patkai, Johannson, and Post, 1974). There is a report of more rapid eye movement (REM) sleep in the premenstrual phase (Hartmann, 1966) but many of the women studied were taking drugs of various kinds. Another study found a greater density of eye-movements in the second half of the cycle and no such change occurred in anovulatory cycles (Petre-Quadens and De Lee, 1974). In a subsequent study confirming these results it was reported that REM density was indeed higher in the luteal phase but the percentage of REM sleep was higher in the follicular phase. The authors believe these variations are a function of oestrogen and progesterone levels, and of age (Hoffmann and Petre-Quadens, 1979). The question of whether dream recall varies with the cycle is an interesting one. In general, recall appears to be related to such factors as short- and long-term memory, verbal skills, motivation, fatigue, cognitive style, presleep experience, and so on. A study of only one subject which investigated dream recall through the cycle found that there was most recall around the time of ovulation and least recall from Day 20 to Day 25 and again during menses (Garfield, 1974). Another study reported an increase in premenstrual contentless dream experience (Cohen, 1972). But one other study found no changes with the cycle, in either the probability of a dream experience occurring, or the reporting of dream content. This was true both of women taking and those not taking a contraceptive pill (Trinder, Van de Castle, Bourne, and Frisbie, 1973). A study of individual differences in intellectual bias and dream recall during the cycle found that 'convergers' recalled more dreams in the premenstrual stage and 'divergers' recalled most in the pre-ovulatory phase (Sheldrake and Cormack, 1974). In a later study the same authors found that women taking various contraceptive pills are more likely to recall dreaming than those who are not taking them (Sheldrake and Cormack, 1976b). In a study of two subjects only, dreams were reported to have the highest sexual content during menstruation and most hostility post menses (Lewis and Burns, 1975). The dreams were rated by the authors. In another study dreams rated by independent judges had highest manifest sexuality and hostility during menses and were judged by the subjects themselves to be most unpleasant during menstruation (Swanson and Foulkes, 1967). Another study found that during menstruation there were increased emotions of attraction and of hate, more preoccupation with male adult figures, themes relating to the mouth and themes of attacking others. Various factors were not controlled for and the authors themselves feel the results need confirmation (Hertz and Jensen, 1975). A finding inconsistent with these last three reports of menstrual variations in emotional content of dreams is reported in a study of young women who had low neuroticism scores and low levels of self-rated menstrual distress. They were found to have no increases in dream affect as a function of the menstrual cycle (Schultz and Koulack, 1980).

There has been very little investigation into the effects of the contraceptive pill on sleeping. There are some indications of less variability in sleep with combination pills than in non-users (Henderson, Nemes, Gordon, and Roos, 1970; Patkai, Johannson, and Post, 1974).

Clearly much more work on the quantity and quality of sleep and dreaming through the cycle is needed. The stage has not yet been reached where unequivocal descriptive accounts of what happens can be given. Until that is achieved, speculation about mechanisms would be premature. It has been pointed out that changes do occur in sleep under the influence of hormones and suggestions have been made about the various central mechanisms which might be involved in this hormonal effect on sleep (Hoffman and Petre-Quadens, 1979; Petre-Quadens and De Lee, 1974).

Conclusions

Sleep and dreaming appear to vary with the cycle but reports of these variations are somewhat inconsistent at present. More detailed descriptions of the changes are needed. The neural, hormonal, and psychological mechanisms have scarcely been speculated upon as yet.

There is a summary of this review of changes at the end of Chapter 4.

CHAPTER 4

Changes associated with the menstrual cycle: II

PSYCHOLOGICAL AND BEHAVIOURAL CHANGES

SEXUAL FEELING AND BEHAVIOUR

Most studies agree that there are cyclical variations in sexual feeling and sexual behaviour but the findings are not entirely consistent as regards the precise pattern of variation. In fact the situation is far from clear and this is due to many factors, notably the limitations of self-report accounts of sexual feelings and behaviour, inadequate identification of the relevant variables and generalizations from unrepresentative groups.

Sexual feeling

Early reports of sexual arousability (that is, feelings, dreams, desires) were of a rise just before and during menstruation (Davis, 1929; Hart, 1960; Kinsey, Pomeroy, Martin, and Gebhard, 1953; Masters and Johnson, 1966; Terman, 1938). A questionnaire study (Moos, 1969) found a peak of sexual arousal at ovulation, another rise premenstrually and then a drop until Day 7. A more recent study (Englander-Golden, Chang, Whitmore, and Dienstbier, 1980) found that self-reported sexual arousal was higher premenstrually, around ovulation, and at the end of menstruation, compared with the luteal phase. Women on a low-progestogen combination pill did not have the luteal dip, but showed a sudden and short (one or two days) decline in arousal at the very end of the luteal phase. In general the contraceptive pill users reported a somewhat higher level of sexual arousal than non-pill users. The study included a group of men who reported higher levels of sexual arousal than both pill and non-pill users; the men presumably showed no cyclical variation. This study reported that, within the non-oral contraceptive and oral contraceptive groups of women, results were somewhat different according to the type of self-report questionnaire used. There is a discussion of this methodological point in Chapter 9. Another recent study (Sanders, and

56

Bancroft 1982) found a significant increase in sexual feelings pre- and post-menstrually.

Two of the authors cited above (Kinsey, Pomeroy, Martin, and Gebhard, 1953; Masters and Johnson, 1966) claimed some physiological basis for their finding of increased sexual feeling in the premenstrual and early menstrual phases. Kinsey reported that 69% of women in their survey recognized that their vaginal secretions during sexual arousal were more abundant premenstrually (11% reported most abundance at ovulation). Masters and Johnson reported that at the premenstrual and early menstrual time there was increased vascularity, which could intensify sexual awareness and responsivity. One study (Schreiner-Engel, Schiavi, Smith, and White, 1981) measured sexual arousal both by photoplethysmographic recordings of vaginal vasocongestion and by self-report. The vaginal measure showed significantly higher levels of arousal from Day 4 to Day 6 and from Day 21 to Day 24 compared with Day 10 to Day 16. The same pattern appeared in the self-report data but without reaching statistical significance. The authors express some reservations about the self-report questionnaire which they used. Levels of certain hormones were measured and correlations with sexual arousability were low. Some relationships were found, though:

1. Oestradiol was negatively related to arousability in the phases Day 4 to Day 6 and 7 to 4 days premenstrually.
2. Any relations between progesterone and arousal became increasingly negative over the menstrual cycle.
3. Levels of testosterone and arousal were positively related during the ovulatory phase.
4. There was evidence suggestive of a relationship between testosterone and sexuality when women were grouped into different levels of testosterone.

Another study failed to find evidence of cyclical variation on three physiological measures of sexual arousability (Hoon, Bruce, and Kinchloe, 1982). Investigations such as the last two, although clearly carefully planned and conducted, took place without a sexual partner. These circumstances are not ideal for the assessment of any variability in physiological arousal with the cycle, which is presumably the outcome of many other psychological and physiological changes, and of life events at the time.

Conclusions about sexual arousal cannot be clear-cut, but there does seem to be some agreement on high levels premenstrually, often during menstruation and perhaps, though less often reported, at ovulation. The considerable methodological problems have to be borne in mind.

Sexual behaviour

Sexual behaviour has not always been adequately defined. It seems essential, in order to understand the behaviour and the underlying mechanisms, to distinguish between intercourse and orgasm. It is also important to know something of female-initiated as well as male-initiated sexual activity. Occasionally these requirements have been met. Kinsey, Pomeroy, Martin, and Gebhard (1953) reported that orgasm occurred more frequently and more precipitately in the premenstrual and early menstrual phases. Kinsey put great emphasis on the increased sexuality of the time just before menstruation. He reported that for some women masturbation was solely confined to that period and that it was the phase when 'most human females are most responsive erotically'. The findings of Masters and Johnson (1966) are in broad agreement and, as mentioned above, the authors provide some evidence of a physiological basis for this rise in sexual activity around menstruation. Udry and Morris (1968) reported maximum occurrence of orgasm and intercourse around ovulation followed by a sharp drop in the luteal phase and then another rise premenstrually. They later found that there was no luteal dip in women using various oral contraceptives (Udry and Morris, 1972). Unfortunately no statistical analyses are given. James (1971) reported the highest rate of coitus immediately after menstruation with only the faintest signs of a minor peak around ovulation. James rightly found much to criticize in the methodology used in this field. He arrived at his conclusions, which are not in agreement with others, by carrying out a new analysis of data from earlier reports combined with new data. The usefulness of combining data gathered in various ways from different sources to give an over-all calculation is doubtful. Adams, Gold and Burt (1978) report a welcome attempt to distinguish between female- and male-initiated sexual activity and between different types of non-oral contraception methods and oral contraceptives. They studied a group of married women who were asked to make daily reports on various aspects of sexual activity. One category of sexual activity was female-initiated, divided into heterosexual and autosexual (masturbation, fantasies, dreams, arousal from books, and so on). The other category of activity was male-initiated. Women not using an oral contraceptive experienced a statistically significant increase in female-initiated sexual behaviour, both heterosexual and autosexual, at ovulation. This peak was not present for male-initiated behaviour, except where non-intrusive contraceptive methods (intrauterine device or male vasectomy) were used. They also found some premenstrual and post-menstrual rise in female heterosexual activity, as well as increases in autosexual behaviour during menstruation. Dividing autosexual activities into consummatory (masturbation) and fantasy-like activity, masturbation increased during the ovulatory phase for women using intrusive contraception (diaphragm, foam, male condom) but decreased in that phase for women using other forms of contraception. Fantasy-like activity was significantly greater during the ovulatory portion of the cycle for all groups, though less so for pill-takers. The authors believe that consistent ovulatory effects of a peak of activity would be obtained if measures of sexual activity determined by the woman were used. The women using combination oral contraceptives did not experience the ovulatory rise in female-initiated sexual activity and, in general, their female-initiated heterosexual activity was unexpectedly low. From their rather low baseline, there were rises in female-initiated sexual activity premenstrually and post-menstrually. The authors' conclusions, and their methods of calculating time of ovulation, have been questioned (Kolodny and Bauman, 1979; Persky, O'Brien, Lief, Strauss, and Miller, 1979; Tersman, 1979). Further investigation of the variables studied by Adams, Gold, and Burt would contribute to an understanding of sexual activity through the cycle.

It seems that women experience troughs and peaks in sexual desire and sexual activity throughout the normal cycle. Most of the recent studies find a peak around ovulation. Equally often reported is a peak premenstrually and also towards the end of menstruation. Any explanations of these variations are necessarily speculative at the moment. They will certainly be found in social as well as in physiological and psychological factors. Authors usually attribute the ovulatory sexual peak to endocrine factors, with the biological purpose of conception. Some favour oestrogens as important in increased sexual activity (Adams, Gold, and Burt, 1978; Udry and Morris, 1968) and progesterone in decreasing it (Englander-Golden, Chang, Whitmore, and Dienstbier, 1980). One study, which did not quantify cyclical variations as such, found no significant relationship between oestrogen (oestradiol) levels and three measures of sexual behaviour including arousal, intercourse frequency, and sexual gratification. Nevertheless the authors suggest a possible role for oestrogens in sexual behaviour (Persky, Charney, Lief, O'Brien, Miller, and Strauss, 1978). Their model postulates that oestradiol stimulates the production of androgens, which they previously indicated were related to enhanced sexual gratification (Persky, O'Brien, and Khan, 1976). Other authors also suggest that androgens, which rise slightly at mid-cycle (see Chapter 2) may be important in the ovulatory rise in sexual activity (Gray and Gorzalka, 1980; O'Connor, Shelley, and Stern, 1974; Speroff, 1977). It is a widely held view that androgens are important in the sexual responsiveness of women (for example Bancroft, 1981) and testosterone treatment has been found effective for sexual unresponsiveness in women (Carney, Bancroft, and Mathews, 1978).

If, as seems highly possible, the ovulatory peak is largely attributable to hormonal factors (with some variations arising from contraceptive considerations) what is the explanation for the premenstrual rise in sexual feeling and behaviour? Kinsey, Pomeroy, Martin, and Gebhard (1953) suggested an evolutionary shift which transferred the period of maximum sexual arousal from mid-cycle to near the time of menstruation. The adaptive purpose of this is not clear, though a possible one is suggested by James (1971). Commenting on his belief that there is no significant increase in sexual activity around ovulation, James quotes a theory of Morris (1967) that in humans sexual activity has, in addition to reproduction, the function of helping to maintain the parental pairbond through the extended period of rearing children. It is interesting that rhesus monkeys have a pattern of copulation through their menstrual cycle (also about 28 days) which is not unlike some of the findings on sexual behaviour in humans. The monkeys have a peak of sexual activity around ovulation, but there is also a rise in the middle of the premenstrual phase, and again at the beginning of menstruation (Michael, Zumpe, Kaverne, and Bonsall, 1972). Cutler, Garcia, and Krieger (1980) point out that primates are alone among mammals in their sexual activity at non-ovulatory times. Cutler suggests that this activity may serve to prime the reproductive system as well as to impregnate it.

The increase in sexual behaviour towards the end of menstruation which is often reported may be plausibly attributed to a reaction to the relative abstinence during the first days of menstruation whether due to cultural and religious taboos, preference, or for reasons of comfort. Sexual abstinence during menstrual bleeding is extremely widespread. It is virtually total in some societies and very prevalent in others. A World Health Organization survey (1981a) revealed that in the United Kingdom, for example, 54% of a sample of 550 parous women said intercourse should be avoided during menstruation. Bancroft (1981) suggests that the proposed explanation of the pre- and post-menstrual peaks being that they precede and follow sexual abstinence is not a sufficient one. He puts forward two other possible factors. The increased pelvic awareness associated with menstruation (reported by Kinsey *et al.* and by Masters and Johnson); also at least in some women the removal premenstrually of a negative effect of progesterone.

Most authors mention the probability that psychological and social factors must play an important part in sexual arousal and behaviour, but there are few detailed suggestions of how such factors operate. More studies are needed of the important variables and of their interactions; for example, the type of variable in the study by Adams, Gold, and Burt (1978) cited above, which explored the differences between male- and female-initiated sexual activity and the influence of different types of contraceptive. One possible, unconfirmed way of construing the findings would be that the active sexual phase around ovulation is not surprising in view of the heightened sensory activity and the feelings of well-being and assertiveness at that time (all presumably originally conducive to conception). As for the other reported peaks before and during menstruation, we have the views of Kinsey, Pomeroy, Martin, and Gebhard (1953) and of Morris (1967) that there has been an evolutionary shift of sexual arousal to the premenstrual phase and that this shift has a physiological and an adaptive basis. If there is a physiological basis the expression of it is undoubtedly enhanced or perhaps even largely determined by psychological and social variables and we might speculate on how these factors combine. Social change has led to increasingly varied, active, and satisfying sexual lives for women; an optimum time for this more uninhibited approach appears to be around menstruation, for a variety of reasons. Physiologically there may be, at least potentially, increased sensitivity; the premenstruum brings feelings of high arousal which may find an outlet in sexual thoughts and behaviour. Menstruation in its turn brings a relief from tension, with an atmosphere of relaxation and, for certain people, towards the end of menstruation, a reaction to sexual abstinence. Such a model is entirely speculative but any attempt to understand human sexual behaviour during the cycle will have to take into account the particularly complex biological, psychological, and social factors which are involved.

Conclusion

Present evidence indicates higher sexual feelings and behaviour at ovulation and in the premenstrual and menstrual phases than in the rest of the cycle. This evidence needs to be amplified by investigation of more of the relevant variables. The limitations of self-report, perhaps especially on sexual matters, have to be remembered. The sexual peak around ovulation probably has a hormonal basis though whether this is predominantly oestrogenic or androgenic is not known. The rise around menstruation possibly also has a physiological basis but this requires confirmation; psychological and social factors may be particularly salient at that time.

MOOD

This is an area where the question of the validity of self-report questionnaires is particularly important since most findings have been collected by that method. The matter of various forms of self-report of menstrual cycle changes is discussed in Chapter 9. For present purposes it is enough to bear it in mind as one of the many problems associated with the investigation of mood through the cycle. Other methodological difficulties in this topic are often related to lack of fine-grained analysis. This is true both of the mood categories and of the menstrual cycle phases. A central shortcoming in this area, often mentioned in this book, is the virtually total lack of research into positive mood changes. We are dealing almost exclusively with studies of negative mood and what are often referred to as psychological symptoms. It is also worth remembering that the reports are mostly of group studies and although a little work has been done on individual characteristics in relation to cycle changes such studies are rare.

The findings on variations in mood with the cycle are not entirely consistent though the great majority of studies do find cyclical effects. The positive results are given first, in terms of the rather gross categories of menstrual, ovulatory, and premenstrual phases with a brief mention of the intervening phases. Afterwards, studies will be cited which found no variation with the cycle in certain moods.

Premenstrual phase

There are frequent reports of increased anxiety premenstrually (Benedek and Rubinstein, 1939; Beumont, Richards, and Gelder, 1975; Golub, 1976;

Ivey and Bardwick, 1968; May, 1976; Moos, 1969; Silbergeld, Brast, and Noble, 1971; Silverman, Zimmer, and Silverman, 1974). Many studies report a premenstrual upsurge in what is referred to as negative affect or mood. This is measured in various ways but usually includes anxiety, irritability, restlessness, and tension (Abplanalp, Donnelly, and Rose, 1979; Benedek and Rubinstein, 1939; Beumont, Richards, and Gelder, 1975; Garling and Roberts, 1980; Golub, 1976; Janowsky, Berens, and Davis, 1973; Kirstein, Rosenberg, and Smith, 1980–81; Moos, 1977; Parlee, 1980; Silbergeld, Brast, and Noble, 1971; Taylor, 1979; Voda, 1980). One of the studies (Beumont, Richards, and Gelder, 1975) found no such increases in a group of women who had had a hysterectomy with conservation of the ovaries. One study (Englander-Golden, Willis, and Dienstbier, 1977) which showed a premenstrual rise in tension found that the cyclical fluctuations in tension did not take place in men. There are reports of a premenstrual increase in feelings of aggression (Moos, 1969; Silbergeld, Brast, and Noble, 1971) and of hostility (Ivey and Bardwick, 1968: Paige, 1971; Silbergeld, Brast, and Noble, 1971).

Reports on depression in the premenstrual phase are not consistent. Some find no change (Moos, 1969; Silbergeld, Brast, and Noble, 1971); one study finds it significantly lower premenstrually than at mid-cycle (Parlee, 1980), others find an increase (Beumont, Richards, and Gelder, 1975; Golub, 1976; May, 1976; Taylor, 1979). This lack of agreement may partly reflect the fact that depression during the cycle is usually measured by questionnaires which were designed to indicate level of clinical depression. They are probably inappropriate as indicators of the more transient type of depression which may be experienced in relation to the menstrual cycle. The usual picture of premenstrual depression does not have all of the characteristic features of current clinical descriptions of depression.

It is negative mood which tends to dominate accounts of changes in the premenstrual phase. The term premenstrual syndrome refers to the reported marked tendency for these feelings, and other manifestations, to recur, at significantly increased levels, in the days before menstruation. The premenstrual heightening of negative mood cannot be seen in a unified way; several different kinds of mood are included and many women experience different combinations of them at different times. A review (Steiner and Carroll, 1977) of all aspects of premenstrual disorder suggests that there are several distinct premenstrual syndromes—of mainly depression, elation, or hostile irritability. Nevertheless the authors conclude that while it may be possible to identify subgroups of women with each of these circumscribed syndromes, it appears that most women experience some combination of the symptoms. Within one premenstrual phase, closer study of the research findings and of clinical reports reveals that although the over-all mood has a dark colouring, it has also a labile tendency. That is, the moods tend to change very easily at this time, so that there are 'high' patches as well. It seems that some women see the premenstrual phase positively. In one study 40% of 30 women rated themselves as very happy (May, 1976) so that perhaps if women were given more opportunity to report on positive aspects of the premenstrual phase, a substantial incidence of good patches might be found. There is also need of more detail of individual difference in the nature of the changes experienced and of a finer analysis of change through the days of the premenstrual phase.

Menstrual phase

There are reports that during menstruation there is an easing of emotional tensions and general relaxation (Benedek and Rubinstein, 1939; Silbergeld, Brast, and Noble, 1971), and a reduction in negative feelings (Janowsky, Berens, and Davis, 1973; Parlee, 1980, on 'Menstrual Distress Questionnaire'; Taylor, 1979). On the other hand, some studies found continuing negative mood during menstruation (Abplanalp, Donnelly, and Rose, 1979; Beumont, Richards, and Gelder, 1975; Englander-Golden, Whitmore, and Dienstbier, 1978; Parlee, 1980, on 'Profile of Mood States'; Wilcoxon, Schrader and Sherif, 1976). This last study found that the cyclical variations in mood were not present in men. One study (Moos, 1969) found anxiety and aggression were high at the start of menstruation but declined sharply thereafter. Paige (1971) found anxiety was highest at menstruation and suggested this was only so for women who experience heavy flow, and that reduced anxiety during menstruation is associated with light menstrual flow. It is possible that any negative feelings found during menstruation are related to physical symptoms (see for example Abplanalp, Donnelly, and Rose, 1979; Beumont, Richards, and Gelder, 1975; Moos, 1977) and this possibility would merit further investigation. This view is put by Golub and Harrington (1981) who found significantly increased negative affect, measured by the Menstrual Distress Questionnaire, in the menstrual phase in a group of adolescents. The authors point out that it may be that this is related to menstrual pain, which was also significantly elevated. Culberg (1972) found that there was a relationship between a decrease in dysmenorrhea and an improvement in mental state. In general, future studies of the determinants of mood during menstruation might profitably explore further the role of pain and discomfort and also that of social and cultural factors. At present a tentative conclusion is that in spite of several reports of lifting of negative mood from the onset of bleeding, there are marked individual differences and that these may be at least partly a function of other (physical) menstrual symptoms and of cultural attitudes and practices surrounding menstruation.

Ovulatory phase

There is some evidence that around ovulation there is an increase in self-confidence, assertiveness, competitiveness and dominance (Bardwick, 1976; Ivey and Bardwick, 1968), feelings of well-being and pleasantness (Moos,

1969) enhanced cheerfulness, energy, outgoingness (Taylor, 1979) and a peak in feelings of elation and vigour (Little and Zahn, 1974). Voda (1980) found that a positive affect grouping (affectionateness, orderliness, excitement, well-being) was at a peak around ovulation. Rossi and Rossi (1977) found that the ovulatory phase was 'uniquely characterized by an elevation of positive moods measured in various ways' and that the cyclical variations did not take place in men. There is just one report of an increase in one type of feeling in the ovulatory when compared with the menstrual phase. Parlee (1980) found that anger/hostility were significantly higher at ovulation than during menstruation. These are the results of studies which specifically explored feelings and mood around ovulation. There is in addition the information which comes less directly, from all of the studies reporting negative mood in the premenstrual and, less often, in the menstrual phase. In these studies, the comparison is usually made with the ovulatory phase which is thus shown to be characterized by significantly lower negative affect than are the other phases. There is still much work to be done on mood during the ovulatory phase of the cycle. It appears from the existing reports that at that time there may be rather subtle changes of mood which are often not measured in questionnaires. Research and clinical reports speak of moods of self-confidence, well-being, outgoingness, competitiveness. These feelings, and behaviour which reflects them, are often not well defined in self-report or in interview assessment.

Intervening phases

It is worth mentioning briefly the impression which comes from a small amount of work on the phases between premenstrual, menstrual, and ovulatory. In the follicular phase there are suggestions of a prevailing mood that is pleasant with feelings of well-being and increasing sexual desire which may be aggressive (Benedek and Rubinstein, 1939); an affectionate mood (Silbergeld, Brast, and Noble, 1971); negative moods (except for hostility) are extremely low (Silbergeld, Brast, and Noble, 1971). In the luteal phase, there seems to be a tendency to a pleasant emotional state and a passive, inward-turning mood (Benedek and Rubinstein, 1939) with negative moods low (Silbergeld, Brast, and Noble, 1971). The investigation of the possibly more subtle mood changes of cycle phases other than the obvious ones of premenstrual, menstrual, and ovulatory would be valuable.

A few studies have failed to find cyclical variations in certain moods. Abplanalp, Donnelly, and Rose, (1979) found no variations in daily self-report of mood on the Profile of Mood States (POMS), including two moods of friendliness and elation which were added in this study. Another author (Parlee, 1980) found no variations with the cycle on the POMS tension/anxiety and vigour and fatigue. These two studies found, as recorded above, variations in mood on the Menstrual Distress Questionnaire. There is a finding of no variation in daily self-report of anxiety, fear, restlessness, and

64

irritability (Zimmermann and Parlee, 1973). Lahmeyer, Miller, and DeLeon-Jones (1982) found no significant variations in Menstrual Distress Questionnaire scores or in State-Trait Anxiety Scale State scores, though the scores were elevated premenstrually. Golub and Harrington (1981) reported no significant fluctuations in depression (on Depression Adjective Check List) and anxiety (on State-Trait Anxiety Inventory) in a group of adolescents. Dan (1980) found no significant change in mood variables over the cycle, with one exception. There were higher scores in the premenstrual phase on self-rated hostility and on hostility outward on a free-associative measure.

The reported effects of the contraceptive pill on the cyclical variations in mood are not easy to state precisely. This is partly because of the complexities of individual differences in response to different types and dosages of pill (see for example Culberg, 1972). Also, the published studies have used a wide range of oral contraceptives, details of which are not always stated. The majority of studies find that the mood variations of the natural cycle are greatly lessened, or eliminated, by the combination pills (Englander-Golden, Willis, and Dienstbier, 1977; Herzberg and Coppen, 1970; Kutner and Brown, 1972; Moos, 1977; Paige, 1971; Rossi and Rossi, 1977; Silbergeld, Brast, and Noble, 1971). One of these authors, in a subsequent study in which the Menstrual Distress Questionnaire was administered in two different ways, retrospectively and daily (Englander-Golden, Whitmore, and Dienstbier, 1978) found similar differences in cyclical variations between pill and non-pill groups on negative affect measured retrospectively. The authors point out that the groups were fairly small and that the differences between their later results and previous ones could be partly accounted for by more recent changes in hormonal concentrations in the oral contraceptives. Bardwick (1976) quotes an unpublished study by Oakes of game-playing behaviour through the cycle. The cyclical variations observed in women with natural cycles was not present in women taking combination contraceptive pills and the latter women in general played less competitively than those with natural cycles. This study also found that women on oestrogen-dominant pills described themselves as higher in assertiveness, aggression, and hostility compared with those on progestogen-dominant pills. The latter described themselves as high in deference, nurturance and affiliation.

The view that women taking contraceptive pills experience more depression than do those with natural cycles is not supported by the findings of controlled studies (Goldzieher, Moses, Averkin, Scheel, and Taber, 1971; Kutner and Brown, 1972; Paige, 1971; Silbergeld, Brast, and Noble, 1971). However, there is evidence of a small number of women being particularly vulnerable to adverse reactions, such as depression, to the contraceptive pills, mainly women who suffered from psychological symptoms prior to taking the pill (Culberg, 1972; Herzberg and Coppen, 1970; Weissman and Slaby, 1973). A number of studies report a temporary negative response to the pill, usually in the first month or so only (see Weissman and Slaby, 1973). Investigations of the effect of the smaller-dose pills on the variations of the natural cycle would be useful. Combination pill-users do not appear to benefit from the positive feelings which predominate around the mid-point of natural cycles. Since, with the combination pill, moods tend to follow an even course through the cycle, there is a tendency for both the positive peak at mid-cycle and the premenstrual trough not to take place (though differences between users and non-users are not always marked enough to be statistically significant (Paige, 1971; Silbergeld, Brast, and Noble, 1971; Wilcoxon, Schrader, and Sherif, 1976). The findings on the effects of contraceptive pills on positive feelings are sparse and no firm conclusions can be drawn.

There is less information on the sequential contraceptive pills. There are some indications that women taking the sequential pills have variations in mood more similar to those of natural cycles than is the case with combination pills, (Kutner and Brown, 1971; Moos, 1977; Paige, 1971). Further studies of the effects on mood of the sequential pill would be of interest but are less likely to appear on a large scale because of the reduction in use of these pills.

Conclusions

Conclusions about cyclical variations in moods have to be tentative because of the methodological problems and because of some inconsistencies in the findings. Nevertheless most of the present evidence suggests a fairly clear picture at least as regards three broad phases of the menstrual cycle. There are premenstrual changes in mood which are predominantly negative. Menstruation is often reportedly marked by relief from the premenstrual mood, but some studies have found continuing negative feelings, possibly dependent on physical symptoms and on culturally related menstrual practices. The middle of the cycle is most often characterized by positive moods and feelings. The indications are that in the other phases, the follicular and the luteal, pleasant moods predominate. It appears that the fluctuations in mood are reduced when combination contraceptive pills are taken. The sequential pill is accompanied by variations which are similar to those of natural cycles. The possible determinants of the mood changes with the natural cycle are explored in some detail in Chapters 5, 8 and 9. It seems that there are observable changes in mood and feelings which closely correspond to known fluctuations in hormone levels and in other phsyiological and physical changes. In addition to those associations, there are undoubtedly a multiplicity of learned and environmental factors which contribute to the ways in which the biologically based changes are experienced (see Chapter 9). A great deal of information is lacking. This lack includes details of individual differences and of different cycles for each woman. It is a matter of common observation that any woman does not experience the same mood variations in every cycle. This would be expected for various reasons; some cycles are anovulatory, prevailing hormone levels will vary from one cycle to the next and physical changes and events at the time will influence the over-all impression of any phase. Methods will have to be devised to measure small, probably cumulative, effects and to record possibly frequent and subtle variations within any one phase. Existing mood or emotion categories may be too gross for some of the changes with the cycle, and the type and magnitude of change may be subject to fluctuation.

PSYCHIATRIC SYMPTOMS

There are cyclical variations in more serious psychiatric disturbances. Smith (1975) reviewed studies which found an exacerbation of 'recurrent mental disturbances of psychotic proportions in the premenstrual phase'. Diamond, Rubinstein, Dunner, and Fieve, (1976) found increased affective symptoms premenstrually and during menstruation in women suffering from both bipolar and unipolar affective disorders; there were significantly more reports of exacerbated affective symptoms premenstrually than menstrually. Admissions to hospital and outpatient contact increase in the few days before menstruation and, less often, during menstruation (Dalton 1959; Diamond, Rubinstein, Dunner, and Fieve, 1976; Glass, Heninger, Lansky, and Talan, 1971; Jacobs and Charles, 1970; Janowsky, Gorney, and Castelnuovo-Tedesco, 1969; Kramp, 1968). One study found a marked association between onset of depressive psychiatric crises and phase of the menstrual cycle (Abramowitz, Baker, and Fleischer, 1982). These authors confirmed previous reports of significantly higher rates of admission of depressed patients in the paramenstruum. They also found a further striking elevation on two particular paramenstrual days, the day before and the first day of bleeding; 41% of the 60 depressed women were admitted on those two days. In a comparison group of schizophrenic patients, some elevation of admission rates in the paramenstruum was observed but there was no additional rise on the day before and the day of onset of menstruation. The authors offer a speculative explanation, that the increased rate of depression may be a result of high levels of monoamine oxidase which are known to coincide with low levels of oestrogen. There is one report of the prevention of recurrent menstrual psychosis in just one patient by administration of an oral contraceptive (Felthous, Robinson, and Conroy, 1980). These authors also suggest the possibility that the modification of monoamine oxidase activity, consequent upon the administration of the hormones, might explain the results. There is an increase during the luteal/premenstrual phases in acute symptoms in psychiatric patients who are already in hospital (see Smith, 1975, for review). There are two reports of some exacerbation (though less than premenstrually and during menstruation) of certain psychiatric symptoms at mid-cycle (Dalton, 1959; Jacobs and Charles, 1970).

Apparently there are no reports which deal specifically with the effect of the contraceptive pill on cyclical changes in serious psychiatric disturbance. It is not within the scope of this book to examine the wider question of the possible effects of the contraceptive pill on mood and psychiatric state in general.

Conclusions

There is some question as to whether some psychiatric illnesses lend themselves more readily to cyclical variations than others, and no firm conclusions can be drawn until more studies are carried out to establish separate figures for various symptom groups. There is also a lack of information on individual differences among patients in their susceptibility to variations in symptoms with the cycle. Until these questions are clarified there is unlikely to be any real under-standing of the worsening in some psychiatric symptoms, most usually starting before menstruation. It is reasonable to assume an additive model in which the usual cyclical changes in mood and physical changes are superimposed on the existing psychiatric disorder, causing a further deterioration in psychiatric state. This view is put forward by for example Zola, Meyerson, Reznikoff, Thornton, and Concool (1979) who provide data which are sugges-tive of an additive effect of psychotic symptoms with the normal fluctuations of the menstrual cycle.

Suicide, which might have been included in this section, is discussed separately as the data are of a different nature than for psychiatric symptoms in general.

SUICIDE AND ATTEMPTED SUICIDE

Many studies have shown a preponderance of suicide attempts during the last part of the cycle and/or into menstruation (Dalton, 1959; Parvathi and Venkoba, 1972; Thin, 1968; Tonks, Rack and Rose, 1968). The largest numbers of telephone calls to a suicide prevention centre were reported to be in the premenstrual and menstrual phases (Mandell and Mandell, 1967). One study (Birtchnell and Floyd, 1974) found that an increase in attempted suicides premenstrually and during menstruation did not reach statistical significance. Wetzel and McClure (1972) carried out a comprehensive review of studies of the relationship between suicidal behaviour and the menstrual cycle since 1900. They found that most of these reports were of suicide attempts in the premenstrual and menstrual phases. As regards completed suicide, the early study of post-mortem reports of the wombs of 102 women, 38 of whom died by suicide was mentioned in Chapter 3. Of these 38 suicides, 34 took place during the last half of the cycle (MacKinnon, MacKinnon, and Thomson, 1959). There is a report by a pathologist in Kenya who carried out necropsies on 22 Hindu women who died by self-immolation; 19 of the 22 were menstruating (Ribeiro, 1962). The review by Wetzel and McClure (1972) found that most studies reported an increase in successful suicides during menstruation, though they are mindful of the fact that the best of the early studies, methodologically (that of MacKinnon, MacKinnon, and Thomson, above) found the increased risk of completed suicide to be in the luteal and premenstrual phases.

Although the amount of agreement between studies is telling, there are considerable problems in demonstrating the precise degree of increased risk at certain times of the cycle. A central difficulty with attempted suicide is in predicting and confirming the exact date of the next menstruation and hence locating the attempt in the current cycle. Also, some suicide studies are not representative of all suicides in the population because of restrictions for various religious and social reasons. One of the reports cited above (Parvathi and Venkoba, 1972) gives an example of one source of bias which affected the earlier studies. Christian burial in consecrated ground was only permitted if the person committing suicide was considered insane. At the time of some of the studies, the concept of menstrual psychosis was accepted and hence burial was granted if the woman had been menstruating at the time of the suicide. As the author points out, this bias in consenting to autopsy and burial would inflate the percentage of menstruating suicides. It would, though, presumably deflate the proportion of premenstrual suicides.

These findings of increased risk of attempted and completed suicide in the last part or at the beginning of the cycle are intriguing and if confirmed have considerable preventive implications. The usual combination of biological, psychological, and social factors must be invoked as a possible explanation. More meaningful speculation will await further studies showing, among other things, the different incidence for different days of the very broad category of the paramenstruum, and for different individuals and groups. There is for instance already one suggestive finding that women who are aware of premenstrual distress and express it verbally attempt suicide less than women who do not acknowledge distress (Tonks, Rack, and Rose, 1968). Also the 'aware' women more often take the preventive action of telephoning a help centre (Wetzel, McClure, and Reich, 1971). It therefore seems that individuals who do not use the cycle as an attributional source of feelings of despair may be more likely to attempt suicide, though there are doubtless other variables at work. (See Chapter 9 for discussion of attribution as a mechanism in the changes with the cycle.)

Conclusions

In spite of methodological difficulties and the lack of more detailed studies, there are signs of an increase in attempted and successful suicides in the paramenstruum. In future studies of the part played by individual characteristics, both biological and learned factors such as attributions of negative feelings will probably be found to be important.

ANTI-SOCIAL BEHAVIOUR

Variations with the cycle in deviant behaviour have to be mentioned because they are constantly included in accounts of the menstrual cycle and its effects. In fact, although the findings are suggestive they are sparse and need confirmation. A higher incidence of crime just before and during menstruation, than in the rest of the cycle, is reported. One study claimed to show that 62% of crimes of violence by women had been carried out during the premenstrual week (Morton, Additon, Addison, Hunt, and Sullivan, 1953). Dalton (1961) has reported a relationship between violent crime and the premenstrual and menstrual phases. A more recent study found that of 50 women charged with crimes of violence, 44% committed the offence during the paramenstruum and there was a significant lack of offences during the ovulatory and post-ovulatory phase (d'Orban and Dalton, 1980). There are reports of an increase premenstrually in offences by prisoners (Dalton, 1964a; Morton, Additon, Addison, Hunt, and Sullivan, 1953) and of recorded offences by schoolgirls (Dalton, 1964a). Dalton showed that the cyclical variations she reported did not occur in men prisoners or in schoolboys. There is a clinical report of one case of premenstrual increase in kleptomania (Lederer, 1963). A clinical report of increased child abuse (Dalton, 1979) just before and during menstruation requires more systematic verification. Dalton (1980) has reported on three women who successfully pleaded diminished responsibility in violent crimes due to premenstrual syndrome.

It is important to remember that none of these studies demonstrates a tendency for each and every woman to commit either serious or trivial crimes in the premenstrual and menstrual phases. They merely suggest that those women who have criminal or antisocial proclivities will tend to express them at that time. As with psychiatric symptoms and suicide, the best assumption seems to be that the increases in tension, irritability, and hostility which are widely observed before menstruation are compounded with a predisposed state. Smith (1975) has pointed out that the work on menstrually-related epilepsy and more general episodic behavioural disorders suggests a possible epileptic basis to aggressive impulses during the premenstrual and menstrual phases. So little is known of the individual biological, psychological, and social characteristics of the women who show this behaviour that it is impossible to be more precise.

It is not known if and how the contraceptive pill affects the findings of cyclical variation.

Conclusions

> There seems little doubt that minor and serious offences committed by women occur much more often in the premenstrual and menstrual phases of the cycle. The precise mechanisms of this cyclical variation cannot be stated. It is probable that premenstrual changes in both neuroendocrine activity and negative feelings are superimposed on a predisposed state to produce the increase in anti-social behaviour.

PERFORMANCE ON TESTS

A large variety of functions, ranging from simple perceptual judgements to critical thinking, have been studied in relation to the menstrual cycle. It is worth noting that the tests have usually been shown to be valid measures of certain aspects of behaviour; nevertheless they can only sample various pieces of behaviour and are therefore imperfect reflections of the over-all performance of any individual in a real situation.

A comprehensive review of studies of cognitive and perceptual motor behaviour with the menstrual cycle reported that no cyclical fluctuations were found in the large majority of studies using objective performance measures (Sommer, 1973). The exceptions were one study of vibrotactile learning (Diespecker and Kolokotronis, 1971) and two studies of school examinations (Dalton, 1960, 1968). It would be interesting to have replication of the last two studies with more rigorous control and statistical treatment. After Sommer's review there were three reports of some premenstrual impairment on simple perceptual motor tests: perception of verticality (Klaiber, Broverman, Vogel, and Kobayashi, 1974); arm-hand steadiness (Zimmerman and Parlee, 1973); perceptual after-effects (Satinder and Mastronardi, 1974). In addition, an increased (damping down) kinaesthetic after-effect which is said to reflect a central effect on the perception of subjective stimulus intensity and is possibly related to personality, has been found in the paramenstruum; this variation was not found in males (Baker, Kostin, Mishara, and Parker, 1979; see Chapter 3). If this test, which is ostensibly a perceptual test is in fact indicative of characteristic methods of dealing with stimuli, it would have wide implications for different responses at various times in the cycle, and in different individuals. A later review (Graham, 1980) reported similar findings to those reviewed by Sommer. In general no evidence was found of cyclical variation in cognitive tasks. The author concludes that menstrually-related variability in performance within or between persons is found only on single tests or subtests. Where any such variability is reported, the trend is to greater speed in the pre-ovulatory phase and greater accuracy in the post-ovulatory. This conclusion of very few over-all fluctuations but slight variations on some particular aspects of functioning appears to be rather accurate and we may expect that more information, based on the preliminary findings, will be forthcoming. Graham, in the same article (1980) reports her own study of cognition related to the menstrual cycle, in terms of a model which relates differences in cognition to sex hormone influences (see Broverman, Klaiber, Kobayashi, and Vogel, 1968; Broverman, Vogel, Klaiber, Majcher, Shea and Paul, 1981). Graham found no over-all significant relationship between oestrogen levels through the cycle and cognitive behaviour; and within women no association between those with high or low oestrogen levels and performance on tasks. Nevertheless, some subtests within the battery of tests gave modest support to the prediction of a relationship. The findings also indicate that when the performance scores of the luteal phase, Days 20–25, are compared with those of the other two phases in the study (Days 3–6 and Days 10–19) subjects do perform better during the luteal phase, with the exception of one subtest. Broverman, Vogel, Klaiber, Majcher, Shea, and Paul (1981) carried out a study on the basis of their model which predicts that sex hormones (oestrogen in women, testosterone in men) will facilitate performance of highly practical, overlearned, automatized tasks and will impair performance on perceptual-restructuring tasks (defined as tasks where initial perceptions are wrong and must be set aside in favour of less obvious stimulus attributes). They found no significant difference in performances on Day 10 and Day 20. But the authors suggest that, if anovulatory cycles are discounted (24% of their group probably did not ovulate) and if testing is conducted at very precise times in the cycle, there are variations in performance related to oestradiol/progesterone levels. This is specific to some categories of task—for example automatization tasks improve and perceptual restructuring tasks worsen from pre- to post-ovulatory phases. This means that it cannot be said that over-all cognitive functioning is better or worse at different stages of the cycle.

Golub (1980) reports that univariate analyses showed differences between premenstrual and intermenstrual testings on an associational fluency test (intermenstrual significantly better than premenstrual in those tested intermenstrually first) and on a possible jobs test (premenstrual better than intermenstrual whether tested premenstrually first or intermenstrually first). Multivariate analysis, however, revealed no significant menstrual cycle effect for the whole cognitive battery. Other results include a finding of no relationship between cycle phase and reaction time performance (Hutt, Frank, Mychalkiw, and Hughes, 1980). Another report is inconsistent with this in that it found that reaction time decreased significantly during the luteal phase to a low point (quickest reaction time) two to four days premenstrually (Wuttke, Arnold, Becker, Creutzfeldt, Langenstein, and Tirsch, 1975). This surprising result may have been a function of criterion factors. The same study also found an improvement on mental arithmetic tests during the luteal phase, continuing into two to three days premenstrually.

Turning to self-report measures of perceptual-motor and cognitive behaviour, a slightly different picture emerges. A small number of women apparently believe that their judgement or their mental faculties are impaired around menstruation. This is both a general methodological problem and a reflection perhaps of a more general tendency to associate reduced competence with feelings of discomfort and unhappiness. Sommer, in the 1973 review already mentioned, found that the self-report studies indicated that 8% to 16% of women feel their faculties are reduced particularly in the premenstrual phase. Self-reported difficulties in concentration appear to be higher during the premenstrual and/or menstrual phases (Garling and Roberts, 1980; Golub, 1976; Kirstein, Rosenberg, and Smith 1980–81; Moos, 1969), though there are one or two reports of no cyclical variations (for example Parlee, 1980; Silbergeld, Brast, and Noble, 1971). These studies measured the Menstrual Distress Questionnaire factor of concentration which includes eight items, some of which are more directly related to cognitive functioning than others. The eight items are insomnia, forgetfulness, confusion, lowered judgement, difficulty concentrating, distractible, accidents, and lowered motor co-ordination. One of the studies, Kirstein, Rosenberg, and Smith (1980–81) also administered a prospective daily self-report Temporal Disorganization Scale (covering five dimensions of cognitive function). The ratings of temporal disorganization were higher premenstrually and menstrually than for the rest of the cycle. Further confirmation is needed of the discrepancies between subjective estimates of ability or judgement and actual performance, and of individual differences in reacting positively or negatively to adverse physiological and psychological states.

Effects of the contraceptive pill on performance have not been adequately explored. One report (Wuttke, Arnold, Becker, Creutzfeldt, Langenstein, and Tirsch, 1975) mentioned above, found that combination pill-users, compared with non-users, had slower reaction times and took longer to do simple arithmetic. This slightly lower level on the contraceptive pill did not fluctuate significantly throughout the cycle whereas there was fluctuation in natural cycles. In the study mentioned above (Moos, 1969) which found more difficulty in concentration in premenstrual and menstrual phases of normal cycles, it is reported that there is no fluctuation in concentration in women taking the combination pill, with rather more fluctuation in sequential pill-users. One other study, using a difficult reasoning task and examination results, found that women taking a combination pill had higher scores than those not taking a pill (Sommer, 1972). Neither group showed cyclical fluctuations. These higher scores in pill-users could of course be due to various factors other than the pill. The author suggests that this group may have slightly higher motivation and/or intelligence and may also be rather more stable and less anxious as a group; or the cycle may affect performance in some as yet unknown way which is prevented by ingestion of an oral contraceptive. It is surprising that more studies on the effects of oral contraception have not been carried out, especially by those theorists who consider that hormonal levels may have important effects on performance, (for example Broverman, Klaiber, Kobayashi, and Vogel, 1968; Broverman, Vogel, Klaiber, Majcher, Shea, and Paul, 1981).

The whole question of cyclical variations in competence needs to be further investigated, in view of the claims and counter-claims which are made about the reliability of women at work. Feelings on all sides run high on this subject. Conclusions from two studies provide examples of noteworthy findings which could be extended to provide useful applications. The first is a finding in a simple experimental task situation, that if menstruating women can attribute arousal and frustration (produced by the task) to menstrual symptoms, they actually perform better than equally aroused and frustrated non-menstruating women. It seems that this advantage of having a focus of attribution of discomfort is particularly effective for women with more severe symptoms and does not work for women who report no, or extremely mild, discomfort while menstruating (Rodin, 1976). The second conclusion with practical implications which would repay further research comes from a study of work and the menstrual cycle which finds that the cycle does affect the capacity to carry out certain tasks, though the extent of this will depend on how much the decreased capacity can be offset by increased effort (Redgrove, 1971). The same author points out that men also experience changes in capacity for various reasons which are largely unknown; the suggestion is made that, if it were possible to accurately forecast changes in performance due to the menstrual cycle it might in fact be preferable to employ women, because their outputs would then probably be more predictable than that of men.

Conclusions

We can conclude that objectively measured performance on perceptual motor, and on more complex cognitive functions, does not change in any well-defined way with the cycle, in women in general. It is possible that certain aspects of these performances do change in subtle ways at very specific times of hormonal change, but this has yet to be fully demonstrated. Also it is probable that the group figures conceal a wide range of individual differences, particularly in the ways in which women respond to perceived impairment of their capabilities.

Here, as in so many areas, there is a lack of detailed information, about the precise effects of the cycle on performance on all aspects of perceptual motor and more complex cognitive tasks, individual differences in these effects, and the ways in which the menstrual effects differ from other fluctuations in the performance of both men and women.

COMPARISONS WITH MEN

A small number of the studies of the menstrual cycle have included men. Comparisons with men may serve three main purposes:

1. The primary purpose of including a group of men is of course as one non-menstruating control group. As control groups in studies of the menstrual cycle, they have limitations. Firstly, if cyclical variation in the men were found, this could be a result of the fact that most men in the age groups studied live in close proximity to a menstruating woman, rather than to any inherent cycles. Secondly, men may have different attitudes to reporting changes in behaviour and symptoms, thus rendering reports from the two sexes not strictly comparable. Thirdly, many of the changes do not apply to them at all, or less so; for example, breast tenderness.

2. Comparison studies contribute to knowledge about the functions, behaviour or symptoms in question. Clearly, male scores cannot alone constitute a baseline measurement for any characteristic, but they can form part of a composite picture with which to compare female scores at any point in the menstrual cycle. It is not possible to construct a female baseline (for example, on visual acuity) by, say, taking the average of premenstrual, intermenstrual, and luteal scores, or by assuming that the scores at any one point are 'normal'. Nevertheless it is highly informative to compare the scores through the cycle with the scores of non-menstruating populations. These are matters of interest, not only in the general study of behaviour, but also in the controversy about the effects of the menstrual cycle on performance on tasks which may or may not be better carried out by non-menstruating individuals.

3. Comparison studies give information about men. Although this would be a useful by-product of the use of male control groups, it is inevitably limited in investigations in which the aim is not the description of male characteristics.

In Table 2 are listed the menstrual studies which found cyclical variations in women and which included a comparison group of men. They are a minute proportion of all menstrual investigations. In addition the numbers of men in the control groups have usually been small, and little detail is given about them. The results of the studies in the table have already been included in the appropriate sections in this and the previous chapter. Table 2 summarizes the available evidence on male groups which have been directly compared with menstruating women; studies of cycles in men in general are outside the scope of this book.

Conclusions

The available studies suggest that, as regards the categories of change listed, there are no indications of a cyclical pattern in men similar to the variations in women. In some cases the male groups are too small to draw firm conclusions, but there is no study which suggests a similar cycle in males.* Further studies, of these and other changes, would be useful.

SUMMARY

From the evidence presented in this chapter and in Chapter 3, it is clear that there are considerable physiological, bodily, and psychological fluctuations which are related to the menstrual cycle, whether demonstrated by objective measurement, observed by outsiders or reported by the women who experience them. The changes are real, whatever the underlying cause. In addition to the neuroendocrine events which define the cycle, there are notable and measurable variations in many aspects of functioning. These include complex changes in sensory responses and fluctuations in fluid retention, weight, carbohydrate and alcohol metabolism, electrolyte levels, gastric function, and allergic reactions. There are cyclical variations in certain types of pain. The incidence of illness, accidents, and death varies with the cycle. Levels of activation in the central and autonomic nervous systems appear to change with the cycle, as do patterns of sleep. Variations with the cycle have also been reported in sexual feeling and sexual behaviour, in mood, and in severity of some psychiatric symptoms. There are indications that the incidence of attempted and successful suicides, and anti-social behaviour, is related to the cycle. The cycle appears to have little impact on over-all perceptual-motor and higher cognitive functions. The determinants of these diverse changes are discussed in Chapters 8 and 9. Some of the claims of cyclical variation require confirmation, or demonstration by more rigorous methods, and the problems entailed in that have already been pointed out.

It is important to note that for some of the changes listed there are occasionally reports of no cyclical variations. Sometimes the variations occur only in specific aspects of any function (for example, not all aspects of all sensory modalities change with the cycle). Any attempt to present an over-all picture necessarily involves over-simplification. There are many physiological, physical, psychological, and behavioural functions which have not yet been studied and which may or may not fluctuate with the cycle. Most of the findings refer to groups and will not apply to every woman in every cycle. We shall see in the next chapter that the few existing studies of individual differences suggest that this is a promising area of research both as regards cause and effect and practical implications. Not enough is known yet about baseline measurements, in women and in men. There are unanswered questions of whether any measure at ovulation or during menstrua-

---

* One study of pitch in two women during the menstrual cycle included a male subject, who was found to have a 20-day cycle (Wynn, 1972). The author points out that the study was carried out during a time of stress (examinations, etc.), and the 20-day cycle in pitch could be related to 17-ketosteroids and corticosteroids. Further confirmation would be needed. The two women showed variations in pitch with the menstrual cycle.

Table 2. Menstrual cycle studies which included men

Category of change (in the order followed in Chapters 3 and 4)	Characteristics studied	Authors	No. of men	Result	Over-all levels in men compared with women	Comments
Senses	Visual sensitivity.	Barris, Dawson, and Theiss, 1980.	3	NCV*	Levels of control group similar to 'normal' levels of experimental group.	Also in control group were two non-ovulating women who showed no cyclical variation.
	Visual sensitivity.	Diamond, Diamond and Mast, 1972.	4	NCV	Male levels higher except that women at mid-cycle are slightly higher.	
	Olfactory sensitivity.	Doty, Huggins, Snyder, and Lowry, 1981.	3	NCV	No specific information.	Authors warn that small number of men precludes definite conclusions about absence of inherent rhythms.
Bodily changes	Pain, water retention.	Doty, Huggins, Snyder, and Lowry, 1981.	3	NCV	No specific information.	See comments on Doty above.
	Pain, water retention.	Wilcoxon, Schrader, and Sherif, 1976.	11	NCV	Male levels lower.	
Alcohol metabolism	Blood alcohol levels after specific doses.	Jones, and Jones, 1976.	10	NCV	In general male levels lower than female after same amount of alcohol (allowing for body weight).	
Nervous system activity	Contingent negative variation.	Abramovitz and Dubrovsky, 1980.	5	NCV	Amplitude values in men similar to the lowest female values.	Presume male levels statistically significantly lower, but not made explicit.
	Kinaesthetic after-effect.	Baker, Kostin, Mishara, and Parker, 1979.	100	NCV	Levels similar except that in paramenstruum women have larger effect, i.e. lower activation.	No statistical analysis of male cyclicity but presume none.

Category	Measure	Reference	N		Result	Comments
	Body temperature, nasal airflow.	Doty, Huggins, Snyder, and Lowry, 1981.	3	NCV	No specific information.	See comments on Doty above.
	Perception of time intervals.	Montgomery, 1979.	10	NCV	Men have longer time perception, i.e. lower activation.	Authors warn that finding of lower levels in men may be due to an artefact in their design.
	Figural after-effects.	Satinder and Mastronardi, 1974.	10	NCV	Differences not significant but men had slightly larger after-effect i.e. lower activation.	
	Shock-aversion thresholds.	Tedford, Warren, and Flynn, 1977.	5	NCV	No significant difference.	
Sexual arousal	Self-report of sexual arousal.	Englander-Golden, Chang, Whitmore, and Dienstbier, 1980.	16	NCV	Male levels higher.	Presume no cyclicity in men but not made explicit.
Mood	Perceived interpersonal tension.	Englander-Golden, Willis, and Dienstbier, 1977.	22	NCV	No significant difference.	A pill group showed cyclical fluctuations between the male level of no fluctuation and that of the normally menstruating women.
	Daily self-ratings of mood.	Rossi and Rossi, 1977.	15	NCV	No specific information.	Men's moods showed some variation with the social week.
	Negative affect; anxiety-dysphoria; happy-sad.	Wilcoxon, Schrader, and Sherif, 1976.	11	NCV	Similar levels of negative affect: male levels lower on positive mood.	
Behavioural	Recurrent bad conduct in school children.	Dalton, 1964.	307	NCV	Similar over-all percentages of recurrence.	
	Recurrent offences in prisoners.	Dalton, 1964.	215	NCV	Similar over-all percentages of recurrence.	
	Stressful events; impaired concentration.	Wilcoxon, Schrader, and Sherif, 1976.	11	NCV	No significant difference.	

*All of the studies found no cyclical variations in men. In all of the studies cyclical variations in women were reported.

tion, or at some other point, is the typical one for an individual woman or group of women. Also, which level most closely corresponds to the more stable levels experienced by men. More details are needed, not only of men and non-menstruating women, but of subjects who are more representative of the whole menstruating population; many of the reports studied only students or women associated with universities. Most important, it is difficult to overstate the extent to which the research has tended to focus a disproportionate amount of attention on the days before and during menstruation, thus distorting the view of the cycle. The neglect of more than two-thirds of the cycle, and of the more positive changes, is manifest both in research, in clinical accounts and in commentaries. There is a great deal more to discover about the changes with the cycle. This is true not only of the greater part of the cycle which has remained unexplored but also of that part of it which is constantly being investigated. There is a lack of detail, for example, about each day of the premenstrual phase. A single, or even daily, sampling of behaviour or mood or bodily functions is unrepresentative of, say, the premenstrual phase when oestrogen and progesterone levels are falling precipitately and when, according to clinical accounts, there are fast changes in experience. More frequent sampling would also take account of the important circadian fluctuations in all aspects of functioning (see Chapter 1) upon which any menstrually-related variations have to be superimposed.

The conclusions from those studies which included a group of men are that they do not manifest the same variations as those associated with the menstrual cycle. Men appear to have no similar monthly fluctuations in visual and olfactory sensitivity, abdominal pain, fluid retention, alcohol metabolism, nervous system activity, sexual arousal, positive and negative mood patterns, tension, negative affect, or anti-social behaviour. Verifications, further details, and information about other functions would be welcome.

As regards the influence of oral contraceptives on the changes with the cycle, the most usual effect of the combination pill appears to be to reduce or eliminate the cyclical variation. This has been shown for visual acuity, breast tenderness, weight gain, alcohol metabolism, allergic reactions, dysmennorhea, various bodily symptoms, nervous system activity, sensitivity to shock, sleep, and mood. There are rare reports of the combination pill having no effect on some cyclical variations, for example, glucose levels and headache. There is less information about the sequential pill, which has been, and is, less frequently used. The studies are of interest, though, and it seems likely that the fluctuations in many measures are similar to those of the natural cycle. The possible effects of the pill on some changes have been briefly reported upon but have yet to be confirmed and conclusions cannot be drawn. This applies to olfactory sensitivity, fluid retention, conditioning, dream recall, sexual feeling and behaviour, and performance on tests. The effect of oral contraceptives on many of the changes has not been investigated at all. Since the number of studies which included an oral contraceptive group is relatively small, and since generally the numbers in these groups were restricted, these particular findings must be considered with some reservations.

CHAPTER 5

Incidence of change and individual differences

There are frequent allusions in this book to the need for more information about individual differences in changes with the menstrual cycle. The bare facts about incidence have implications for aetiology, attitude change, and treatment only when they are illuminated by details of individual variation. What, for instance, are the characteristics of women for whom the menstrual cycle is an entirely positive experience, or of those who invariably undergo several days of discomfort or distress? Can we discern meaningful subgroups in that vast majority of women who are not really aware of the positive influence of the cycle and who experience the negative aspects to varying degrees in different ways at different times? There are no definite answers to these questions yet, but there are some indications of what they might be. In this chapter the estimates of prevalence of change are discussed, followed by a closer look at individual variation within those figures.

INCIDENCE

We are again faced with the fact that nearly all of the reports of prevalence are of the premenstrual or menstrual phases and nearly all are about negative changes. The remarkable fact is that women are virtually never asked in any systematic way about any feelings and behaviour during the cycle other than at the paramenstruum. Nor are they generally asked about positive responses. Most of the questionnaires relating to the cycle are in fact symptom scales. Inevitably, because the cycle has until now been approached in a clinical context the greater portion of it has remained unexplored as have the positive aspects. It has to be remembered therefore that the incidence figures which are available are almost entirely concerned with the prevalence of negative changes in the premenstrual and menstrual phases of the cycle. This is also true of any findings on individual differences.

The problems in obtaining incidence figures are considerable. There are differences both in the extent and the intensity of changes, and even where fine gradations of choice are presented on a questionnaire the answer represents the subjective judgement of each individual about the mildness or severity of the change she is reporting. Comparisons between incidence studies is difficult because of different methods of eliciting reports of change and magnitude of change, different definitions and categories, and diverse delineations of phase of the cycle. In view of all this, it is not surprising that there is a wide range of figures which emerge from the different sources. They nevertheless reveal certain extremely widespread effects of the cycle.

Incidence refers to reported prevalence of some of the changes associated with the cycle. These do not of course include the changes in Chapter 2 which define the cycle and are common to all normally menstruating women. Incidence studies, that is those which seek to establish the rate of occurrence in a given population, are rare. Most studies are not concerned with this and simply aim to establish that a change is present or absent in a significant number of subjects at one phase compared with another phase. For example, several people have found a significant change in sensory acuity around ovulation compared with other phases of the cycle, but the prevalence of this effect in the general population has not been investigated. Table 3 shows the findings of the studies of incidence from 1969 onwards. In the table are listed those changes which have been included in at least two studies of incidence. There are also two items which have only appeared in one study, energy and well-being, these are included because they provide figures on the inter-menstrual phase. Table 3 is doubtless an inadequate reflection of the actual situation for the reasons given and especially because of the small number of reports of incidence. Apparently, with one exception (Golub, 1976) the studies did not exclude women taking the contraceptive pill and they do not give separate detailed breakdowns of incidence figures for non-pill and pill groups. Sheldrake and Cormack (1976a) do give separate incidence percentages of contraceptive pill-takers but not of those not taking a pill. Because of the wide definitions of cycle phase used in the studies, the incidence figures are here discussed in broad terms of intermenstrual, premenstrual, and menstrual phases. In fact, only one of the eleven studies in Table 3 reports on the intermenstrual phase.

Incidence of reported change intermenstrually

As we have said, specific information on reported incidence of change in this phase is almost entirely lacking. Just one study (Moos, 1969), aimed at the construction of a questionnaire on menstrual distress and therefore not primarily planned to elicit reports of positive feelings through the cycle, reports, intermenstrually, a reduced incidence of most of the, mainly negative, changes which were investigated. Percentages of women reporting intermenstrual increase in the specified items are depression 9.2%; energy 27.6%; irritability 10.0%; mood changes 16.1%; headache 14.0%; abdominal pain 4.2%; backache 6.6%; tension 12.0%; weight 5.4%; swelling 4.8%; well-being 35.3%. Judging from this single study, there are indications that compared with the premenstrual and menstrual phases very few women

Table 3. Percentage incidence of change with the menstrual cycle.* See also Tables 4 and 5 for two cross-cultural reports of incidence figures

STUDY	Anxiety ▲†	Anxiety □†	Anxiety ●†	Depression ▲	Depression □	Depression ●	Energy ▲	Energy □	Energy ●	Fatigue ▲	Fatigue □	Fatigue ●	Irritability ▲	Irritability □	Irritability ●	Mood Change ▲	Mood Change □
Clare. 1977. UK. 521 patients from 25 general practices. Age 18–45.																	
Golub, 1976. USA. 50 college-educated subjects. Age 30–45.	64			72													
van Keep and Haspels, 1979. Netherlands. 143 subjects from national probability sample. Age unspecified.																	
van Keep and Lehert, 1981. France. 2,501 subjects recruited by medical branch of national opinion poll. Age 15–50.				18						25						37	
Moos, 1969. USA. 839 wives of graduate students. Mean age 25.2.				9.2	42.9	34.6	27.6	26.6	23.9				10.0	52.2	48.9	16.1	44.3 4
Paige, 1973. USA. 298 unmarried university women. 181 Protestant, 54 Jewish, 63 Catholic. Age unspecified.					22									27			
Schuckit, Daly, Herrman, and Hineman, 1975, USA. Students interviewed once in first college year (105) and in second (98). In first year, mean age 18.4	Yr.1 18.1 Yr.2 17.2			Yr.1 33.3 Yr.2 42.5									Yr.1 45.7 Yr.2 43.6				
Sheldrake and Cormack, 1976a. UK. 3,298 students (including 756 taking the contraceptive pill). Age unspecified					31	15.4					16.0	25.4		32.5	21.6		
Timonen and Procopé, 1973. Finland. 748 students. Most aged under 27.	11			35										67			
Wetzel, Reich, McClure and Wald, 1975. USA. 558 students (92 had attended psychiatric clinic). Age unspecified.																	
Wood, Larsen and Williams, 1979a. Australia. 2,343 subjects at a health-check foundation. Aged 15–60.																	

* Percentages refer to an increase in the symptom or state.
† ▲ = Intermenstrual □ = Premenstrual ● = Menstrual.

Pain			Premenstrual syndrome			Tension/ nervousness			Weight/fluid retention			Well-being			Comments
▲	□	●	▲	□	●	▲	□	●	▲	□	●	▲	□	●	
				75											Premenstrual phase only was investigated. Percentage complaining of 'at least one of 34 symptoms'.
															Premenstrual phase only was investigated. Author points out that changes were not of great magnitude.
	17 Head			47											Premenstrual phase only was investigated.
	31 Abdomen 31 Back						18			24					Premenstrual phase only was investigated. Authors grouping of moodiness, irritability, aggression is here called mood change.
Head 14.0	29.4	35.5 Abdomen 4.2 14.2 46.6 Back 6.6 24.4 40.0				12.0	41.2	42.6	Weight 5.4 33.9 22.9 Swelling 4.8	35.5	35.4	35.3	25.5	28	Percentages are of women reporting the symptoms, whether mild, moderate, strong or severe.
	Head 22 Abdomen 57 Back 33							24		Weight 25					Questions referred only to whether symptom was present 'at menstruation'.
															Premenstrual phase only was investigated.
	Head 24 12.4 Abdomen 20.8 44.2 Back 12.1 26.2						11.8 10.4								No separate incidence figures given for non-pill subjects. Premenstrual and menstrual phase only were investigated.
Head 23 17 Abdomen 65 92 Back 42 65							52								Premenstrual symptoms were the focus of the study but some information on menstrual phase was also obtained.
				40											Premenstrual phase only was investigated. 'Premenstrual syndrome' includes various physical and psychological symptoms.
		43				Usually 45.8 Occasionally 29.1			Weight 30 Swelling 51						Premenstrual and menstrual phases only were investigated.

report depression, irritability, mood change, pain, tension, weight gain, and swelling at mid-cycle. Rather more women report increased energy and well-being at this time than in the other phases. No other incidence study reports on any part of the cycle other than premenstrual and/or menstrual.

Incidence of reported change in the premenstrual phase

Ten of the eleven studies in the table report on premenstrual change (Paige, 1973, investigated symptoms at menstruation only). These studies, using different definitions, various methods of questioning and so on, yield the following ranges of increases: anxiety 11–18.1% and, in an over 30s group, 64%; depression 18–42.9% and, in an over-30s group, 72%; energy 26.6%; fatigue 16–25%; irritability 32.5–67%; mood change 37% and 44.2%; headache 17–29.4%; abdominal pain 14.2–65%; backache 12.1–42%; premenstrual syndrome 40–75%; tension/nervousness 18–52%; weight increase 24–33.9%; swelling 35.5% and 51%; well-being 25.5%. Any positive changes premenstrually are reported in only one study (Moos, 1969): 26.6% of the women surveyed reported high enery and 25.5% feelings of well-being in the premenstrual phase.

Incidence of reported change in the menstrual phase

The wide variety of definitions and methods of the nine studies reporting on this phase produce the following ranges of increases: depression 15.4–34.6%; energy 23.9%; fatigue 25.4%; irritability 21.6–48.9%; mood change 27% and 40.81%; headache 12.4–35.5%; abdominal pain 44.2–92%; backache 26.2–65%; 'pain' 43%; tension/nervousness 10.4–42.6%; weight increase 22.9–25%; swelling 35.4%; well-being 28%. Again only one study mentions incidence of positive change during menstruation (Moos, 1969). Of the women asked, 23.9% reported high energy and 28% feelings of well-being during menstruation.

Not included in Table 3 is a study of menstrual problems in psychiatric patients which also gives incidence figures for a control group of 14 non-psychiatric menstruating women. Women reporting symptoms were: premenstrual depression 57%; premenstrual hypomania 21%; menstrual depression 29%; menstrual hypomania 7% (Diamond, Rubinstein, Dunner, and Fieve, 1976).

Some general points about incidence are worth noting. Figures on the precise prevalence in the general population of many of the changes in Chapters 3 and 4, such as sexual behaviour, sleep, anti-social behaviour, are not available. The reported figures are largely based on reports of percentage of women responding to questions about whether or not they experience certain selected changes. Little is known about the frequency of such changes in any individual. The findings of one study suggest that as regards symptoms there is a tendency for any woman to experience these consistently from one menstrual cycle to another (Moos, 1969), and in another study in which daily moods were rated the majority of women reported that their mood during the rating time was typical for them (Rossi and Rossi, 1977). One study (Markum, 1976) suggests that possibly menstrual symptoms do fluctuate slightly from month to month but that women tend to report, reasonably enough, their average experience of the symptoms. It may be that most women do tend to experience certain cyclical changes fairly regularly. It also appears that several different patterns of change can be distinguished. Steiner and Carroll (1977) for example reported that some of the studies they reviewed suggest the presence of several distinct sets of premenstrual mani-festations, see Chapter 4. These authors nevertheless feel that most women experience some combination of these manifestations. Moos and Leiderman (1978) analysed the replies to Menstrual Distress Questionnaire questions about one cycle only. They suggest the existence of several distinct configura-tions of menstrual cycle symptoms. Of the 579 women, 49% fell into clusters reporting in only one of the possible eight areas of change. Another 45% were in clusters reporting changes in more than one area. The other 6% 'remained unclustered'. There are no incidence studies which provide figures for different clusters of change. The study by Moos just mentioned, though, suggests that it might be possible to identify different groups of women in terms of type and pattern of change with the cycle. There will nevertheless be women who do not show clear-cut patterns, and in all women there will doubtless be some variation in magnitude and type of change from one cycle to another. A wide range of factors will contribute to this variation. If some different patterns of change can be identified, possibly with different underlying causes, and if women tend to show some consistency in the pattern they experience this would have important implications for adaptations and treatment.

It is not possible to give an accurate picture of the magnitude of the changes given in the incidence figures. Brooks, Ruble, and Clark (1977) pointed out that the size of the differences between changes intermenstrually and premenstrually is often quite small with most women reporting only mild symptoms premenstrually. Golub (1976) found that premenstrual and menstrual increases in anxiety and depression although significant, did not reach the level found in psychiatric groups. There are indeed differences, experienced by most women, but the symptoms may not always be experi-enced as strongly as is often suggested.

Bearing in mind these various points, the figures suggest at mid-cycle a low incidence of negative, and the highest incidence of positive, reports. Premenstrually, with the exception of pain, there is the highest rate of negative change, which tends to decrease at menstruation. There are slight indications, in these figures and elsewhere, that questionnaires which included a wider range of positive feelings and behaviour might indicate the existence of more of these, throughout the cycle. Heczey (1980) for example, in a study of the treatment of dysmenorrhea, used a questionnaire which included positive states as part of the menstrual experience. She found there was considerable reporting of positive mental and emotional states. It is also possible that information about each day of the cycle phases would transform the incidence figures. For example, if there is a relationship between pain and other physical symptoms and mood change during menstruation (see Chapter 4), if women were asked about their mood on Day 2 or Day 3 of bleeding when pain and discomfort are less a greater number might give positive answers.

The two cross-cultural studies shown in Tables 4 and 5 suggest that the reported incidence of various premenstrual changes is high in many different countries and that a large number of women throughout the world report physical discomfort and mood changes associated with menstruation. There are nevertheless considerable variations in the patterns of change reported in the different countries. This suggests socio-cultural influences, either in the actual experience of change and/or in the ways in which the questions about change are interpreted and responded to. It is also possible that there is some genetic influence, especially on cycle characteristics which in turn determine other manifestations, see 'Other factors', below.

INDIVIDUAL DIFFERENCES

What are the main individual characteristics which might determine patterns of incidence of changes associated with the menstrual cycle? The published work on individual differences has concentrated mainly on the possible relationship between changes with the cycle and the following variables: age, cycle characteristics, personality, emotional adjustment, psychiatric illness and, more occasionally, other factors such as individual hormone levels, physiological responsiveness and genetic influences. Each of these categories will be discussed briefly. Attitudes are obviously also important both to the prevalence of change and to the ways in which change is experienced and they are discussed in Chapter 9.

AGE

It is sometimes said that negative changes with the cycle increase with age but a closer look at the evidence suggests that this view is not entirely accurate. There are very few controlled studies from which to draw conclusions. One study (Moos, 1968) aimed at eliciting reports about menstrual distress, compared two groups of women, one age 21 and under and the other age 31 and over. The younger women had higher mean scores than the older women on seven of the eight scales, in the menstrual phase. In the premenstrual phase, they had lower scores on all but one of the scales. Unfortunately it was not possible in this study to separate the variables of number of children and of age. The pattern of correlations between parity and changes with the cycle was similar to that between age and cycle changes,

Table 4. Incidence of change before and during menstruation in 14 cultural groups. Reproduced by permission of the Population Council from the World Health Organization Task Force on Psychosocial Research in Family Planning, 'A cross-cultural study of menstruation: Implications for contraceptive development and use,' *Studies in Family Planning*, **12**, no. 1 (January 1981): Table 3

Changes	Egypt n = 500	India, Hindu High Caste n = 266	India, Hindu Low Caste n = 280	Indonesia Javanese n = 199	Indonesia Sudanese n = 200	Jamaica n = 574	Korea n = 499	Mexico n = 501	Pakistan Sind n = 351	Pakistan Punjab n = 349	Phillipines n = 522	United Kingdom n = 550	Yugoslavia Non-Muslim n = 166	Yugoslavia Muslim n = 335
Physical discomfort prior to or during menstruation	58	58	55	65	70	61	53	51	68	50	62	57	60	69
Mood changes prior to or during menstruation	42	44	40	34	23	42	52	38	58	39	48	71	65	73
Decreased work during menstruation	10	58	46	12	7	19	14	7	14	11	19	15	12	18
Increased rest during menstruation	21	72	43	18	15	29	28	11	36	22	27	22	21	41

Percentage of respondents reporting physical, psychological, behavioural changes associated with menstruation.
All parous women, any age up to menopause.

Table 5. Incidence of premenstrual syndrome* in six cultural groups. Reproduced by permission of the Academy of Psychosomatic Medicine from Janiger, Riffenburgh, and Kersh, 1972, *Psychosomatics*, **13**, 226–235

Symptom	American n = 135	Japanese n = 100	Nigerian n = 35	Apache n = 28	Turkish n = 51	Greek n = 50
Lower abdominal pain	59	54	83	64	76	60
Irritability	70	29	40	54	62	32
Fatigue	54	41	70	54	76	78
Depression	58	42	36	54	66	56
Fullness and bloating of abdomen	63	26	14	32	60	66
Eruption of face	67	26	40	29	60	40
Tension (nervousness)	57	31	43	64	60	22
Backache	59	4	78	71	88	78
Soreness and tenderness of breasts	56	13	83	36	62	46
Easily upset	60	18	37	61	54	24

* Premenstrual syndrome: Percentage of each nationality group reporting the most frequent symptoms. Given by the authors as the most frequent symptoms in the entire sample. Listed in order of frequency from high to low.
Women recruited via schools, hospitals, anthropological field workers. Ages not given.
Self-report on the week prior to the most recent menstruation.

indicating that the effect of these two variables would have to be separated before drawing firm conclusions. For instance, one study (Coppen and Kessell, 1963) which did separate the two variables found that age and parity had similar relationships to some menstrual changes, but not all. In general, there is a need for studies of large numbers of women to enable separation of age, marital state, and parity which are of course all related to each other.

Two studies found no relationship between age and negative menstrually-related mood (Coppen and Kessell, 1963; Little and Zahn, 1974). There were some differences between older and younger women on some measures of autonomic nervous system activity through the cycle; older women had higher temperatures, less heart-rate variability and somewhat lower skin conductance resting levels in the luteal phase (Little and Zahn, 1974). Head-aches were related to age (older women had more) and menstrual pain was negatively related to age (Coppen and Kessell, 1963). A report of a significant increase in suicide premenstrually found no difference between younger and older women as regards this tendency (Tonks, Rack, and Rose, 1968). One questionnaire study (Rouse, 1978) found a tendency for older women to report more symptoms in the premenstrual and menstrual phases than younger women, but details of which symptoms are not given. Timonen and Procopé (1973) in a study of 748 students in Finland observed increased premenstrual depression in those over 26 years old. They also found that premenstrual headache and abdominal swelling increased with age. There was no relationship between age and the many other psychological and physical symptoms investigated in the study. One study (Gough, 1975) found a significant correlation between age and reported distress in the premenstrual phase. This was not true of the menstrual and intermenstrual phases. A report from France on the epidemiology of the premenstrual syndrome (van Keep and Lehert, 1981) found a different pattern of premenstrual symptoms in women under and over 33 years of age, notably that up to 33 women rarely reported symptoms related to water retention, general uneasiness and fatigue. Golub in 1976 reported that in a group of women, mainly graduates, mean age between 36 and 37, premenstrual anxiety and depression scores were significantly higher than at mid-cycle. The same authors (Golub and Harrington, 1981) later reported on 158 high-school students ages 15–16 years. In this younger group there were no significant changes in mood with the cycle. In addition to the mood scales, the Moos Menstrual Distress Questionnaire was administered and the adolescents' scores on this, menstrual, questionnaire were significantly higher during menstruation than in the rest of the cycle. The authors' suggestion, already mentioned in Chapter 4, is that the tendency for younger women to report symptoms in the menstrual phase, whereas older women report them premenstrually, may be related to menstrual pain (which the adolescent girls rated as the highest symptom).

Conclusions about the relationship of age to the cycle changes are difficult to draw. As usual the small amount of work that is available is largely concerned with symptoms and distress. So far it shows no clear-cut picture of more negative changes with age, though older women appear to have more symptoms premenstrually, which is the phase most often reported upon. Younger women report more symptoms during menstruation. It does seem that there are different patterns of change in younger and older women, with certain symptoms being more or less predominant at different times of life and in different phases of the cycle. It may also be that some of the clinical reports of a change in menstrual symptoms with age were not always able to make a clear distinction between menstrual and menopausal changes in the older women. The menopausal changes begin gradually several years before the cessation of bleeding, see Chapter 6. Another factor to be noted is the fact that the proportion of anovulatory cycles is related to age, see Chapter 2, and studies of cyclical changes have rarely taken account of this. Metcalf and Mackenzie (1980) report that only 62% of women aged 20–24 ovulate in every cycle whereas the figure is 90.9% for women aged 30–39 (see Table 1). As anovulatory cycles lack the pre- and post-ovulatory variations in oestrogen and in progesterone and doubtless in other hormones, this will contribute to the patterns of other cyclical changes with age. More information about the association between age and the manifestations of the menstrual cycle would lead to a better understanding of the bases of the changes and would have important implications for adaptive and therapeutic measures.

CYCLE CHARACTERISTICS

Information on the precise relationship between menstrual changes on the one hand and regularity and length of cycle and intensity and length of menstrual flow on the other, is once again concerned only with symptoms and distress. Length of cycle seems to have some association with symptoms in the premenstrual and menstrual phases. Sheldrake and Cormack (1976a) reported on 2,542 students, not taking a contraceptive pill, who replied to a questionnaire about the presence premenstrually of a variety of physical and psychological symptoms. They found that women with longer than average cycles, of 31–40 days, were the most frequent reporters of most of the symptoms, both premenstrually and menstrually. Those with cycles of longer than 40 days tended to have a low rate of reporting most of the symptoms. At least two studies have failed to find a relationship between length of cycle and reported menstrual distress (Brooks, Ruble, and Clark, 1977; Moos, 1968). The influences which bear on the length of the cycle are complex and are discussed in Chapter 8.

Irregular cycles are more strongly related to premenstrual and menstrual symptoms than regular ones (Brooks, Ruble, and Clark, 1977; Hain, Linton, Eber, and Chapman, 1970; van Keep and Lehert, 1981; Moos, 1969; Sheldrake and Cormack, 1976a). There may of course be an interactive effect of length and regularity. Sheldrake and Cormack (1976a) found that as regards the premenstrual phase the long and irregular group are the least likely to report all symptoms. The short and irregular group have a high incidence of depression, tension and irritability. The long and regular group report more stomach ache, back ache and lethargy. During menstruation, women with long and regular cycles have the lowest rate of reporting most of the symptoms. The short and irregular group have a high incidence of all symptoms.

Length and intensity of the menstrual flow appear to be related to at least some of the menstrual symptoms (Brooks, Ruble, and Clark, 1977; Moos, 1969; Paige, 1971), but further clarification of details is needed. A World Health Organization report has shown cross-cultural differences in the reported number of days of menstrual bleeding and it would be useful to know whether these differences are in turn related to the different patterns of menstrual symptoms reported in different cultures (see Tables 4 and 5).

We can conclude, as regards cycle characteristics, that there appears to be some association between premenstrual and menstrual symptoms and length and irregularity of cycles, possibly in interaction with each other. The number of days and perhaps the intensity of bleeding are also possibly related to some menstrual symptoms. These suppositions have still to be confirmed. As with age, the incidence of anovulatory cycles is doubtless one factor in any relationship between changes with the cycle and cycle characteristics, particularly length of cycle, which appears to be related to anovulation (Cutler, Garcia, and Krieger, 1979a; Metcalf and Mackenzie, 1980).

PERSONALITY

There is ambiguity in some of the published work as regards the distinction between personality on the one hand and emotional adjustment and psychiatric disorder on the other. It nevertheless seems worth making this distinction in attempting to accurately assess the factors which may be related to individual differences in the way in which the cycle is experienced. Only menstrual symptoms and distress have so far been investigated. Many authors report an association between certain personality variables and some menstrual symptoms. There are inconsistent results about which personality factors correlate negatively or positively with menstrual experience. Likelihood of menstrual distress is said to be positively related to personality variables such as physically and socially active, sexually orgasmic, maternal (Rossi and Rossi, 1977), neurotic and paranoid tendencies, lack of understanding of motivations and feelings, unwholesome menstrual attitude (Levitt and Lubin, 1967); and indirectly related to trait anxiety (Awaritefe, Awaritefe, Diejomaoh, and Ebie, 1980), neuroticism (Ladisch, 1977), and femininity (Gough, 1975). Others have reported a negative association between menstrual symptoms and femininity (Berry and McGuire, 1972); and most scores on the California Personality Inventory, such as dominance, sociability, well-being, and tolerance (Gough, 1975). James and Pollitt (1974) and

Moos, Kopell, Melges, Yalom, Lunde, Clayton, and Hamburg (1969) found a positive relationship between high and low scores on premenstrual symptoms and certain personality or mood variables. Coppen and Kessell (1963) and Lamb, Ulett, Masters, and Robinson (1953) had earlier found an association between irritability (Coppen and Kessell) and activity scores (Lamb *et al.*) and premenstrual tension. Bloom, Shelton, and Michaels (1978) reported that dysmenorrhea sufferers were different from non-sufferers on various personality measures, but that the sufferers did not have 'maladjusted' scores. Most of the reviews of the published work report the inconsistencies or at least the variety of the findings (for example Brooks-Gunn and Ruble, 1980). They also point to the finding that any psychological factors will interact with a great many physiological variables and with different levels of individual responsiveness to these variables (Culberg, 1972; Friedman, Hurt, Arnoff, and Clarkin, 1980; Moos and Leiderman, 1978; Reid and Yen, 1981). Other methodological problems have not gone unnoticed. Brooks-Gunn and Ruble (1980) note that often the personality variables chosen are too global, or only indirectly relevant to the menstrual experience. Some people feel this last point may be an advantage. Gannon (1981) suggests that any association between personality tests and, for example, the much-used Menstrual Distress Questionnaire, may be due to the fact that they reflect similar questions. Coppen and Kessel (1963) took account of this and eliminated some questions from the Maudsley Personality Inventory. They found that many psychological symptoms were still significantly correlated with scores on neuroticism. Of course the inventory was then no longer the standardized version. Gannon (1981) also questions the statistical analyses of some of the studies, and some of the interpretations put upon them. There is also the familiar problem that in almost all of the studies cited above, the subjects were students, and hence unrepresentative of women in general.

The attempts to discover a relationship, or lack of it, between personality variables and menstrual experience are bedevilled by the well-known problems of studying personality traits and their varying relationships with other variables on the one hand, and by those of measuring a wide range of reported negative menstrual changes on the other. It is therefore not surprising that the results are inconsistent and that we are unable to draw definite conclusions. Although all of the studies find some associations, positive or negative, between certain aspects of personality and some of the elements of menstrual distress, there are doubts about the conceptual and methodological accepitibilty of some of the work. Until these are resolved it seems best to assume that personality variables possibly contribute, not surprisingly, to a woman's menstrual experience but that the nature of this contribution is by no means clear at present. It also has to be remembered that, if any associations are found, the direction of causality is not known. Women with early experience of menstrually related distress may well have developed certain characteristic feelings, attitudes, adjustments, and so on.

EMOTIONAL ADJUSTMENT AND PSYCHIATRIC ILLNESS

Several studies find an association between emotional adjustment and menstrual distress. Wood, Larsen, and Williams (1979b) report a relationship between premenstrual tension and menstrual pain and four indices of emotional health. Sheldrake and Cormack (1976a) found some indication that those who were more susceptible to emotional disorder were more subject to menstrual disturbance. Hain, Linton, Eber, and Chapman (1970) found a similar relationship. Halbreich and Kas (1977) showed that women suffering from premenstrual syndrome had significantly higher scores than a control group on the Taylor Manifest Anxiety Scale and this was so during the entire cycle. Gruba and Rohrbraugh (1975) found that some of the symptoms of the Menstrual Distress Questionnaire (premenstrual pain, menstrual behaviour change, premenstrual negative affect, and premenstrual and menstrual autonomic reactions) were positively related to Minnesota Multiphasic Personality Inventory scores but there was no association between other menstrual symptoms (water retention and allied symptoms, and activity, excitement, and affection) and the inventory. Golub (1976, 1981) whose work is cited in Chapter 4 considers that her findings with younger and older women do not support the view that premenstrual mood changes are a function of personal adjustment. One other study (Clare, 1977) obtained results which suggest an absence of a clear-cut relationship between neurotic and premenstrual status, but the author states that further investigation is required.

The evidence is slightly in favour of there being some relationship between emotional adjustment and menstrual distress. Nevertheless the methodological problems are great, the studies are few, and conclusions cannot be drawn with any certainty.

As far as more frank psychiatric disorder is concerned, the evidence tends to support the view of a relationship between some menstrual symptoms and affective illness, (Coppen, 1965; Kashiwagi, McClure, and Wetzel, 1976; Wetzel, Reich, McClure, and Wald, 1975). Schuckit, Daly, Herrman, and Hineman (1975) found a similar but non-significant trend. Kashiwagi, McClure, and Wetzel (1976) reported that no relationship was found between non-affective psychiatric disorders and premenstrual psychological syndrome. One study of women with a history of affective illness failed to find a significantly higher rate of premenstrual complaints though these women were more likely to be hospitalized for their affective illness during the premenstrual and menstrual phases. The authors conclude that women who have affective disorders but who are not actually in an episode of the illness experience menstruation much as other women; those who are in the middle of an episode may experience a worsening of the illness premenstrually (Diamond, Rubinstein, Dunner, and Fieve, 1976). The conclusion seems to be that there is probably some relationship between affective illness and likelihood of some menstrual symptoms.

94

If a relationship between the manifestations of the menstrual cycle and emotional adjustment and/or more definite psychiatric disorder does exist, the direction and nature of causality remain a matter for speculation. Much of the evidence for a relationship between menstrual complaints and psychiatric illness now centres on premenstrual depression, but the usual picture of premenstrual depression is quite unlike 'psychiatric' depression, with few of the characteristic features such as early morning sleep disturbance, diurnal variation of mood and so forth. Furthermore, we have seen in Chapter 4 that depression is not in general a consistently reported feature of the premenstrual and menstrual phases. It may be that the relationship between a predisposition to affective illness and the onset of depressive symptoms with the premenstrual phase is highly specific to these patients and has no causal implications for the generality of women. Certainly it might be predicted that a normal amount of menstrual mood change, superimposed on high existing levels of psychological problems, would be perceived as greater than the same change on a background of no affective illness. It would be interesting to know whether any association exists between pyschiatric disorders and positive changes with the cycle, whether for instance the hypomanic phases of bipolar affective illnesses are heightened at mid-cycle. As usual, no-one has systematically explored the rich pastures of the majority of the cycle days which are not premenstrual or menstrual.

OTHER FACTORS

It is worth mentioning very briefly three other sources of individual variation in menstrual experience.

Individual hormone levels

The question of the role of individual hormone levels in determining other changes with the cycle is a vital area of enquiry which has hardly been tackled. Only a few studies have carried out direct measurement of the relationship of hormone levels in individual women with other menstrual changes. There is an increasing number of investigations which include the measurement of one or more hormone levels, but there are indications that it is the over-all pattern of hormones which is of most interest. The decisive work would entail measurement of the combination of the various relevant hormones which pertains at any one time in any individual and the correlation of these with other changes with the cycle. The exploration of the association between such complex sets of variables presents formidable problems of methodology. Most of the few studies which have measured the levels of certain hormones and related them to other changes in groups of women have dealt with the premenstrual phase. These studies are cited in the appropriate sections of this book. Also included, in Chapters 3 and 4, are the few studies which appear to have carried out correlational analyses (this is not always made entirely clear in the studies) between individual hormone levels and measurements of other change (Backstrom, 1976; Doty, Huggins, Snyder, and Lowry, 1981; Persky, Charney, Lief, O'Brien, Miller, and Strauss, 1978; Schreiner-Engel, Schiavi, Smith, and White, 1981; Voda, 1980; Webster, 1980). With the exception of one study, (Voda, 1980) which measured progesterone and aldosterone, these few studies show some relationship between certain hormones and certain, but not all, of the other changes which they have investigated. As regards correlations between premenstrual syndrome and levels of various hormones, the results are inconsistent (see for example Backstrom and Aakvaag, 1981; *British Medical Journal*, Editorial, 1979). There is certainly not enough evidence yet to be able to discern direct relationships between individual hormone levels and experience of other changes with the cycle. This will not be possible until intensive studies of the individual configurations of many hormones and of the other changes are carried out.

Physiological responsiveness

One important area of individual differences, general phsyiological responsiveness, has not been explored in relation to the menstrual changes. [Just one study, Friedman and Meares (1979) refers to a small but significant positive correlation between oestrogen level and point of habituation to an auditory stimulus which the authors take to indicate higher central nervous system arousal.] Given the importance of the central and autonomic nervous systems in every aspect of physical and psychological functioning, an individual's habitual and temporary levels of reactivity in those systems will presumably be fundamental in determining her experience of the menstrual cycle. There is a general discussion of this point in the context of mechanisms of learning, in Chapter 9. The difficulties of measuring physiological responsiveness were referred to in Chapter 3 and these doubtless account for the lack of work. Nevertheless, psychophysiological measurement techniques are improving and progress in applications to the menstrual cycle can be expected.

Genetic influences

Genetic influences are doubtless at work in many sources of individual differences already mentioned. There is only a very small amount of work which has specifically investigated the possible contribution of genetic factors to the experience of the menstrual cycle. Any such studies encounter the general problems of attempts to establish the relative contributions of heredity and environment to any human behaviour or experience. Interpretations of the findings have to be made with considerable reservations. The findings are few and can be briefly summarized. Widholm and Kantero (1971) in a large survey in Finland found a significant relationship between mothers and daughters, and between sisters, on age of menarche; length of cycles; duration of flow; dysmenorrhea and premenstrual tension. Chern, Gatewood, and Anderson (1980) report significant correlations between mothers and daughters, and sisters, on age at menarche; menstrual interval and duration of flow. The same authors give some preliminary results which show that daughters of mothers with extremely long or short cycles have a higher than normal chance of having cycles of extreme length. Metral (1981) carried out a simulation study which suggested the operation of natural selection on menstrual cycle length, which in turn is apparently related to premenstrual and menstrual symptoms, see 'Cycle characteristics', above. Clearly, we are not at present justified in drawing conclusions about genetic influences on individual experience of the menstrual cycle. The work which does exist gives some indication of genetic contribution to certain aspects of the cycle.

SUMMARY

This chapter on incidence and individual differences in menstrual changes indicates that most women experience some degree of change with the cycle in some aspect of their physical, psychological, and behavioural functioning. There are no prevalence figures on many of the cyclical changes which are known to occur. Incidence figures are almost entirely lacking on changes other than those occurring just before and during menstruation. We therefore have only a very incomplete picture of the prevalence of changes throughout the cycle.

As regards the characteristics of the individuals who do and who do not experience any particular change, there is a similar loading of information on the symptoms and distress of the days around menstruation. There are nevertheless indications that age, cycle regularity, length and intensity of menstrual flow, personality, emotional adjustment and psychiatric disorder, patterns of hormonal levels, physiological responsiveness, and genetic factors are all worth exploring as possible correlates of certain patterns of change with the cycle. In the meantime, we can make a few tentative suggestions. Different patterns of change are found with age, mainly, as regards some negative aspects, with a tendency for younger women to report symptoms in the menstrual phase and for older women to report them premenstrually. There are indications that length and regularity of the cycle, as well as certain features of the menstrual flow, are related to some premenstrual and menstrual symptoms. It is difficult to comment on the role of individual differences in personality, emotional adjustment, and psychiatric illness in the experience of the cycle. This is because, although there are some indications that they may be contributing factors, there are methodological problems which have not yet been satisfactorily overcome. Even if the indications are confirmed, the unanswered question of direction of causality will remain. Three factors have scarcely been explored and are undoubtedly important. They are individual hormone levels, physiological responsiveness, and genetic factors. Real progress in this area will depend on large longitudinal studies which examine a wide range of variables. It will also depend on further clarification of the different types of change which actually take place. The present categories such as feelings of well-being, negative affect, premenstrual tension, premenstrual dysphoria, need closer definition. Magnitude of change should be taken more into account. Also important would be information on how, for any individual, each part of a cycle is related to every other part of it; whether there are individual patterns of change throughout the cycle with, say, the level of change mid-cycle being systematically related to level of change premenstrually. Investigation of the question of individual propensity to experience anovulatory cycles will also provide crucial information about the factors which determine the individual's experience of the cycle.

The discussion so far has centred on the years of full reproductive life and we now turn to the menopause when procreative ability is coming to an end.

CHAPTER 6

The ending of the reproductive cycle: I

THE MENOPAUSE

It is not within the scope of this book to give an exhaustive account of the menopause and the post-menopausal years. This chapter is concerned to describe the events of the menopause and to outline the mechanisms which bring about the ending of the menstrual cycle. The next chapter sets out the main changes and symptoms which are associated with the menopausal years.

The immense upsurge of interest in the climacteric in recent years is the result of a combination of developments. Probably the most important factor is the relationship between the age at which the reproductive years end and life expectancy. In modern times the younger age of menarche has prolonged the fertile period. Nevertheless the reproductive years represent a smaller proportion of the lifespan because of the much increased life expectancy. At least 55% of women now live to 75 years or more, and therefore spend a third of their lives after the menopause. The post-menopausal era is no longer a negligible part of life, as it was a century ago, when the average life expectancy was 48 years. Social factors have greatly contributed to the present concern with the climacteric years. They centre largely on the declared aim of more varied lives for women, with interests and challenges outside as well as inside the home. This has focused attention on the need to attenuate any ill-effects of the ending of the reproductive cycle and to render the considerable number of subsequent years free from the repercussions of changes which occur at that time. Finally, improved techniques, especially in hormonal measurements, have combined with the demands brought about by longer life and by changing social attitudes to create around the climacteric a thriving area of fundamental and applied research.

METHODOLOGICAL ISSUES

We shall see that the whole topic of the climacteric is somewhat unwieldy and that the problems of definition are formidable. Menopause, or the last menstruation, although identified retrospectively, is a fixed point and relatively easily agreed upon as a criterion. The delineation of the menopausal or climacteric years defies any simple approach. The changes which mark the ending of the reproductive process are gradual, long-lasting, and extremely difficult to measure in large numbers of women. They have no clearly marked beginning and an even less definite end. The climacteric years comprise several stages, each one differing widely from the other in many ways. There is a case, for instance, for differentiating as the premenopause a period of at least six to eight years before the date of last menstruation, during which time there are irregular menstrual cycles and a decline in fertility (Kopera, 1979). Similarly several marked and far-reaching changes take place after the menopause. In this book the concern is with the process of the ending of the menstrual cycle, that is the transitional years which are physiologically a time of change and instability, as opposed to the clearly post-menopausal years, which are more stable. The duration of the complete menopausal transition varies greatly among women. No very clear distinctions of the different stages in the long and variable climacteric phase emerge from the published work. Many clinical studies frequently cover an age range of as much as 30 years, sometimes including younger artificially menopausal women with those who are completely post-menopausal. These groups are too heterogeneous to give rise to any solid conclusions (McKinlay, Jefferys, and Thompson, 1972).

Some of the other methodological problems are similar to ones we have already encountered in the rest of the menstrual cycle. Accurate information must be obtained from large numbers of women. This entails identification, on the part of each woman for a prolonged period of time, of significant vaginal bleeding. They must also judge the magnitude of various changes and must often exercise a level of memory for detail which few people are capable of. As regards measurement, excellent techniques for the assessment of hormonal levels have been developed in recent years, including methods for investigating sources other than the ovaries for production of steroids after the menopause. Details of conversion and interconversion of androgens and oestrogens have also become known, thanks to the development of isotopic techniques (Hutton, Jacobs, and James, 1979). All this opens up immense possibilities of understanding, but the measurements nevertheless entail obtaining blood and urine samples from large numbers of women regularly, often daily. Another problem, already encountered, is the variety and 'partiality' of the questionnaires or other methods of eliciting information. They are necessarily incomplete and often entirely angled towards one restricted aspect of the menopausal years. Particularly familiar is the fact that the majority are clinically orientated and therefore concerned only with symptoms and distress. The problem of meaningful control groups looms large when it comes to demonstrating the specificity of some of the changes associated with the climacteric. Clearly, control groups could come from women who are for natural or for artificial reasons pre- or post-climacteric. All of these differ from the climacteric group on many other variables.

This becomes particularly crucial in attempts to establish specificity to the climacteric of such features as memory impairment, which could be more generally attributable to age. Ideally information would come from various groups of women studied from well before the onset of the climacteric, and through it, on many variables including detailed physiological changes. This kind of information is rarely available. The question of direct comparisons between climacteric women and groups of ageing men has hardly been broached in the published work. There is a rather hazy picture of what happens to men during these years of life and appropriate mention will be made of this at various points. Certainly it is not yet justified to say whether there is, or is not, a male equivalent of the 'climacteric syndrome' since the whole question has simply not been investigated, and men have rarely been asked for their subjective reports of the time when hormonal levels are changing, testicular function is declining, and so on.

In addition to the general problems of investigating the years of menopausal transition it will be seen that there are often particular difficulties in attempting to describe and explain some of the changes.

AGE AT MENOPAUSE

The ovarian failure which ultimately brings the reproductive process to an end does not happen suddenly and in fact begins long before menopause, perhaps as much as ten years before. There is a gradual breakdown in the functional relationship between the hypothalamus, the pituitary gland, and the ovaries. The term climacteric refers to the time of transition between the fully reproductive years and the non-reproductive stage of life. Menopause is, strictly speaking, a much narrower term which indicates the last menstruation, occurring on average at around 50 years of age. Establishing the precise facts about age at menopause is beset with difficulties. There are as yet only tentative answers to questions about the average age and the ways in which it varies. When it comes to actually dating the last menstrual period the gathering of information has relied on the memory of the women surveyed. Not only does the memory of older people tend to be imperfect but there is the related finding, already mentioned in Chapter 2, that in dating their menopause women tend to round off to five-year intervals; there is also a tendency, particularly in those who are further away from it, to understate the age at menopause. Since the reported dates of menopause are therefore not reliable, calculations of the mean age are not accurate, and use of the median is preferable. In order to arrive at the median the information required from each woman surveyed refers only to events in that particular year, and from that the percentage of post-menopausal women in each age group is calculated. A survey of London women revealed a median age at natural menopause of 50.78 years, and around 51 years can be considered typical of the approximate median age in industrialized societies (McKinlay, Jefferys, and Thompson, 1972). In Chapter 2 the prevailing view was expressed that the age of menopause has not changed appreciably for at least a century and possibly much longer, or at all. This is in contrast to the age of menarche which has gone steadily down, presumably largely as a function of nutritional changes. There are no obvious explanations for the age of menopause being so firmly fixed through the centuries, in spite of changing physical, social, and psychological conditions. In evolutionary terms, the basis for the continued, and still extending, survival of women after the fixed and unchanging end of reproductive life is not clear. Facts such as the stable age of menopause and of the maximal lifespan have raised the possibility, mentioned in Chapter 1, of genetic control of fixed timing of these events. The practical approach is to assume that the changes which follow ovarian failure are unselected consequences of increasing survival beyond reproductive life and must be dealt with as constructively as possible (Worley, 1981a). In considering the variables which appear to be related to the age at which reproductive life ends for any individual there are considerable methodological difficulties, not the least being the close inter-relationships between many of the variables. At present, the following factors are thought to have some association with age at menopause.

Smoking

Smoking, and having smoked in the past, is associated with age of menopause. The more cigarettes smoked per day, the earlier the menopause (Jick and Porter, 1977). This variable could be related to weight. Since there is some evidence that an increased amount of fat tissue may delay the age of menopause, and non-smokers as a group are heavier than smokers, it might be thought that this could at least partly explain the precocious menopause of smokers. One study, however, indicates that the toxic effects of smoking *per se* is the more important factor in an early menopause (Lindquist, 1979).

Height

Height, investigated separately from weight, is related to menopausal age; taller women have a later age (Brand and Lehert, 1978).

Marital status

Women who are currently married reach the menopause later than those who are widowed, divorced/separated, and unmarried (Brand and Lehert, 1978; McKinlay, Jefferys, and Thompson, 1972).

Occupation

It is difficult to assess the variable of working outside the home because, among other things, it is associated with marital status, but it appears to be related to an earlier menopause (Brand and Lehert, 1978).

Socio-economic class

Any association between menopause and socio-economic class is apparently not statistically significant (McKinlay, Jefferys, and Thompson, 1972) though one study found a very low income group had a significantly earlier menopause than a very high income group (Ernster and Petrakis, 1981).

Parity

It is possible that nulliparous women have a later menopause than parous women (Ernster and Petrakis, 1981).

Oral contraception

Prolonged oral contraceptive use, sometimes thought to be associated with a later menopause, may not be a significant factor when large numbers of long-term users have been studied (Brand and Lehert, 1978).

Age of pregnancy

There appears to be some relationship between pregnancy after the age of 40 and a later menopause though one study found this relationship was not significant (Ernster and Petrakis, 1981).

The possible role of race, familial patterns, geographical factors and disease in menopausal age is not yet clear (Flint, 1976).

In general, there is a great deal of inconsistency in the reports of factors related to age at menopause. Further confirmation of all the findings is needed. At present it seems that in any individual and in certain groups various cultural and other factors influence, in both directions, the age at which reproductive life ends, though the normal age range remains fairly stable. Premature menopause has to be defined arbitrarily. There is not enough information available from epidemiological studies to permit the calculation of meaningful parameters in a relevant population. Details of aetiology, characteristic features, individual differences and so on are therefore lacking. It is generally defined as a primary ovarian failure before a certain age (45, for example), and the accepted important diagnostic feature of premature menopause is the primary ovarian failure, rather than any other cause of permanent amenorrhea. The complete hormonal pattern in premature menopause is in fact identical to that of the normal menopause. The clinical implications, especially the problems of precocious oestrogen deficiency, are obvious (Jacobs and Murray, 1976).

HORMONAL CHANGES

The hormonal and organic events which take place at the end of the reproductive years are common to all women and define the climacteric. They are being rapidly documented, though details of all the inter-relationships are not yet known.

Oestrogens

During reproductive life, the main oestrogen secreted by the ovarian follicle and the corpus luteum is oestradiol. Since both of these sources decline during the menopausal transition, oestradiol deficiency is the main characteristic at that time. Oestrone, another oestrogen compound secreted by the ovary before the menopause, afterwards becomes proportionately the major circulating oestrogen, by conversion from other hormones. The third oestrogen compound, oestriol, is biologically weaker and not secreted by the ovary at all. In the post-menopausal woman levels of both oestrone and oestradiol fall and the cyclical variations of the reproductive years disappear. Although it is generally agreed that there is a greater decrease in the oestradiol fraction and that oestrone then becomes the comparatively major oestrogen because of its alternative sites of production, it is possible that there is an increase in oestradiol levels in the late climacteric (Chakravarti, Collins, Forecast, Newton, Oram, and Studd, 1976). Also to be noted is wide individual variation in hormonal changes through the climacteric including, in the case of oestrogens, differences according to amount of fat tissue, which appears to be a major determining factor of oestrogen levels. Greater fat mass is related to higher production of oestrogen (Peters, 1979).

Progesterone

Comparatively little is written about the course of progesterone levels through the menopause, but it seems that early in the menopausal transition there are normal concentrations of this hormone. As the frequency of ovulatory cycles decreases, the secretion of progesterone declines, until cycles become anovulatory and there is essentially no ovarian production of progesterone (Vaughn and Hammond, 1981). It is thought that in post-menopausal women any progesterone secretions have an almost exclusively adrenal origin (Vermeulen, 1976).

Androgens

There is no clear evidence of androgen deficiency during the climacteric. Testosterone levels in post-menopausal women remain essentially unchanged and the main source is probably the adrenal glands, through a process of conversion from another androgen, androstenedione (Studd, Chakravarti, and Oram, 1977).

Gonadotrophins

As regards gonadotrophin levels during the menopausal transition the situation is more complex than was previously thought. FSH appears to rise more, and earlier, than LH. Also, the exact timing of the gonadotrophin changes does not always reflect the presence of a simple feedback relationship with ovarian hormones. As women approach menopause, increased FSH and LH excretion is often found with normal oestrogen (oestradiol) levels and high and sustained FSH and LH levels are even present when there is evidence of follicular maturation and corpus luteum function, that is, of ovarian activity. One report (Sherman, West, and Korenman, 1976) emphasizes the complexity of the hypothalamic-pituitary-ovarian regulatory system and the authors suggest that their findings indicate that FSH and LH are modulated, independently of each other, at pituitary level. They offer a further, more speculative, explanation that there may be another, as yet unknown, ovarian regulatory hormone that would decrease with increasing age and with a reduced number of follicles. The main contender at present is a hormone analogous to inhibin, a non-steroidal substance which is also thought to exist in men. This 'inhibin-like' material has been shown to suppress preferentially the secretion of FSH (Ben-David and van Look, 1979). Certainly the levels of FSH and LH during the climacteric do not simply rise together in a uniform fashion. As ovarian failure progresses and the menopause approaches, levels of both of these hormones increase, but there is an earlier and greater rise in FSH than in LH, suggesting that FSH is relatively more sensitive to the suppressive effect of oestrogen. The maximal levels of FSH are recorded three to five years after the menopause when they may be as much as 15 times higher than their highest value in the menstrual cycle. With increasing post-menopausal age the FSH levels again fall towards premenopausal levels. LH levels also peak, but less markedly, at about five years after the menopause, and decrease with advancing years (Chakravarti, Collins, Forecast, Newton, Oram, and Studd, 1976).

ORGANIC AND BODILY CHANGES

Organic changes through and after the female climacteric have been fairly extensively described. Though we are interested here in changes which are specific to the ending of the reproductive cycle, rather than changes which take place later on, it will be evident that it is not always possible to make a clear separation.

Urogenital tract

There are marked changes in the genital organs which manifest themselves only gradually after the menopause. The ovaries begin to decrease in size from the age of 30 and the rate accelerates after the age of 60. Each ovary contains about 700,000 small follicles at birth, and these are reduced to half by the first onset of menstruation. The numbers continue to decrease throughout reproductive life and only a small number are left at menopause (Peters, 1979). Primordial follicles are found in post-menopausal women (Costoff and Mahesh, 1975) but through the menopausal years the remaining ones are less responsive to pituitary gonadotrophin stimulation (Studd, Chakravarti, and Oram, 1977). There are changes in the walls of vessels in the ovaries and increased deposits of lipids (Beard, 1976). With age there is a marked proliferation of the surface epithelium of the ovary leading to cysts and deep invaginations. There is an increase in pigment-bearing phagocytes, also nodules and ducts appear (Peters, 1979). The vaginal skin becomes atrophied with the oestrogen deficiencies of the climacteric. The vaginal wall becomes thin and dry with decreased vascularity and elasticity (Studd, Chakravarti, and Oram, 1977). The vagina shortens and narrows (Vaughn and Hamond, 1981). The cervix shrinks and atrophies and the cervical canal decreases in size. The uterus, including the endometrium, becomes atrophied and diminishes in size. The labia majora and minora become less prominent, the vulval skin becomes extremely thin and there is a loss of pubic hair. Muscle tone in the pelvis is reduced. The general decline in the pelvic region includes changes in bladder mucosa and in urethral tone (Studd, Chakravarti, and Oram, 1977).

All these changes are the inevitable outcome of the menopause. There is nevertheless marked variability in the onset and severity of atrophy of the urogenital tissues (Vaughn and Hammond, 1981). There are also individual differences in the tendency to develop symptoms as a result of these urogenital changes. Symptoms are by no means universal, and they are discussed in the next chapter.

Skin

There is difficulty in assessing which of the changes in the skin with old age are specific to the climacteric. It is still not known whether the skin is a true target organ for oestrogens, since it has not been shown to possess the requisite specific receptor molecules (Marks and Shahrad, 1977). The epidermis tends to become thinner with increasing age, in both sexes. A decrease in the rate of epidermal cell proliferation is also characteristic of old age (Shahrad and Marks, 1976). It may be that the main results of oestrogen deficiency are reflected in other changes which make the skin look old. For example it may affect water retention in the skin. Oestrogen therapy seems to have, in some women, a beneficial effect on the circulation and moisture of the skin (Rauramo and Kopera, 1976). Many older men complain of skin atrophy, but it is not known whether this is specific to declining endocrine function (Nieschlag, 1979).

There are important metabolic changes with the menopause, notably in bone and lipid metabolism.

106

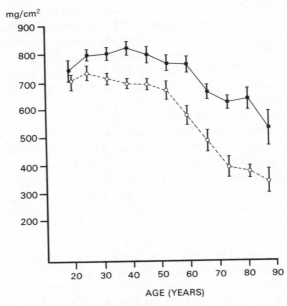

Figure 10. Bone mineral mass (mean ± s.e.) of the
radius in 305 normal men (●) and 308 normal
women (○). Reproduced by permission of Israel
Journal of Medical Science from Meema and
Meema (1976). Menopausal bone loss and estrogen
replacement. *Israel Journal of Medical Science*,**12**,
601–606

Bone

Bone is lost at the rate of 1–2% per year, after the menopause, possibly
more rapidly in the first six years. In men, there is a slower bone loss, it also
starts later and never reaches the same degree: 50% in women, 25% in men,
(Utian and Gordan, 1979). In both sexes, bone mass reaches its peak between
25 and 35–40 years of age (Meema and Meema, 1976; see Figure 10). The
peak level stays on a plateau for several years, then begins to decline, and
the rate of loss is much greater for women than for men (Vaughn and Hammond, 1981). While it seems certain that bone loss in women is a result of
oestrogen decline there is as yet no clear account of the mechanism by which
this happens. In women, demineralization of bone is more closely related to
ovarian failure than to age. One study found that women over 50 who were
still menstruating had no loss of bone mineral mass, whereas women after
the menopause, regardless of age, lost bone mass in proportion to the number
of years after menopause (Meema, Bunker, and Meema, 1965). Clinical
studies have also shown the importance of ovarian production of oestrogen
in maintaining normal bone mass (Worley, 1981b). Oestrogen therapy
prevents the menopausal acceleration of bone loss (Vaughn and Hammond,

1981) and this effect is almost certainly due to an inhibition of bone resorption (Hammond, Jelovsek, Lee, Creasman, and Parker, 1979a). Since men have a significant bone loss it is surprising that detailed comparisons between men and women in this respect have not been carried out. The contrasting course of oestrogen levels with age in the two sexes, and the differing patterns of bone loss, might be expected to throw some light on the causal relationship between oestrogen level, bone resorption and calcium balance. It has been pointed out that a plausible case can be made for a link between the oestrogenic hormones and bone in men. Plasma oestrogen levels are generally higher in men than in post-menopausal women and the oestrogen levels fall in men at about age 60. This later onset of oestrogen decline in men than in women may explain the later loss of bone in men (Crilly, Francis, and Nordin, 1981). Amplification of the findings on administered progestogen and bone loss would also cast light on the mechanisms involved. Progestogens do seem to be effective in reducing bone loss and it is thought that this is achieved in a different way from that of oestrogen (Lindsay, Hart, Maclean, Garwood, Aitken, Clark, and Coutts, 1978). The repercussions of the bone loss which starts at menopause are discussed in the next chapter.

Blood lipids

In the post-menopause there are changes in the blood lipid profile. In particular the levels of cholestrol and triglyceride rise by up to 20% of premenopausal levels (Oliver, 1976).

Musculo-skeletal changes

Muscular strength declines and ligaments show increasing laxity after the menopause, but it is impossible to say whether these are a result of the menopause or part of the ageing process. There have been no controlled studies designed to establish causation (Studd, Chakravarti, and Oram, 1977).

NEUROENDOCRINE MECHANISMS IN THE MENOPAUSE

The neuroendocrine mechanisms of the menopause are known in outline though many details have yet to be confirmed. During the premenopausal years, the increasing failure of the ovaries, due to the reduction in the number of follicles, disrupts the feedback relationship between the ovaries and the hypothalamic-pituitary unit. Although there are no satisfactory means of measuring hypothalamic GnRH levels, they are assumed to be raised in the menopausal and post-menopausal years. These high levels stimulate secretion of gonadotrophins from the pituitary. Also, hypothalamic neurotransmitter metabolism is probably implicated in the events of the climacteric, and more information is needed about this (Ben-David and van Look,

1979). In addition to the hypothalamic effects, the pituitary is also affected by the absence of negative feedback from the ovaries. Part of the normal feedback action of ovarian hormones on gonadotrophin secretion is exerted directly at pituitary level. The pituitary shows very little impairment of secretory activity with age and indeed FSH and LH are higher in post-menopausal than in regularly menstruating women, due to the absence of ovarian feedback. Thus the activity of the hypothalamus and also the activity of the pituitary, indirectly by GnRH from the hypothalamus, and directly by ovarian failure, are markedly affected by the menopausal ovarian changes; the indications from clinical administration of oestrogen are that the negative and positive feedback mechanisms of these structures remain functionally intact during the climacteric (Ben-David and van Look, 1979). Hence it is ovarian failure, rather than any hypothalamic or pituitary change, which leads to the end of the feedback relationship with the ovaries.

The mechanisms of the menopausal transition can be very briefly summarized in the following way. It is apparent that the initial change is in the ovary and that the ovarian involution gives rise to elevations in gonadotrophin secretion. The number of follicles in the ovary are reduced to between 5,000 and 20,000 by age 45. Also, as already mentioned, the remaining follicles are less responsive to gonadrotrophin stimulation (Studd, Chakravarti, and Oram, 1977). When the number of follicles remaining in the ovaries becomes markedly reduced the interval between successive waves of follicle growth increases and menstrual bleeding becomes progressively more irregular. In this transitional phase there is an irregular pattern of periods of relative inactivity in the ovaries with low levels of oestrogen secretion and somewhat raised levels of FSH and LH which are intermediate between the normal and the post-menopausal range. These inactive periods are interspersed with normal levels when follicles start growing. The anovulatory cycles which are common during this phase are doubtless due to inadequate follicular oestrogen secretion (Ben-David and van Look, 1979). The levels of gonadotrophins finally rise towards the post-menopausal levels with depletion of gonadotrophin-sensitive follicles from the ovaries and a concomitant decline in oestrogen. There is also a virtual end to ovarian production of progesterone (Sherman and Korenman, 1975).

The precise role of the neurotransmitters in the hormonal changes of the menopause has not been explored. This is surprising in view of their importance in gonadotrophin release (Shaw, 1978) and of their interactions with ovarian steroids (Coulam, 1981).

HORMONAL AND ORGANIC CHANGES IN MEN

Apart from its intrinsic interest, information about hormonal and organic changes in middle-aged men is important for understanding the specific effects of the menopause in women. The amount of available information is notably less for ageing men than for women. Nevertheless, changes with age in male hormonal levels, as opposed to the wider question of a male climacteric syndrome, are now relatively well documented. Comparison of some detailed results from many studies is difficult, since widely different samples have been used, but some fairly clear findings do emerge. All studies find considerable individual differences in the lifespan hormonal changes. The concentrations of testosterone which prevail from about puberty start to decline steadily from about 40 years of age, and decrease significantly from 50 years of age. With this decline in levels, there is an increase in amount,

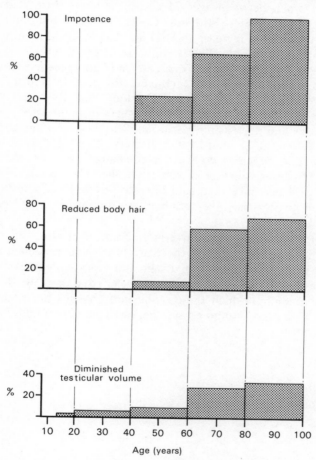

Figure 11. Frequencies of impotence, reduced body hair and diminished testicular volume (<15 ml.) as a function of age in men. Adapted from Baker, Burger, de Kretser, Hudson, O'Connor, Wang, Mirovics, Court, Dunlop, and Rennie, (1976). Changes in the pituitary-testicular system with age. *Clinical Endocrinology*, **5**, 349–372, and reproduced by permission of Blackwell Scientific Publications Limited

and in binding capacity, of testosterone binding globulin (Baker, Burger, de Kretser, Hudson, O'Connor, Wang, Mirovics, Court, Dunlop, and Rennie, 1976). Also many men have a decrease in the metabolic clearance rate of testosterone (Vermeulen, Reubens and Verdonck, 1972). With this decrease in testosterone there is a concomitant increase in oestrogen (oestradiol); this is not a large increase and the difference between the levels in young and old men is relatively small. There is a gradual rise in FSH and LH levels starting about age 40 such that the levels in men over 50 are significantly higher than in men between ages 21 and 50 (Baker, Burger, de Kretser, Hudson, O'Connor, Wang, Mirovics, Court, Dunlop, and Rennie, 1976). The relatively moderate increase in FSH and LH levels in men may be due to the limiting factor of only slightly rising oestrogen levels.

Testicular volume and body hair decrease and impotence increases steadily with age, as shown in Figure 11 (Baker, Burger, de Kretser, Hudson, O'Connor, Wang, Mirovics, Court, Dunlop, and Rennie, 1976). The degeneration in testicular function with age, which includes decelerating spermatogenesis and decreasing sperm mobility, is almost certainly attributable to the testes rather than to the pituitary. There are clear indications that pituitary function shows no age-related changes, whereas the involution of testicular functions with age is well established (Nieschlag, 1979). These mechanisms of senescence therefore operate primarily at a testicular level and the whole process is rather gradual, starting after 40 and progressing through old age.

In this chapter changes which invariably occur at or after the menopause have been discussed. In addition, there are other changes which are associated with the menopausal transition to a greater or lesser degree and these are the subject of the next chapter. It will be apparent that there are difficulties in deciding the extent to which these associated changes are specific to the menopause. There is a combined summary of Chapters 6 and 7 at the end of Chapter 7.

The ending of the reproductive cycle: II

CHANGES AND SYMPTOMS ASSOCIATED WITH THE MENOPAUSE

There are systematic changes with age which begin early in life and which affect all bodily systems. These changes are not specific to old age, although they become more apparent then. There are wide individual variations in the ageing process. Contrary to widespread belief, the endocrine system makes a relatively unimportant contribution to the manifestations of old age (Calkins, 1981). The belief that the effects of ageing reflect endocrine decline has probably arisen because of ideas about the menopause. Yet, as is clear from the discussion in the previous chapter, the specific and invariable changes of the climacteric in women, and the changes with ageing in testicular function in men, are a result of degeneration of the ovaries and the testes respectively, rather than of the endocrine system as a whole. The widely-held views of ageing in general and of the menopause in particular are not accurate yet they tend to be perpetuated. Age-related changes proceed throughout the whole of the lifespan, the endocrine system being rather less affected by the changes than most other systems. The ending of the female reproductive cycle is indeed an outstanding feature in the ageing process but it is important to remember that the menopause does not reflect a sudden or severe decline in the whole endocrine system. The only relatively abrupt event of the menopause is the end of menstrual bleeding. All other changes, hormonal, organic, bodily, are spread over a large number of years, both before and after the end of menstruation. There are problems in considering the specific role of the menopause in changes which occur in women after about 50 years of age. It is interesting, and often vital for clinical purposes, to distinguish symptoms resulting from hormonal changes from those due to more general ageing. Nevertheless the menopause is itself a part of the ageing process, and the question really becomes that of which parts of ageing are mediated by the menopause.

The concern in this book is specifically with the mechanisms and the effects of the ending of the reproductive cycle, not with ageing as such. Great care is needed in any attempt to attribute physical and psychological changes to the menopause because the manifold effects of general ageing become increasingly apparent at the same time as the climacteric. Here, as with the rest of the cycle, there are in addition to a vast mythology a great deal of many unsubstantiated anecdotal accounts, clinical impressions and inadequately controlled studies. A constant theme, in ascribing specificity of reported changes and symptoms to the menopause is the scarcity of studies of non-clinic groups of women. Even data from well women's clinics are not of course typical of the whole population. It is a curious fact that many of the forces which have combined to make the reproductive cycle appear to be a matter for gloom and despondency combine again to make the ending of the cycle appear to be an even greater catastrophe. It is rarely acknowledged that there are certain physical and psychological advantages to be gained from the ending of the menstrual cycle and that many negative changes are wrongly attributed to the menopause. Mistaken attribution of symptoms to the menopause has many unfortunate results not the least being that it leads to therapeutic measures based on a false rationale. The fact is that, as we shall see, some changes are an extremely likely outcome of the menopause whereas many others, commonly attributed to it, have their origins elsewhere. In many cases, on careful investigation, the changes and symptoms are found to occur at a similar rate at other times of life. Once again, only rigorous adherence to properly established facts about the complexities of the menopausal transition will lead to improved personal, social, and therapeutic approaches.

In talking of changes with the climacteric we are actually dealing with reported negative changes, mainly symptoms, since any benefits which may accrue from the ending of the reproductive cycle have not been documented. At least one study gives some clue as to what the findings might be if women were asked explicitly about the positive aspects. In a questionnaire survey aimed at eliciting information on aspects of the 'menopausal syndrome' two questions on attitude were included. The majority of premenopausal respondents (77%) did not anticipate any difficulties. Only about 13% of premenopausal and 9% of post-menopausal women expressed regret at the cessation of menses (McKinlay and Jefferys, 1974). When negative states are investigated, they are found to be low in the older groups. A large study of women of all ages found that tension decreased steadily from about age 35 to a minimum at ages 50–59. Menstrual pain continued a steady decrease with age throughout the menopausal transition (Wood, Larsen, and Williams, 1979b; see Figure 12). Another study compared women of all ages on a large number of physical and psychological symptoms. In spite of the fact that currently menopausal women scored higher on physical symptoms, it was the adolescent group (age 13–18) which scored highest on psychological symptoms and the lowest scores were in the post-menopausal (age 55–64) group. The authors suggest that although physical symptoms are high at the two times of great hormonal change (adolescence and menopause) the older women because of their experience and maturity have learned to cope more

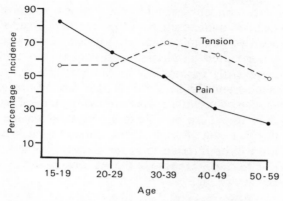

Figure 12. Percentage incidence of premenstrual tension and menstrual pain as a function of age in 2,343 women attending a health testing centre. Reproduced by permission of The Australian and New Zealand Journal of Obstetrics and Gynaecology Pty Ltd from Wood, Larsen, and Williams (1979). Social and psychological factors in relation to premenstrual tension and menstrual pain. *Australian and New Zealand Journal of Obstetrics and Gynaecology*, **19**, 111–115.

effectively, at the psychological level, with biological changes and stress (Neugarten and Kraines, 1965). This bonus that comes with experience and maturity obviously manifests itself fully when the menopause is over. If surveys were to include questions about positive states, some of the advantages of later life would doubtless be apparent in the replies. Even in response to negatively worded statements, a majority of women show positive attitudes to the menopause, though there are wide cultural differences. An International Health Foundation Survey (van Keep, 1970) of attitudes to the menopause in several European countries included the statement 'the menopause marks the beginning of old age'. 74% of women in Britain disagreed with this. In other countries the amount of disagreement was less, but overall the majority did not concur. Kahana, Kiyak, and Liang (1980) have reviewed, and provided, evidence that in response to various kinds of survey women consider menopause as requiring little readjustment when compared with other life events. From the study of Kahana *et al.* it appeared also that the menopause is not viewed with trepidation by younger women, nor remembered as a stressful period of change by the elderly. In fact negative stereotypes of the menopause are less prevalent among women than among men. The climacteric is viewed by men as a major life change. In addition to these views of the people involved, many of the research workers are of the opinion that it is inaccurate to see the menopause as a serious deficiency state which gives rise to a wide variety of symptoms. One report even argues that the menopause might be seen as adaptive in that, for example, it limits the duration of secretion of oestradiol, the biologically most active form of oestrogen which, if unopposed by progesterone, is supposed to have carcinogenic properties (see this chapter). Viewed in this light, the menopause is not a major feature in physiological decline, but could be seen as an adaptive process partly responsible for the greater longevity of women (Alington-MacKinnon and Troll, 1981). There are nevertheless changes, many of them negative, which often occur around the time of the menopause, whether or not they are all attributable to it, and these changes will now be discussed. The small amount of reliable information which is available about men in middle life will be referred to at the relevant points. Although it is sparse, it may serve to clarify the role of the menopause in the changes which women experience at this time.

HOT FLUSHES

This is the most frequently reported menopausal symptom and is thought to occur to some extent at some time in about 75% to 85% of women. Subjectively, the hot flush is characterized by a feeling of heat in the face, neck, and chest, followed by acute perspiration and sometimes shivering. Frequently there are palpitations. Although the onset of the hot flush itself is sudden, there is often an awareness of an impending flush just before it occurs. The flushes vary, both in duration, from 1 minute to 4 minutes, and in intensity (Sturdee, Wilson, Pipili, and Crocker, 1978). In spite of the high incidence of this symptom there has been little systematic investigation of it; and the aetiology is still not entirely clear (Hutton, Jacobs, and James, 1979). The evidence indicates that oestrogen levels are not a sufficient explanation. There is not a direct relationship between the flushes and oestrogen concentrations. Various clinical groups with low oestrogen levels, excluding those with abrupt oestrogen decline after surgery, rarely experience this symptom (Studd, Chakravarti, and Oram, 1977). Flushing attacks are not markedly correlated with levels of any hormone, though recent evidence suggests that the onset of the hot flush immediately follows a pulsatile release of pituitary LH. This probably does not denote a causal relationship, but rather that LH release and hot flush are both mediated by a suprapituitary mechanism (Bates, 1981). It has been thought that women who experience flushes have hormone profiles which are indistinguishable from those of women without the symptom (Hutton, Jacobs, and James, 1979). It had however been suggested that more extensive study of 24-hour hormonal profiles of women with and without flushes might lead to somewhat different conclusions (Campbell, 1976). A recent study found that women with severe flushes had significantly lower levels of oestrogen than women who had never had flushes. The women with the symptom also had significantly lower ideal body weights, leading the authors to suggest that the known effects of body weight on oestrogen levels in post-menopausal women may be important factors in hot flushes (Erlik, Meldrum, and Judd, 1982). Men treated with oestrogen for prostatic cancer report hot flushes soon after oestrogen withdrawal (Bates, 1981). The hot flush is one of the few menopausal symptoms which is directly and significantly improved by oestrogen therapy (Bates, 1981; Hutton, Jacobs and James, 1979).

Doubtless hot flushes are due to a combination of factors, including the rate of withdrawal of oestrogen (Studd, Chakravarti, and Oram, 1977). One strong possibility is that an interaction of oestrogen metabolites and alterations in certain neurotransmitters may be involved (Hutton, Jacobs, and James, 1979), though there is not direct evidence of this as yet (Bates, 1981). There have been a few welcome attempts to measure the magnitude of physiological change during menopausal hot flushes. The subjective sudden feeling of heat in the face, neck and chest is associated with changes in temperature (Bates, 1981), electrocardiographic baseline, skin resistance, and heart rate (Sturdee, Wilson, Pipili, and Crocker, 1978). Figure 13 shows changes in heart rate during a hot flush. In the last study similar changes in heart and skin variables did not occur in a control group of premenopausal

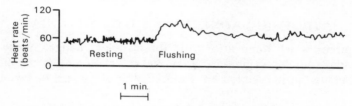

Figure 13. Physiological recording of heart rate (beats/minute) from one menopausal woman before and during a hot flush. Reproduced by permission of British Medical Journal from Sturdee, Wilson, Pipilli, and Crocker (1978). Physiological aspects of menopausal hot flush. *British Medical Journal*, **ii**, 79–80

women with induced vasodilation and sweating. A technique which measures elevations in skin temperature and provides an objective index of hot flushes has recently been developed (Meldrum, Shamonki, Frumar, Tataryn, Chang, and Judd, 1979). This type of work promises to lead to a greater understanding of the mechanisms underlying this most ubiquitous of menopausal symptoms. Not only is it ubiquitous, it also generates serious secondary effects. Hot flushes, and sweating at night, create other problems by disturbing sleep and personal, domestic, and working life and can easily lead to other symptoms (Campbell and Whitehead, 1977).

OTHER VASOMOTOR SYMPTOMS

Other vasomotor symptoms, mainly migrainous headaches and palpitations, have been reported. It has not been demonstrated that these are primary symptoms of the menopause. An extensive survey of 20 symptoms in five-year age groups of women from 20 to over 65 years revealed that headaches actually decrease from 45 years. Palpitations remained stable from age 40 to after 55, when there was a slight increase, not statistically significant (Wood, 1979). Another study (Bungay, Vessey, and McPherson, 1980) found a similar decrease in headaches from age 40, in women and in men. Another survey of several symptoms commonly associated with the menopause found that palpitations (and indeed all other symptoms apart from hot flush and night sweating) showed no direct relationship to the menopause (McKinlay and Jefferys, 1974). The International Health Foundation survey mentioned above of 2,000 European women aged 46 to 55 found reports of palpitations in 24% of the women. Since younger women were not asked to report, there is no way of assessing the possible role of the menopause in this figure (van Keep, 1970). Also, future studies might perhaps profitably make a clear distinction between the palpitations which are a frequent feature of the hot flush and those which occur independently of it.

Some older men complain of hot flushes, sweating, and tachycardia (Nieschlag, 1979), but this needs further documentation.

ATROPHIC VAGINITIS AND DYSPAREUNIA

The symptoms which often arise from the atrophic changes in the vagina and the vulva, notably vaginal irritation and infection and dyspareunia, are discussed below, in the section on sexual feeling and sexual behaviour.

URINARY SYMPTOMS

It has been noted in Chapter 6 that there is considerable variability in the onset and severity of atrophy of the urogenital tissues. Any increase in urinary symptoms will presumably follow a similar pattern. This is an area where it seems useful to distinguish between non-patient and patient groups. When non-patient groups have been studied, there is apparently no rise with the menopause in incidence of frequency (Bungay, Vessey, and McPherson, 1980; Osborne, 1976; Wood, 1979) and urgency (Osborne, 1976). One study (Bungay, Vessey, and McPherson, 1980) included reports on frequency and urgency in both women and men, and whereas these symptoms did not increase through the menopausal and post-menopausal years in women there was a steep rise in the same age groups in men, presumably reflecting prostatic problems. There is one quantified report of increase in nocturia in women. The post-menopausal figure was significantly higher than the premenopausal at the 0.05 level of significance (Osborne, 1976). This rather small rise could be a secondary outcome of waking with night sweating. On the other hand, studies of women who attend a clinic report an increased incidence of frequency, urgency, infections of various kinds, and incontinence with the menopause. The rise in the incidence of these symptoms in clinic patients is assumed to be a result of the atrophic changes in the urethra and the bladder which in turn are thought to be the outcome of oestrogen deficiency. The symptoms all respond well to oestrogen treatment (Campbell, 1976; Kopera, 1979; Vaughn and Hammond, 1981).

OSTEOPOROSIS

It has been amply demonstrated that accelerated loss of bone follows failure of ovarian function (see Chapter 6). Insufficient bone mass leads to increased porosity and brittleness, and a rarefaction of normally mineralized bone, which predispose to bone fracture. Osteoporosis and the related fracture becomes a problem in women from about 60 years of age. This age group is not within the scope of this book, though the bone loss starts at the menopause and early remedial steps are sometimes vital (Worley, 1981b).

Bone loss takes place in ageing men, though later and to a lesser degree than in women. Rigorous studies comparing the incidence of osteoporosis and bone fractures in the two groups would be useful.

MUSCULAR SYMPTOMS

Various aches and pains during the climacteric have not often been systematically investigated. As with other symptoms, comparisons should be made between women of all ages. Statements about the percentage of climacteric women experiencing a symptom, without similar information for other age groups, are of limited usefulness. One study already mentioned which investigated symptoms in women of all ages found a small increase from the menopause onwards but this was not statistically significant (Wood, 1979). Another study reported that aches in joints, bones, and muscles were observed in 30% of women who were menstruating normally. There was a rise to a maximum of about 46% through the menopause, with a subsequent decline to 33% at five to ten years after the menopause (Jaszmann, van Lith, and Zaat, 1969). A third study which compared different age groups found that specifically low backache decreased from about 48 years of age in women, whereas in men the same symptoms increased slightly from about age 57 (Bungay, Vessey, and McPherson, 1980). Since it is not known to what extent age changes in muscle and in ligaments are due to the hormonal changes of the menopause (see Chapter 6) it is impossible to attribute causative factors in any reported symptoms. One study of the effects of administered oestrogen found that joint pains and backache were not among the symptoms significantly improved by oestrogen treatment, when compared with placebo (Campbell and Whitehead, 1977).

CORONARY HEART DISEASE

The rise in cholesterol and triglyceride levels after the menopause, by up to 20% of premenopausal levels, has already been noted in Chapter 6. Most authors also report an increased risk of coronary heart disease with the menopause. The exact nature of the relationship between all these changes is not clear. As regards changes with age, up until 50 years mortality from cardiovascular disease is many times higher among men than women. Non-smoking women enjoy virtual immunity from coronary heart disease before the menopause. High levels of cholesterol and triglycerides, together with smoking and hypertension, are associated with the development of coronary heart disease in men. In post-menopausal women the same links exist and after age 45 there are reports of a rise in levels of cholesterol and triglycerides and an increased incidence of coronary heart disease (Oliver, 1976). It is assumed that in women ovarian hormones have a protective effect. This assumption led to the use of administered oestrogens, both in men who had already suffered myocardial infarction and in post-menopausal women. In the men, the administered oestrogens were unfortunately associated with an increased risk of recurrence (Coronary Drug Project Research Group, 1973). As regards the post-menopausal women, the results are conflicting, with findings of detrimental effects (Gordon, Kannel, Hjortland, and McNamara, 1978), beneficial effects (Hammond, Jelovsek, Lee, Creasman, and Parker, 1979a) or no effects (Nachtigall, Nachtigall, Nachtigall, and Beckman, 1979; Pfetter, Whipple, Jurosaki, and Chapman, 1978) on the development of coronary heart disease. Results of the oestrogen treatment are not only clinically vital, they would also throw light on the mechanisms of coronary heart disease. Elevated levels of lipoproteins and cholesterol (assumed to be associated with risk of atherosclerotic disease) can be reduced by oestrogen administration (Ryan, 1976) but not all lipoprotein fractions are uniformly influenced by any oestrogen preparation. The new occurrence of hypertension is said to be significantly reduced by oestrogens (Hammond, Jelovsek, Lee, Creasman, and Parker, 1979a). Nevertheless, as already pointed out, the assumption that the risk of atherosclerotic disease is reduced by administered oestrogens has not been verified (Vaughn and Hammond, 1981).

The inconsistent findings may reflect some faulty assumptions. One report of an analysis of the Registrar General's data on mortality from coronary heart disease in men and women for a five year period challenges the view that women lose protection from the disease after the menopause (Heller and Jacobs, 1978). On the other hand a large longitudinal study which avoided many of the methodological pitfalls, found a clearly increased risk of coronary heart disease immediately after menopause. This increase appears to be abrupt and restricted to a short time span and is therefore probably not attributable solely to the expected rise in incidence with age. After 55 the risk augments only slowly, if at all. This study also indicates that most premenopausal coronary heart disease presents in the milder form of angina pectoris or coronary insufficiency. This is in contrast to the figures for men under 55 in whom only about 25% of coronary heart disease presents as angina (Gordon, Kannel, Hjortland, and McNamara, 1978). The present conclusion has to be that there is a widespread belief in the protective effect of the functioning ovary, probably through blood lipid levels, against coronary heart disease. More detailed demonstration of this belief would be welcome. The effect of administered oestrogens on the incidence of coronary heart disease is quite uncertain. This last point is discussed further in the section on treatment at the end of this chapter.

SLEEP

Insomnia does not appear to be a distinct symptom directly related to the menopause in spite of several anecdotal reports to that effect. There is some increase in reported insomnia in older women but this is not marked and is probably not specific to the menopause (McKinlay and Jefferys, 1974; Wood, 1979). Some older men also complain of sleeplessness (Nieschlag, 1979), and in both men and women it is probably related to age. In some women any additional insomnia appears to be a by-product of the hormonally-related hot flushes and night sweating (Campbell and Whitehead, 1977).

MEMORY FUNCTION

Memory function, as everyone knows, declines with age, in both men and women. One study (Campbell and Whitehead, 1977) found that poor memory in menopausal women responded to oestrogen replacement therapy and this did not appear to be a secondary benefit of reduction in vasomotor symptoms. Although there is an increasing incidence with age of memory dysfunction in men, it may be that a similar increase in women is somewhat exacerbated by ovarian failure, or by its effects. The question has not been rigorously investigated.

SEXUAL BEHAVIOUR AND SEXUAL FEELING

Sexual behaviour and sexual feeling in the climacteric phase have been widely studied, but it is an area where methodological difficulties are particularly great. The findings have to be interpreted with caution, based as they are on the questionnaire replies of people willing to take part in surveys. As regards sexual behaviour, there appears to be a pattern of declining sexual activity with age in men and in women. In all age groups the frequency of sexual intercourse is lower for women than for men (Pfeiffer, Verwoerdt, and Davis, 1972). Masters and Johnson (1966) noted a significant increase in sexual activity in middle-aged women, described as casting around for new partners or for new sexual variation, but they do not provide quantified evidence to support this claim. Neither is this view supported by other work. A study of middle and upper socio-economic groups found that women and men experience a significant decline in sexual intercourse with increasing age. Men had more frequent intercourse at all ages but the rate of decline in both groups reached the same level of significance (Pfeiffer and Davis, 1972). There is nothing in these findings to suggest an upsurge in sexual activity in women through the climacteric years, but neither do women have more of a proportional reduction in intercourse than do men. The author of one study does not agree with this last point. In a survey of perimenopausal women in Sweden (Hallstrom, 1977) the data confirm a decline of sexual activity in women from 38 years to 54 years. The author then concludes that women's interest declines more than that of men, but this conclusion is not supported in the study, which reports no comparable data for men in the same age group. As regards sexual feeling or interest, a survey in Britain of men and women aged 30–64 years, taken from a selection of general practitioners' lists, shows that at all ages women have less interest than men in sexual relations. From their respective baselines, though, whereas in men there is a decline from about 48 years, in women at that age there is a slight, probably not significant, reversal of a previous trend towards loss of interest (Bungay, Vessey, and McPherson, 1980). An American survey of middle and upper socio-economic groups also showed a significant decline in interest with age in both men and women. Again from their respective baselines, the amount of decline in interest from age 46 years in men and in women is at the same level of significance (Pfeiffer, Verwoerdt, and Davis, 1972). The study in Sweden already mentioned found that the majority of women report moderate sexual interest beyond age 50, and many well beyond that (Hallstrom, 1977).

Determinants of sexual behaviour and feelings with age

There is general agreement that sexual feelings and sexual behaviour decline with age and most authors feel that the rate is somewhat similar in women and in men. It is difficult to identify all the determinants of this decline. In the sexuality of women, the specific influence of the menopausal hormonal changes does not seem to be great. During the normally menstruating years the patterns of sexual arousal and behaviour does not correspond to a particular hormonal profile, see Chapter 4. Likewise, in a controlled study of men complaining predominantly of sexual impotence (disturbed erection existing for one year, organic causes excluded, acute partner problems absent) there were no endocrinological differences between these men and a control group (Nieschlag, 1979). At the menopause, it does not seem likely that loss of libido is primarily a result of hormonal changes, since there is no correlation between them (see for example Studd and Thom, 1981). Menopausal oestrogen therapy in women does not have a significant effect on libido or sexual behaviour, as reflected by masturbation, orgasm, frequency of intercourse, and satisfaction (Campbell and Whitehead, 1977). From the present state of knowledge, menopausal endocrine changes do not seem to be a prime, specific factor in the declining sexual functioning. Nevertheless they may well combine with other variables to play some part. The role of secondary effects of ovarian failure, especially atrophic vaginitis and painful intercourse (dyspareunia) in reduced sexual behaviour and

interest cannot be doubted, though apparently it is not of enormous significance. One study (Hallstrom, 1977) showed that indeed women whose
sexual interest declines tend to suffer more from dyspareunia but very few
women in fact suffer from that symptom—5% occasionally, 1% usually, and
2% at every sexual intercourse. Another study (Studd, Chakravarti, and
Oram, 1977) showed that only about 43% of patients who were actually
referred with sexual symptoms had both loss of libido and dyspareunia; the
rest had only one or the other. Another study (Campbell and Whitehead,
1977) found that relief of atrophic vaginitis by oestrogen therapy did not
result in an improvement in libido. In the British survey already mentioned
(Bungay, Vessey, and McPherson, 1980) men reported a similar, or slightly
higher increase in difficulty with intercourse, from age 55, as women. Baker,
Burger, de Kretser, Hudson, O'Connor, Wang, Mirovics, Court, Dunlop,
and Rennie (1976) have reported a considerable increase in impotence in
men by age 60, (see Figure 11). A study of the determinants of sexual
behaviour in men and women from 46 years to 71 years of age (Pfeiffer and
Davis, 1972) found that a much larger number of variables influenced
sexual behaviour in men than in women. The sexual functioning of the men
through middle life to old age was influenced independently by factors of:
age (negative), health (positive), social class (positive), treatment for hypertension (negative), life satisfaction (positive), physical functioning (positive),
and excessive concern over physical function findings (negative). Only a small
number of factors made independent contributions to sexual functioning in
women. They were mainly marital status (intact marriages were positively
correlated) and age (negatively correlated). Only small contributions were
made by educational level (positive), being employed (positive), and being
post-menopausal (negative). A highly salient feature emerged from a
separate analysis of the relationship between past sexual experience and
present sexual functioning. In women and in men past sexual experience is
an extremely important feature of present sexual enjoyment and interest.
This, and other previous studies, show that continued sexual activity in older
age groups is positively related to previous enjoyment of sexual behaviour
and experience. This means that with changing social attitudes a different
pattern can be expected in women's sexual behaviour with age. Presumably,
now that in general women are leading more sexually active lives their
interest in and enjoyment of sex will, throughout life, be greater than
previously, and a correspondingly higher level will be maintained into old
age.

Another important determinant in the continued sexual interest and
behaviour in ageing women is, not surprisingly, the presence of a partner
and the continuing sexuality of that partner. In the earlier work Kinsey,
Pomeroy, Martin, and Gebhard (1953) reported that whereas sexual activity
in unmarried women remained fairly constant up to 55 years of age, in
unmarried men it declined gradually but steadily from adolescence onwards
(the rather constant rate in unmarried women was, at that time, extremely

low and would doubtless not be applicable now). On the other hand, the frequency of intercourse for married men and for married women largely parallel each other (though the male curve drops somewhat more steeply). Kinsey inferred that any decreasing frequency of intercourse for women might be a result of the partner's ageing. (They could of course also both be a result of similar forces operating on married people.) Masters and Johnson (1966) indicated that despite changes in the reproductive organs the ageing woman is fully capable of orgasm if she is exposed to regular effective sexual stimulation. The American study already mentioned (Pfeiffer and Davis, 1972) found that most women attributed the cessation of intercourse to their husbands, and that men in general also attributed the responsibility to themselves. Confirmation of such findings are needed, but it does seem that, to accurately assess the course of sexuality in women, it is important to take account of their partner's sexuality. Various other factors make some contribution to the sexual life of women and men in middle and old age (Hallstrom, 1977; Pfeiffer and Davis, 1972), as they undoubtedly do throughout the lifespan.

The conclusion to be drawn at present seems to be that many women experience some decline in sexual interest and sexual behaviour through the climacteric years. Men have a similar rate of decline (from a higher baseline) throughout the same years of life. In women, the general effects of ageing probably combine with the menopausal endocrine changes and their secondary effects, and with various psychological and social factors to bring about the changes in sexuality that are observed. Particularly important are past sexual enjoyment and the sexuality of the partner.

PSYCHOLOGICAL CHANGES

We have seen that there are many neurophysiological and bodily changes with the ending of reproductive life and that these are compounded with the general effects of ageing. It would be surprising if there were not psychological overtones to such fundamental events. It is important to know what these are and also, as a basis for effective action, to know the origins of the psychological manifestations. Which of them are closely related to the hormonal changes and their secondary effects and which are largely a function of social and environmental factors, and of ageing in general. A particular problem in assessing presence and magnitude of psychological symptoms during the menopause is to find measuring instruments which are sensitive enough. Many studies have used standard clinical measures and it seems likely that these are not always appropriate for monitoring psychological changes in menopausal women most of whom do not have a psychiatric disorder (Campbell and Whitehead, 1977). Since this probably applies to women who have been referred because of the existence of definite presumed menopausal symptoms it must be even more true for women in whom changes are not marked enough to provoke referral. Another difficulty is that the vast majority of reports have considered only patient populations, that is women presenting with some symptoms presumed to be menopausal and who are therefore not typical in many respects (McKinlay, Jefferys, and Thompson, 1972). Gradually, though, more information on well women is being collected and this will be a useful addition.

The assumption that for most women the climacteric is a time of distressing symptoms and feelings is extremely prevalent. Included in this assumption is the notion that a variety of specific psychological problems and disturbances accompany the undoubted physiological and bodily changes. Not only has the assumption of widespread psychological symptoms not been verified, it has rarely been investigated at all. When adequate studies are carried out, the consensus view seems to be that there is no evidence of a specifically menopausal psychological syndrome (Dominian, 1977; McKinlay, Jefferys, and Thompson, 1972; Thompson, Hart,and Durno, 1973; Wood, 1979); or that, if one can be discerned, only a small proportion of women, especially vulnerable for various reasons, suffer from it (Ballinger, 1977). In one survey using a multivariate analysis technique life stress in general was shown to have more influence than did the menopause on psychological and somatic symptoms. Moreover there was no significant increase in total life stress at the time of the menopause and the highest levels of both psychological and somatic symptoms were found in the 35–44 year old group, after which age there was a steady decline (Greene and Cooke, 1980). Menopausal depression has been given the most credence, especially under the name of involutional melancholia. If this illness existed in the past, it is doubtful that it still does. A review of the evidence failed to find support for the validity of involutional melancholia as a distinct diagnostic entity. In addition a review of the research findings does not support the idea of increased prevalence of depression around the menopausal years (Weissman, 1979). The same author reports a study of a group of women diagnosed as suffering from major non-bipolar depression. There was no increase in depressive symptoms in the menopausal years, compared with the pre- and post-menopausal years. The same review includes the findings of a Swedish survey which showed no significant change in rates of mental illness in general with the menopause; nor were there any characteristic personality or emotional changes during the menopausal years, (Hallstrom, 1973). Another ten-year prospective study in Sweden also found no evidence of an increase in mental disorders during the climacteric. In fact the peak for mental disorders was age 35 to 44 years, after which there was a decrease (Hagnell, 1966) which agrees with the Greene and Cooke findings, above. A comprehensive survey in Australia of women of all ages found no increase with age (including the menopausal transition) of the psychological symptoms investigated and indeed found a decline with age in headaches and irritability (Wood, 1979). In a British survey, also, irritability significantly declined in women at about age 48, whereas it did not decline in men (Bungay, Vessey, and McPherson, 1980). The same is true of depression requiring admission to hospital. Incidence figures for first admissions in England and Wales for 1965–66 show no increase in depression of any kind in women from age 35 to 65, after which it declines. In men, depression of all kinds rises quite sharply from age 50 to about age 60 after which it declines (Spicer, Hare, and Slater, 1973).

None of this means that women do not react to the very real changes of the climacteric with anxiety and/or depression. On present evidence, though, this appears to be no more true of the climacteric than of other times of life which bring certain stressful events and the events of the climacteric phase are no more stressful than some with other causes. It now seems likely that there is no clearly defined set of psychological symptoms which women in general develop around the menopause. There are nevertheless doubtless some women who experience distressing psychological manifestations in response to the particular stresses brought about by the physiological and physical changes of the menopause in combination with their past experience and their individual life events. A recent report already mentioned presents a convincing case for believing that women with psychological problems frequently seek help at gynaecological clinics, at any age (Wood, 1979). Another study which compared women, aged 40–55, referred to a gynaeco-logical clinic with a non-clinic group found a higher proportion of psychiatric morbidity in the clinic group. Also their psychiatric disorder was more severe and more depressive in nature (Ballinger, 1977). This means that women attending the clinics are a biased sample of the whole menopausal population in respect of psychological symptoms. This overlap between gynaecological and psychiatric problems would partly explain why clinicians often assume a causal relationship between ovarian failure, hot flushes, and psychological problems (Wood, 1979). There may also be some women who are particularly vulnerable to hormonally-related pscyhological changes, especially at times of sudden decline in hormone levels, but very little is known about this. It is not known whether the particular combination of hormones through the climacteric is reliably associated with psychological change. From the evidence available at the moment it appears that no such specific pattern does emerge. The great variety of symptoms which are reported (Furuhjelm and Fedor-Freybergh, 1976) suggests, rather, psychological difficulties associ-ated with problems of ageing and personal and social change, and these have often not been properly separated out in the published work. Reports of effectiveness of oestrogen therapy on psychological function would provide some clue to the origins of any psychological symptoms at this time but the existing studies, which are necessarily of clinic groups, have often not employed a double-blind procedure and indeed many have included no placebo group at all. Some have included women who have undergone a surgical menopause which is not comparable in several important respects with a natural one. The results of the properly controlled studies suggest that psychological benefits from oestrogen therapy are secondary to the relief of physical symptoms, mainly hot flushes and the attendant insomnia and other difficulties (Dennerstein, Burrows, Hyman, and Sharpe, 1979; Wood, 1979).

The possibility nevertheless remains of some direct therapeutic effect on brain functioning (Campbell and Whitehead, 1977). A large controlled study of the effects of long-term oestrogen replacement therapy showed that incidence of psychiatric illness (anxiety and tension state, depression and 'other') was unaffected by administered oestrogen (Hammond, Jelovsek, Lee, Creasman, and Parker, 1979a). Further investigation of a possible direct and specific effect of oestrogen therapy on psychological symptoms would be welcome, since it would have implications for causation and would also provide guidance for treatment. This kind of analysis of the present evidence has therapeutic implications which are similar to those for any situation where certain unavoidable physical and personal factors may give rise to psychological difficulties. Alleviation is aimed both at attenuating the effects of primary causes and at rational ways of dealing with the attendant distress. For example when the anxiety, agitation, or depression tends to be centred around hot flushes, since that symptom is significantly improved by oestrogen therapy (Campbell and Whitehead, 1977) the psychological symptoms will also be improved by the treatment of the primary factor.

The most reasonable conclusion (necessarily oversimplified in the absence of detailed evidence) about psychological manifestations of the menopause seems at present to be that there are no clear-cut built-in psychological elements with the physiological and physical changes of the menopause. The hormonal and bodily changes and their effects (such as insomnia from hot flushes) nevertheless combine with certain personal and social patterns to occasionally produce in some women new or more marked psychological difficulties; or, perhaps more frequently, the menopause becomes the scapegoat for previously existing problems. Where the aetiology of the primary changes is known and is effectively treated by specific treatment a more or less direct effect on the psychological manifestations can be expected. Where the primary causes are less clear and specific treatment is therefore less successful, therapy aimed more directly at the psychological symptoms will be necessary (Dominian, 1977).

If in effect the presence of a psychological syndrome specific to the menopause does not emerge why has the notion of such a syndrome been so prevalent? Allusions to the 'change of life' usually include the idea of particular psychological stress. That view can probably be explained by the fact that a focus is provided by the very real hormonal and bodily changes which, as we have said, as in similar circumstances at other times, elicit certain understandable reactions on the part of the woman. The whole phase therefore tends to appear to the outside world as one of special psychological and emotional strain, as well as of physical problems. It is more difficult to explain the persistent more specialized beliefs, particularly in the disorder of involutional melancholia. We have already mentioned the frequency with which women with predominantly psychological problems present in gynaecological clinics, which is doubtless one explanation. In addition there was possibly a factual basis in the past. It may be that increased awareness of the menopause and its effects, on the part of the women and of clinicians, and the increasing availability of effective treatments has somewhat removed a diagnostic entity which formerly may have been justified. An added factor in the disappearance or lessening of some previously observed symptoms might be the changing lives of women in our society. There is a little evidence that menopausal symptoms bear at least some relation to work attitudes and indeed to the wider social framework in which the menopausal changes are experienced (Flint, 1979). The author of an Australian survey cited above suggests ways in which psychological symptoms may become associated with the menopausal phase. Firstly, psychological symptoms may have preceded the climacteric, may be occurring secondarily to hot flushes or may be a result of new stresses which may occur at any age. Secondly, the propensity to link many psychological symptoms with the menopause may provoke new anxiety; or it may turn the menopause into a scapegoat for patients with chronic anxiety or depressive states. Finally the author rightly suggests that more information about the general effects of ageing, favourable and unfavourable, would put the menopause in a better perspective (Wood, 1979).

INCIDENCE

Incidence figures have been referred to at various points in this chapter and this section will serve to draw together the findings on prevalence. There is little precise, direct information on incidence of the changes which are often associated with the menopause in the general population. Most of the reports on prevalence are of groups of women who have been referred for treatment of menopausal symptoms. Exceptions are an early study, in 1933, of 1,000 women by the Council of Medical Women's Federation of England which reported that 15.8% were free of symptoms at the menopause, 62.3% had no symptoms other than hot flushes, for an average duration of two years, and that 89.7% carried on their daily activities without any interruption. In 1969, 2,000 women aged 46–55 were surveyed by the International Health Foundation in several European countries (van Keep, 1970); this report has already been mentioned above. In the survey many symptoms were included which may well be experienced at other times of life, and we do not know what percentage would have been reported by younger or older women. These figures are therefore not percentages of menopausal complaints over and above figures that might be reported at any other time. Although 22% of the sample were reported to be still experiencing normal regular menstrual cycles, it is doubtful whether this whole group can be considered as clearly outside the climacteric years and hence as a valid comparison group. Since 20% of those still experiencing regular cycles reported hot flushes, it seems likely that many of them were already in the perimenopausal phase where various climacteric changes are already taking place. Also, since the regularly menstruating group were over 45 they are probably not typical of menstruating women in general. For instance, a study already mentioned (Greene and Cooke, 1981), found that the highest levels of psychological and somatic symptoms in women was in the 35–44 year old group, after which there was a marked decline. Certainly, groups for comparing symptom incidence figures in menopausal women would have to include age groups below 45. The International Health Foundation survey gives percentages of symptoms most frequently experienced in their age group (46–55) as: hot flushes 55%, tiredness 43%, nervousness 41%, headaches 38%, insomnia 32%, depression 30%, irritability 29%, joint and muscle pain 25%. Another study (McKinlay and Jefferys, 1974) of over 600 women also included a group of regularly menstruating women but the age range was 45–64. Hot flushes ranged from about 18% among normally menstruating women through a maximum of 75% during the climacteric to about 29% among women who were at least nine years post-menopausal. Percentages of some other symptoms in the group of most interest to us, the menopausal transition group, are reported as headaches 38.3% (compared with the 45% of women before menopause); sleeplessness 45% (compared with 20.9% before menopause); depression 55% (compared with 38.8% before menopause). Again, it would be easier to assess the implications of these figures if a much wider age range had been included. A rather large incidence survey of women at various stages of menopausal transition, as well as a normally menstruating group, defined as having had normal menses during the year preceding the survey, precise age range not given but mean 45.3 years, was carried out in the Netherlands, (Jaszmann, van Lith, and Zaat, 1969). Hot flushes rose to a maximum of 65% one to two years after cessation of menses and declined thereafter. Muscle and joint aches were reported in 30% of women who were regularly menstruating and this rose to 50% three years after menopause. Depression was not a feature of the menopausal years. The same is true of irritability though it increases slightly in the menopausal transition, from 28% in normally menstruating women to 37% during the climacteric. The authors believe that only hot flushes, sweating, and muscle and joint aches can be seen as typical climacteric complaints. The incidence of hot flushes has been reported by Thompson, Hart, and Durno (1973). 74% of post-menopausal women in a general practice in Scotland reported hot flushes. Of these 17% had been having them for over one year, 50% for two to five years and 19% for more than five years.

As regards incidence of change in sexual interest and behaviour during the menopause precise information is very sparse. One study, which did not aim to separate age effects from menopausal effects, showed that, by age 50, 58% of women and 49% of men reported some decline in their sexual interest and activity; 79% of women and 72% of men reported a decline by the age of 60. In terms of actual interest (as opposed to decline from former level) the percentage of men reporting absence of sexual interest was zero at age 50, rising to 11% by 65; 7% of women reported absence of interest at age 50 rising to 51% by age 65 (Pfeiffer, Verwoerdt, and Davis, 1972).

Another study of 800 women gives percentages for preclimacteric as well as menopausal women. Percentages of women expressing moderate sexual interest at different ages are: 38 years, 72%; 46 years, 70%; 50 years, 62%; 54 years, 48%. As regards sexual behaviour the figures for women reporting no change in capacity for orgasm are: 38 years, 70%; 46 years, 62%; 50 years, 66%; 54 years, 50% (Hallstrom, 1977).

The conclusion from the incidence figures on changes associated with the menopause (not those which we have called the defining changes), although they need amplification, is that they support the view that, apart from hot flushes, there is no clear-cut set of related changes which appear consistently in the majority of women at menopause. More detailed incidence studies, with comparison groups of younger women, and of men, would be of interest.

HORMONE TREATMENT

Detailed discussion of treatment, except where it has implications for the description and explanation of changes, is not within the scope of this book. Since hormone therapy during and after the menopausal transition, in addition to its practical applications, does cast some light on the understanding of some of the manifestations and mechanisms of the climacteric, a summary of the present position is included here. The discussion will centre on oestrogen therapy but there is increasing interest in the use of progestogens usually, but not always, in combination with oestrogens, and mention will be made of this. It has to be noted that the prescribed oestrogens provide different approximations from the hormones which are produced naturally in the body. Menopausal hormone therapy now often consists of so-called natural oestrogens. These drugs produce oestrogens fairly similar to the endogenous ones, but with a wide range of variation of effects. Conjugated equine oestrogens are also much used but they are not as 'natural' because the biologically predominant hormone from them is equilin, a highly potent oestrogen that does not normally occur in humans (Hutton, Jacobs, and James, 1979). Also to be noted is that the method of administration (oral, the most usual; intramuscular; intravenous; vaginal) will determine the relative concentrations of oestradiol and oestrone which ultimately result (Hutton, Jacobs, and James, 1979; Rigg, Hermann, and Yen, 1978). It has been pointed out that the term hormone replacement therapy is imprecise since the doses of oestrogen which are required for effective relief of symptoms are higher than natural levels; also oestrone rather than oestradiol becomes the predominant oestrogen compound. The levels of FSH and LH are not decreased to pre-menopausal values and prolactin is not increased to those levels. The treatment therefore does not reinstate the hormonal milieu which existed before the menopause (Whitehead, McQueen, Minardi, and Campbell, 1978).

A progestogen is now usually added to the oestrogen treatment. This practice was instituted mainly to reduce the risk of endometrial cancer (see below). It also seems likely that there may be other clinical advantages in the use of progestogens (Gambrell, 1982).

Treatment can be aimed at symptoms which occur during the climacteric or it can have long-term prophylactic aims. Long-term therapy poses particular problems of safety, and its effectiveness in retarding or reversing degenerative processes specifically attributable to oestrogen loss has been a matter of controversy. Our main interest here is in the years which mark the ending of the reproductive cycle, but in fact summarizing the effects of oestrogen therapy during these years cannot be entirely dissociated from the frankly post-menopausal years.

BENEFITS

The beneficial effects of oestrogen therapy on some of the climacteric symptoms are relatively well-documented.

Vasomotor symptoms, particularly hot flushes and night sweating, are relieved by the administration of oestrogen (Studd, Chakravarti, and Oram, 1977). Symptoms which are probably secondary to these symptoms, such as insomnia and poor concentration are also helped (Studd, Chakravarti, and Oram, 1977). Since the precise aetiology of vasomotor symptoms is not known, the method of action of oestrogen therapy is not fully understood (Hutton, Jacobs, and James, 1979). Oestrogen appears to be the most specific therapy and is thought to be more effective than other treatments (Vaughn and Hammond, 1981). Progestogens may also reduce vasomotor flushes (Schiff, 1982).

The accelerated bone loss of the menopause is prevented by oestrogen therapy (Worley, 1981b). Calcium supplementation also prevents bone loss, but to a lesser extent (Recker, Saville, and Heaney, 1977). It is not certain whether oestrogen therapy also significantly decreases the incidence of fractures in oestrogen deficient women (Vaughn and Hammond, 1981). It does, however, seem likely. One study of younger women (mean age about mid-40s) who received oestrogen replacement after loss of endogenous oestrogen production for various reasons, including menopause, gives some evidence that both osteoporosis and fractures are decreased (Hammond, Jelovsek, Lee, Creasman, and Parker, 1979a). Various other accounts, notably a prospective 10-year study of post-menopausal women, found that oestrogen therapy had a significantly preventive effect on the fracture rate (Nachtigall, Nachtigall, Nachtigall, and Beckman, 1979). The mechanisms involved in the beneficial effects of oestrogen are not fully understood though various suggestions are being investigated (Worley, 1981b). Oestrogen therapy does not appear to noticeably reverse any bone loss which has already occurred (Heaney, 1976). A great disadvantage in the use of oestrogens for prevention of bone loss is that if the treatment, no matter how prolonged, is ended there follows an alarming decline in bone mass (Lindsay, Maclean, Kraszewski, Hart, Clark, and Garwood, 1978). Figure 14 shows the extent

130

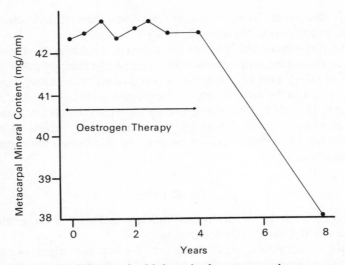

Figure 14. Effects of withdrawal of oestrogen therapy on bone mineral content after four years of treatment. Reproduced by permission of The Lancet Ltd, from Lindsay, MacLean, Kraszewski, Hart, Clark, and Garwood (1978). Bone response to termination of oestrogen treatment. *Lancet*, **i**, 1325–1327

of this effect and makes it clear that, in the present state of knowledge, oestrogen therapy for bone loss must be continued indefinitely. Preliminary results indicate that progestogens may be effective in preventing bone loss (Lindsay, Hart, Purdie, Ferguson, Clark, and Kraszewski, 1978). More studies will be needed to know whether the now more usual oestrogen/progestogen combination will be as, or more, effective in prevention (Mandel, Davidson, Erlik, Judd and Meldrum, 1982).

Vaginal dryness, dyspareunia, and in certain cases, presumably where it is secondary to vaginal changes, loss of libido, are improved by oestrogen therapy (Campbell and Whitehead, 1977; Studd, Chakravarti, and Oram, 1977). Various urinary symptoms are improved by administration of oestrogens (Brown, 1977; Kopera, 1979). Since the urethra and the vagina have a common origin in the urogenital sinus, they are very similar with regard to the squamous epithelium and the effects of oestrogen on both can be assessed by cytological investigation. It can be shown that oestrogens have a proliferative effect on the vaginal and the urethral epithelium and on elastic and connective tissues, (Vaughn and Hammonds, 1981). Hence the mechanisms of the therapeutic effect of oestrogens on the symptoms of urogenital atrophy seem clear.

Observed decreases in blood pressure and pulse rate with oestrogen therapy seem to be secondary to a reduction of anxiety, since they are also obtained with placebo (Campbell and Whitehead, 1977).

There is no firm evidence that oestrogen therapy has a direct beneficial effect on most psychological symptoms, though these may improve in the wake of a reduction in distressing physical symptoms and a general increase in well-being with the therapy (Campbell and Whitehead, 1977; Studd, Chakravarti, and Oram, 1977). Doubts have already been expressed earlier in this chapter as to the existence of a psychological syndrome which is specific to the menopause. Nevertheless whatever psychological problems exist during the menopause, arising from the physiological ageing process and environmental factors, may be exacerbated in some women by oestrogen deficiency and its effects. Since the nature and extent of the possible role of oestrogen decline has not been demonstrated, hormonal therapy is likely to be effective only when other possible origins of psychological symptoms have been excluded (Coulam, 1981).

HAZARDS

Some hazards associated with oestrogen therapy are now becoming relatively clear. Increased risk of cancer of the uterus is associated with administrations of oestrogens unopposed by progestogens. Moreover, some of the mechanisms by which oestrogens can lead to hyperplasia of the endometrium, and hence to greater likelihood of cancer, are known. Natural progesterone limits the impact of oestrogen on the endometrium by two different actions. It increases the rate of conversion of oestradiol to oestrone which, being a weaker oestrogen, does not give rise to proliferation and hence to hyperplasia in the endometrium. Progesterone also directly inhibits the synthesis of oestrogen receptor proteins (Jacobs, 1979). There is now good evidence that with the periodic addition of progestogens and with careful dosage of 'natural' oestrogens the increased risk of cancer of the uterus is reduced or abolished (Hammond, Jelovsek, Lee, Creasman, and Parker, 1979b; Thom, White, Williams, Sturdee, Paterson, Wade-Evans, and Studd, 1979). However, more needs to be known about whether progestogens are fully protective, and also about their long-term systemic effects (Campbell, McQueen, Minardi and Whitehead, 1978; Jacobs, 1979; Schwarz, 1981). In addition to the clinical studies, there have been investigations of the possible mechanisms of the protective effect of progestogens. One study for example found that a group having oestrogen unopposed by progestogen had changes in cytoplasmic oestradiol and progesterone receptors, whereas a progestogen-opposed group were no different from controls (Natrajan, Muldoon, Greenblatt, and Mahesh, 1981). Now, more information is emerging on the differing effects of various types and amounts of progestogens, see Whitehead, Townsend, Pryse-Davies, Ryder, Lane, Siddle, and Krip (1982).

The weight of the evidence as regards an association between oestrogen therapy and other cancers suggest no increase in prevalence (Hammond, Jelovsek, Lee, Creasman, and Parker, 1979b). There were fears that the incidence of breast cancer may increase with the use of synthetic oestrogen, since endogenous oestrogen is implicated in that disease. In fact, as regards post-menopausal oestrogen preparations, the majority of studies show neither an increase nor a decrease in the risk of breast cancer (Nisker and Siiteri, 1981). There is some preliminary evidence that progestogens may reduce the likelihood of carcinoma of the breast (Lobo and Gibbons, 1982).

The doubts about the effects of oestrogen therapy on coronary heart disease have been mentioned earlier in this chapter. The assumption is, though it needs further substantiation, that the menopause brings a considerably increased risk of coronary heart disease as an outcome of oestrogen deficiency. Initially it was hoped that oestrogen therapy would prevent the increased risk but this promise did not appear to be fulfilled and in fact the question was raised as to whether administered oestrogen actually increased the risk. As far as presumptive mechanisms such as lipid metabolism are concerned, it seems that the type and dose of oestrogen replacement are important. Natural oestrogens are probably more effective in conferring an atherosclerosis-protective effect than are the synthetic ones. Not only do different oestrogens have different effects on blood lipids but in some cases there may be an adverse response (Utian and Gordan, 1979). The occurrence of another intermediary mechanism, hypertension, is as already noted, reduced by oestrogen therapy (Hammond, Jelovsek, Lee, Creasman, and Parker, 1979a). As regards the effect of oestrogens on the risk of post-menopausal coronary heart disease, this does not seem to be increased by administration of oestrogens (Bain, Willett, Hennekens, Rosner, Belanger, and Speizer, 1981; Rosenberg, Slone, Shapiro, Kaufman, Stolley and Miettinen, 1980) and is probably reduced (Bain, Willett, Hennekens, Rosner, Belanger, and Speizer, 1981; Hammond, Jelovsek, Lee, Creasman, and Parker, 1979a). There is, though, at least one report, already mentioned, of detrimental effects of oestrogens on the disease (Gordon, Kannel, Hjortland, and McNamara, 1978) but the women in this group possibly had large doses of oestrogen replacement. Final conclusions about the effect of administered oestrogens on the post-menopausal rise in coronary heart disease await further studies on different types and doses of oestrogens, as well as possible revision of the general question of the development of the disease after menopause. The role of progestogens also needs to be clarified.

There appears to be a risk of impaired glucose tolerance with oestrogen therapy, though the degree of risk depends on type of oestrogens and dosage (Studd, Dubiel, Kakkar, Thom, and White, 1978). This risk, however, does not appear to lead to greater risk of diabetes, at least with 'natural' oestrogens (Rauramo and Kopera, 197). With no therapy, there is no disturbance of carbohydrate metabolism with the menopause.

There has been a considerable amount of research on the possibility of increased risk of thrombosis with oestrogens. Interpretation of the information so far available is complex and will require still further clarification. The complexity arises from the fact that the data come largely from two very different sources (i) measurement of blood-clotting factors in women receiving oestrogens for various reasons and (ii) epidemiological studies.

Both methods of inquiry must consider the normal age-related changes in thrombosis and in coagulation factors. Although there is a positive association between increasing age and thrombosis, very little is known about the relation of age to changes in coagulation. It appears likely for instance that of the several indices of clotting mechanisms more are changed with age in men than in women, but magnitude of change in certain factors is greater in women, though all this needs verification. Neither is it clear that individual coagulation characteristics *per se* predispose to thrombosis (Notelovitz, 1977). The scarcity of information on the precise relationship between thrombosis and clotting factors in the individual not taking drugs is a central problem in assessing the effects of administered oestrogens. When certain oestrogens do produce change in various blood clotting indices the significance of the changes for risk of thromboembolism is far from clear. It may be that only certain women are vulnerable, by virtue of a combination of factors, and that preliminary screening might identify those women (Ambrus, 1976). The supposition of increased risk of thrombosis with oestrogens arose from findings with the contraceptive pill in younger women. The data on oestrogen therapy in menopausal women are relatively clear as regards clotting factors. The synthetic oestrogens accelerate certain coagulation indices (Aylward, 1978; Notelovitz, 1979). As we have said, this does not necessarily predispose to thrombosis. These changes in the coagulation system usually level off in three to nine months. The natural and conjugated oestrogens induce relatively little change in most of the coagulation factors (Notelovitz, 1979). This is rather an over-simplified view since within the two categories of synthetic and natural oestrogens different types and doses of the hormones have different effects on clotting mechanisms (Aylward, 1978; Studd, Dubiel, Kakkar, Thom, and White, 1978). Many authors also point out that more long-term prospective studies are needed since increased risk may take many years to become evident (Aylward, 1978; Notelovitz, 1979). Route of administration may also have a significant effect (Notelovitz, 1979). Regardless of these findings of some effects of some oestrogen preparations on certain coagulation factors, the same is not true for the actual occurrence of thrombosis. The reports on change in incidence of thrombosis with oestrogen therapy so far recorded show no evidence of increased risk (Hammond, Jelovsek, Lee Creasman, and Parker, 1979a; Notelovitz, 1977, 1979).

The effects of added progestogen on the findings outlined are not yet entirely clear. At present it appears that progestogen combined with 'natural' oestrogens does not produce changes in either direction in blood-clotting and platelet activities. More work needs to be done on the relation between coagulation factors and progestogen, and also on incidence figures, with the increasingly used combination therapy (Aylward, 1978). The tentative conclusion at present seems to be that with careful choice of type and dosage of drugs and with haemotological screening to eliminate susceptible individuals there is no significantly increased risk of thrombosis with oestrogen therapy. It does not appear that added progestogen alters the

134

blood-clotting findings but long-term epidemiological studies on the effects of progestogen are needed.

SUMMARY

The menopause is easily defined as the last menstruation. The climacteric is a long phase of wide variations, among individuals and in any one individual, in many aspects of functioning. Although the upper age limit of menopause has not changed, there are many factors which appear to be related to the age at which the reproductive years will end for any individual. Smoking, height, and marital status are the most firmly established variables so far. There are methodological problems in eliciting all the details of the climacteric years. The technical developments in hormone measurement, however, have provided improved possibilities for understanding the endocrine changes. The progressive decline of ovarian functions brings about changes in the feedback relationship between the ovaries and the pituitary and hypothalamus. This is a gradual process. It is difficult to establish which of the organic changes observed are specific to the menopause. There are gradual but marked changes in the urogenital tract and in bone which result from the menopause. Changes in skin and in the musculature are probably part of the ageing process. All of these changes show considerable variations in rate and in magnitude.

As regards changes and symptoms which are frequently associated with the menopausal transition, many are probably not specifically menopausal and are part of the ageing process. Also there is no information on any positive aspects, although there are some indications that they do exist. The most consistently reported menopausal symptom is hot flushes. Several other symptoms are probably secondary to this. It is doubtful that impaired memory function is specific to the climacteric, though a decline in memory may be somewhat aggravated by the menopausal events. There is some decline in sexual feelings and behaviour during the menopausal transition but this is probably mainly a function of age. It is also related to the sexuality of the partner. For a small group of women there is a decrease in sexual interest associated with atrophic vaginitis. There is no good evidence of a psychological syndrome which is specific to the menopause. The primary changes of the climacteric can give rise to psychological difficulties but this is true of other times in the lifespan. Nevertheless the possibility remains that hormonal changes with the menopause may exacerbate the effects of any stress.

Incidence figures of changes associated with the menopause need amplification. Such as they are, they support the view that, apart from the universal hormonal and bodily changes, hot flushes and atrophic vaginitis are in most women the only changes specifically associated with the menopause.

Careful choice of type and dosage of hormonal treatment can provide effective treatment of primary and secondary menopausal symptoms. With appropriate screening for vulnerable individuals and with the use of so-called natural oestrogens combined with progestogens and with regular checks for possible harmful effects, the hazards of hormonal therapy appear to be low, but more long-term studies are needed.

Very little quantified information is available on changes in men during the same years of life. The main findings of interest, based on remarkably few studies are as follows. In men, from about 50 onward, there is a significant decrease in testosterone levels with a small increase in oestrogens and a moderate increase in FSH and LH. There is decreasing testicular function, starting gradually after 40 and progressing through old age. Men experience a decline in sexual activity with increasing age, especially from about the mid-40s onwards. Reports of vasomotor and various related symptoms in older men need further verification. Bone loss starts later in men than in women and proceeds more slowly. There are reports of skin atrophy with age in men, but this needs quantification. From age 50 to 60–65, there is in men a rise in depression of all kinds, after which there is a decline.

CHAPTER 8

Cause and effect: I

The mechanisms of change through the cycle are beginning to emerge. They will provide the key to improved adaptations to the cycle and to effective treatment of menstrual distress. Clearly the problem is to identify not only the origins of those changes which are an inevitable outcome of the reproductive process but also of those changes which are learned in response to the cycle. This means attempting to go beyond description and interpretation and searching for possible explanations. There are some indications of what these might be: some of the evidence is entirely convincing, some is no more than reasonable conjecture.

Many explanations of the menstrual changes tend to emphasize either hormonal or psychological factors. Let us start with what seems to be the reasonable very broad assumption that both of these influences are operating. Also, let us assume that the psychological factors operate in two ways, firstly as part of the natural process and secondly as a result of learning and of environmental factors. That is, that on the one hand there are psychological influences in the specific sense that it would be remarkable if the whole panoply of natural apparatus and mechanisms for the reproduction of human beings excluded any provision for appropriate feelings and behaviour. No-one doubts that with the hormonal and organic changes of pregnancy and maternity, for example, there are fundamental and relevant changes in feelings and behaviour. There is no obvious reason to doubt that similarly, related to the hormonal and organic changes of the earlier stages of the procreative process, that is of the menstrual cycle, there are appropriate psychological and behavioural concomitants. The 'natural' psychological factors are the strong predispositions to certain feelings and behaviours which are the outcome of the neuroendocrine processes acting at the time. As Friedman, Hurt, Arnoff, and Clarkin (1980) have suggested, the variations in the intensity of certain psychological states occur because of cyclical fluctuations in the biological activities of substances which have an impact on parts of the central nervous system that regulate the psychological states. In addition, there is an acquired psychological and social overlay to the reproductive cycle, as there is to any set of bodily and physiological changes, and there are also environmental factors constantly operating.

What is the evidence for the assumptions that we have made, namely that the hormonal fluctuations are directly related to other changes and that the psychological factors are of two kinds, as part of the natural design and as responses and attitudes learned by each individual? In general, there is evidence of some of the relationships between the endocrine system, the central and autonomic nervous systems, and feelings and behaviour. Beach (1975) has pointed out that, once correlations have been reliably established, the next step is to identify the mediating mechanisms in order to understand how the behavioural consequences of hormones are brought about. In humans, there is still much detailed work to be done. The concern here is not with the large amount of evidence showing that hormones affect behaviour in various and fundamental ways. The aim is to review the neuroendocrine events of the menstrual cycle which may be expected to provide a basis for the physical, psychological, and behavioural manifestations of the cycle. In the present state of knowledge it is not always possible to spell out specific routes but there is abundant evidence of close and powerful relationships.

The discussion of mechanisms can conveniently be divided into two parts. Firstly, the neuroendocrine processes in the physical, psychological, and behavioural manifestations of the cycle and also the variables which may influence those processes. These are presented in this chapter. Secondly, the mechanisms of the learned factors which determine the individual's experience of the cycle. They are the subject of the next chapter.

NEUROENDOCRINE PROCESSES IN THE PHYSICAL, PSYCHOLOGICAL, AND BEHAVIOURAL MANIFESTATIONS OF THE CYCLE

STEROID HORMONES AND THE NERVOUS SYSTEM

There is ample demonstration that the brain is a target area for endocrine hormones. Steroid hormones are known to be metabolized and transformed in specific brain areas (Ball, Haupt, and Knuppen, 1978), to have effects on individual brain cells (McEwen, 1976; O'Malley and Schrader, 1976), and to accumulate mainly in the pre-optic hypothalamic area, the pituitary, the amygdaloid region, septum, hippocampus, and cerebral cortex (see Backstrom, 1977; McEwen, 1976). These brain structures are presumably important in the functional integration of hormones, and are said to be the substrates of certain specific behaviours. According to Gray and Buffery (1971) and Gray (1972), for instance, parts of the hypothalamus and the midbrain, and also the amygdala, and the stria terminalis participate in aggressive and dominant behaviour; the hippocampus, parts of the frontal cortex and the septal area serve in submissive and fearful behaviour. It is highly probable that the effects of the steroid hormones in these brain areas could be one basis for the contrasting behaviours observed through the cycle when levels of oestrogen, progesterone, androgens, and the adrenocortical hormones are undergoing fluctuations. Steroid hormones have profound effects on sexual development and behaviour by acting on nerve cells in the brain and these effects are not only evident to systematic observation but can now be demonstrated experimentally. It is probable that hormones such as oestradiol and testosterone which are central in the establishment of sexual differentiation during development, then go on, during adult life, to modulate sexual activity (McEwen, 1976). Although in humans it is clear that many psychological and social factors contribute to the determination of sexual activity, the steroid hormones regulate the functioning of the neural circuits which have been structured during development. As regards methods of action of the steroid hormones, Abramovitz and Dubrovsky (1980) have made the point that in the course of evolution instead of the creation of new compounds new receptor sites developed. This means that the mechanisms may be acting by different routes for different purposes. For example, specific mating mechanisms may be affected by the steroid hormones acting through established receptor sites; more general control of excitability of the central nervous system may be achieved through membrane effects on regions of the brain stem reticular formation.

OVARIAN AND PITUITARY HORMONES

A general observation is that oestrogens seem to have a central nervous system activating effect and progesterone, or oestrogens plus progesterone, have the effect of depressing central activity (Vogel, Broverman, and Klaiber, 1971). Many studies have shown the direct effects of oestrogens and progesterone on the amount of excitability in various parts of the brain (Abramovitz and Dubrovsky, 1980; Backstrom, 1977). There are also some indications of a general effect on brain activity of hypothalamic and pituitary hormones, namely of GnRH (McAdoo, Doering, Kraemer, Dessert, Brodie, and Hamburg, 1978) and of LH and FSH (Friedman and Meares, 1979; Houser, 1979). A welcome addition to the work on cyclical changes in nervous system activity, cited in Chapter 3, would come from studies of precise relationships between those changes and levels of the various hormones. It is clear that with the fluctuation in concentrations of circulating hormones there will be variations in baseline levels of nervous system activation. Details of this association would be of practical value, given the influence of nervous system activity on feelings, behaviour and symptoms. It is possible that oestrogens, and perhaps other hormones, may act in a permissive role in some menstrual cycle changes which are primarily controlled by the central nervous system. For example, Doty, Huggins, Snyder, and Lowry (1981) have suggested that in the case of cyclical changes in olfactory sensitivity, although these may not be directly dependent on fluctuations in ovarian hormones, it is likely that oestrogens may be necessary for the variations to occur. Work with animals has shown that cyclical changes in a number of behavioural or neurological rhythms associated with the oestrous cycle, although eliminated by removal of the ovaries, are restored with administration of non-cyclic oestrogens.

ANDROGENS

There is very little work specifically on the interaction of androgens with other endocrine and neural processes during the cycle. Women not only have lower over-all levels of androgens than men, they also have different proportions of the various androgens. In contrast to men, women have dihydrotestosterone as a significant though still small fraction of total circulating androgens (Yen and Jaffe, 1978). In both sexes, testosterone is transformed in the brain into one of two hormonal steroids—dihydrotestosterone and oestradiol. Androstenedione is the other precursor of dihydrotestosterone. The sources of androgens are the ovary and the adrenal cortex and their relative contributions vary in the course of the cycle as do the fluctuations in the various androgens. Testosterone appears to be higher mid-cycle than in other phases. Androstenedione levels rise before the onset of the LH and FSH surges and remain elevated until after ovulation (Judd and Yen, 1973), see Chapter 2. Androgens are thought to lower monoamine oxidase activity (Bardwick, 1976; Broverman, Klaiber, Kobayashi, and Vogel, 1968); more detailed demonstration of how this takes place during the female cycle is required. More generally, the neuroendocrine processes underlying the role of androgens in the cycle and its manifestations are still to be fully elucidated. It is nevertheless clear that the various androgens, which have known powerful influence on feelings and behaviour, particularly on aggressive and hostile responses and on sexual activity, fluctuate systematically through the cycle.

ADRENOCORTICAL HORMONES

The course of the hormones of the adrenal cortex during the cycle is important in a number of ways. In general they are involved in sexual functioning, mood, and reactivity to stress. Also in fluid and electrolyte balance, as well as in the metabolism of carbohydrate, protein, and fat. They are in close interaction with the hormones of the adrenal medulla, adrenaline and noradrenaline, which facilitate arousal of the sympathetic nervous system and which are so heavily implicated in mood and in emotion. The influence of the adrenocortical hormones on the brain is not as well understood as that of the ovarian hormones but they do appear to significantly affect brain function. They are found in the septum and also in the hippocampus where they probably play a role in rapid eye movement sleep and/or dreaming. There are experiments showing that the administration of adrenal steroids to human volunteers depresses rapid eye movements during sleep, possibly by the action of corticosterone on hippocampal nerve cells (McEwen, 1976).

There is considerable clinical evidence that adrenal steroids are involved in sensory detection (McEwen, 1976).

Aldosterone concentrations are higher in the second half of the cycle than in the first and within that pattern there is a peak around Day 20, falling a few days later. In most women the luteal rise is thought to be the result of increased activity in the renin-angiotensin system (Steiner and Carroll, 1977). There is evidence that levels of aldosterone secretion are related to progesterone, levels of both hormones increasing somewhat in parallel after ovulation (Voda, 1980). The details of any relationship between aldosterone, sodium, and potassium levels and physical and psychological changes during the cycle are not clear (see Chapter 3). In particular there is need of more studies in which ingestion and rest/activity are controlled before the role of aldosterone in cyclical fluid retention and weight gain is known. Similarly the part played by aldosterone in the mood changes of the cycle, whether through the renin-angiotensin-aldosterone system or in some other conjunction, with for instance ovarian hormones, has still to be clarified.

Cortisol levels are said to be somewhat lower during the follicular than during the luteal phase (Steiner and Carroll, 1977), though some studies have found them to be relatively stable over the course of the cycle (Marinari, Leshner, and Doyle, 1976). It may be adrenocortical reactivity to stress and its influence on mood, rather than levels, which varies, being greater premenstrually than at other times (Marinari, Leshner, and Doyle, 1976). One study (Abplanalp, Livingston, Rose, and Sandwisch, 1977) found an association between increased levels of cortisol and emotional arousal in general but no significant variations in cortisol levels and response to stress with the cycle. More information on individual differences in reactivity to stress with the cycle is needed. The rhythmicity of cortisol secretion may be related to emotional changes with the cycle. Patients suffering from endogenous depression show loss of cortisol rhythmicity. Also patients with cortisol secretion disturbances experience depressive symptoms (Anders, 1982).

The adrenal cortex produces small amounts of oestrogens, progesterones, and androgens and in fact after the menopause becomes the principal source of oestrogens and androgens (Hutton, Jacobs, and James, 1979). The androgens secreted by the adrenal cortex are apparently important, in men and women, in maintaining sexual desire, ideation, sensitivity, and responsiveness (Gray and Gorzalka, 1980).

PROSTAGLANDINS

The synthesis and release of prostaglandins in the brain may be partly mediated by oestrogens. In turn prostaglandins may play an intermediary role in the integration of neuroendocrine function. They have been shown experimentally to have central nervous system effects and though they do not themselves act as transmitter substances they may regulate the action of such substances (Coulam, 1981). It has already been pointed out that prostaglandins are implicated in the volume and duration of menstrual bleeding and hence in dysmennorrhea. They are similarly implicated in ovulation and in mid-cycle pain. Amplification of the work on prostaglandins may indicate that they are important links in the neuroendocrine processes underlying many other changes with the cycle.

PROLACTIN

Prolactin is doubtless one of the more important endocrine mechanisms in the manifestations of the cycle. It has widespread action on osmoregulation, metabolism, and on reproductive functions and has numerous specific receptor sites throughout the body (Yen and Jaffe, 1978). It has already been said that, contrary to previous reports, careful measurement of prolactin levels shows that they do vary with the cycle in many women, with wide individual variations; they are higher in the luteal phase than in the follicular phase (Steiner and Carroll, 1977). Dopamine inhibits prolactin (McGeer and McGeer, 1980) and other transmitters are probably involved, notably melatonin, via LH inhibition (Cutler and Garcia, 1980). Monoamine oxidase, through its blocking effects on dopamine, increases prolactin levels (Brush, 1977). Oestrogen promotes the synthesis of prolactin and its release by the pituitary (Yen and Jaffe, 1978). Prolactin levels are also related to testosterone, possibly due to the conversion of testosterone to oestrogen in the hypothalamus. Prolactin appears to have a mutually antagonistic relationship with progesterone and, like progesterone, it can affect fluid balance (Brush, 1977). Levels of prolactin rise markedly during sleep and after stress (Yen and Jaffe, 1978). It seems likely that prolactin is implicated in some aspects of premenstrual tension doubtless in conjunction with other hormonal and with neural processes (Brush, 1977).

NEUROTRANSMITTERS

There are considerable reciprocal transactions between reproductive hormones and neurotransmitters. The content and the turnover of neurotransmitters are selectively affected by different hormones (see Coulam, 1981) and neurotransmitters are involved in the release of hormones. Details of these feedback effects are beginning to emerge. For example, dopamine, noradrenaline, and serotonin are all found within hypothalamic neurones and although experimentally none of these neurotransmitter substances alone can induce LH and FSH release their additive effect stimulates release of GnRH. There is ample evidence that these three neurotransmitters aid in the regulation of the pituitary secretion of gonadotrophins and also that the effect of dopamine, for example, on LH levels varies with the cycle (Yen and Jaffe, 1978). Adrenaline may also be involved in some steroid feedback mechanisms (Shaw, 1978). There appears to be an interplay between inhibition of serotonin and excitation of monoamines in gonadotrophin release

(Cutler and Garcia, 1980) and it is oestrogen that modulates this process of neural control of gonadotrophin release (Ojeda and McCann, 1973). So that neurotransmitters exert their influence on hypothalamic releasing factors which influence pituitary hormones which influence ovarian hormones which in turn regulate the neural control. It is worth noting here that the catecholamine neurones which serve broad and diffuse pathways in the brain have considerable potential influence on other brain cells. In addition, noradrenaline for example has a diffuse distribution peripherally as well as in brain and is one of the principal effector mechanisms of sympathetic innervation (McGeer and McGeer, 1980). Noradrenaline levels are probably higher premenstrually than at other times, whereas adrenaline is unchanged (Patkai, Johannson, and Post, 1974; Wiener and Elmadjian, 1962). Also important, especially for premenstrual state, is the growing body of evidence that catecholamines are involved in the regulation of salt and water balance (Reid and Yen, 1981).

The intermediary role of monamine oxidase in these interactions has been scrutinised. The effects of oestrogen and progesterone and probably testosterone on monoamine oxidase activity, and hence on levels of catecholamines and of serotonin are well established both clinically and experimentally (Backstrom, 1977; Coulam, 1981; Warren, Tedford, and Flynn, 1979). Serotonin, like dopamine and noradrenaline, is metabolized primarily by monamine oxidase. Oestrogens are known to affect the precursor of serotonin, tryptophan. Tryptophan is an amino acid which is related to levels of pyrodoxine, Vitamin B_6. These relationships doubtless have bearings on mood and on affective disorders during the menstrual cycle (Coulam, 1981) and on the effects of some contraceptives (Brush, 1977). They are also probably involved in the lowering of pain thresholds after ovulation to the end of menstruation, through the action of oestrogen and progesterone on monamine oxidase and on serotonin (Tedford, Warren, and Flynn, 1977). The findings on levels of monoamine oxidase activity through the cycle are slightly equivocal (see for example Asso, 1978). The majority of studies find rather higher levels premenstrually than at other times but a few studies report no such increase. One study reports higher levels before ovulation than after, but rising from a low eight days premenstrually to the high pre-ovulatory levels at menstruation (Baron, Levitt, and Perlman, 1980). Further information is required before the precise role of monamine oxidase in the cycle is clear.

Melatonin inhibits ovulation through the effects of light on endocrine processes. It can therefore be crucial to the occurrence or not of ovulation, the timing of cycles and hence to many other characteristics of any cycle. There is also evidence of various kinds that melatonin secretion seems to be controlled by sympathetic neurones (see Lewey, Wehr, Goodwin, Newsome, and Markey, 1980). This implication of the autonomic nervous system, which is so important in emotional responsiveness, in the activity of melatonin with all its ramifications is doubtless important in the psychological and behavioural changes with the cycle. Also of importance is the part played by the sympathetic nervous system, via melatonin, in ovulation (Cutler and Garcia, 1980). Since increased activity in this nervous system is an accompaniment of augmented emotional response, this may provide an explanation for any effect of emotional factors on ovulation.

The comprehensive and continual involvement of neurotransmitters in every aspect of the reproductive cycle is beyond doubt. These transmitters are likewise known to be vital in the physiological, psychological and behavioural manifestations of mood, emotion, sleep, sexual activity, general motivation. They are also involved in heat regulation, pain sensitivity, and locomotor activity. All these associations have been amply demonstrated (see for example McGeer and McGeer, 1980).

The role of some neurotransmitters, other than those mentioned, in the menstrual cycle is unknown. It will be of great interest to know how the peptides, for example the endorphins, may affect the manifestations of the cycle. They are found in high concentrations in some of the neural structures which have already been mentioned in the context of the cycle—septum, hippocampus, amygdala, hypothalamus (McGeer and McGeer, 1980). The manner in which peptides may participate in the modulation or integration of mood, behaviour and the varied manifestations of the premenstruum has been suggested by Reid and Yen, (1981). The more specific possibility of a relationship between changes in levels of endorphins and premenstrual dysphoric symptoms is discussed by Halbreich and Endicott (1981).

AUTONOMIC NERVOUS SYSTEM

The autonomic nervous system also has reciprocal interactions with endocrine processes. Although still relatively unexplored, there is some evidence of the mutual influences. Noradrenaline is widely distributed both in the brain and in the periphery; it is, as already mentioned, one of the principal effector mechanisms of autonomic, sympathetic division, innervation and hence is a major mediating influence on emotional response. Most postganglionic fibres of the sympathetic division secrete noradrenaline. In addition, all autononic preganglionic fibres, sympathetic and parasympathetic, secrete acetylocholine. This is also true of the postganglionic fibres of the parasympathetic division. Various indices of the autonomic nervous system fluctuate with the cycle and these fluctuations are thought to be related to the cyclical variations in mood and in emotion and possibly in the propensity to acquire conditioned responses (see Chapter 3). In view of the importance of the autonomic nervous system in emotion and mood and in the learning of behaviour and symptoms, it may be one intermediary mechanism in some of the more overt manifestations of the neuroendocrine changes of the cycle.

SENSATION AND PERCEPTION

Sensory and perceptual mechanisms are altered by hormones which are in turn affected by the sensory/perceptual responses. A point of particular interest in understanding the manifestations of the menstrual cycle is that some hormones, instead of changing sensory thresholds, appear to affect perception and thus to alter or even to reverse preferences. For example, a deficiency in certain adrenocortical hormones evokes a craving for the taste of salt. Male rats prefer the odour of oestrous females to that of females not on heat (Beach, 1975). In humans there is some evidence that vaginal odours are judged to be slightly less unpleasant by men and women in the preovulatory and ovulatory phases (Doty, Ford, Preti, and Huggins, 1975). So that there are some preferences created by hormonal processes which may have implications for behaviour.

GENERAL CONSIDERATIONS

There are some general points which are worth stating or reiterating in considering the neuroendocrine mechanisms in the physical, psychological, and behavioural changes of the cycle. The present limited amount of detailed knowledge of the complexities of the neuroendocrine processes, obvious from even the brief account above, make it difficult to give a clear delineation of precise mechanisms in any manifestation of the cycle. In addition to the interactions between the various neural and endocrine systems, any component may act in more than one way. They may act directly to affect physical and psychological processes, or indirectly through another component of the neuroendocrine system. They may also affect different systems via different intermediary routes.

There are wide individual differences in the relationships between neuroendocrine processes and physical, psychological, and behavioural factors even where group associations have been repeatedly found. The importance of individual factors such as transient phsyiological and psychological state, personality differences, genetic differences, and environmental variables can hardly be overstated, and these are discussed in various parts of this book.

It has been pointed out (in Chapter 5) that attempts to correlate hormone levels with other menstrual changes in individual women are rare and the results are not conclusive, partly no doubt because none of the studies has yet been able to investigate fully the various combinations of hormones throughout the cycle. Group relationships between hormonal levels and various changes in mood and behaviour have been demonstrated, but there are individual differences in hormone levels and in sensitivity to the various hormones, as well as different amounts of learned influence. In spite of the fact that the exact nature of the effect of individual characteristics awaits demonstration, observable, and marked changes in feelings and behaviour at times of specific hormonal changes have been shown in suitably controlled group studies. In addition, the psychological, behavioural and bodily changes which accompany the phases of great hormonal fluctuations such as puberty and pregnancy are evident to all, and cannot be attributed solely to the life events at those times. This view, in which certain combinations of hormonal levels are related to various moods, feelings and behaviours is further supported by the findings on the contraceptive pill, given in Chapters 3 and 4. The use of a combination pill, which maintains more stable levels of hormones, is accompanied by less variations in, particularly, mood and sexual arousal than with no pill whereas there are indications that the sequential pill, which creates a hormonal climate more similar to the natural cycle at least as regards fluctuation in levels, gives rise to variations which are closer to those reported with the normal cycle. What is more, reports of variations in feelings, symptoms, and behaviour tend to vary systematically according to the actual amounts of hormonal substances in the contraceptive pill. The more oestrogen there is in the pill, the less depression is reported; with high progestogen pills, more depression and lowered sexual desire are reported. Women on oestrogen-dominant pills feel more aggressive and hostile compared with women on progestogen-dominant pills, who report strong feelings of deference, nurturance, and affiliation (Bardwick, 1976). One study which demonstrated differences in negative affect between naturally menstruating women and women taking contraceptive pills also showed that these differences were not attributable to self-selection, prior expectations or reduction of physical discomfort in the pill-users. Only anxiety was considered to be possibly due to social factors. This study was not based on self-report methods but on interviewers' assessments of women's verbal material (Paige, 1971). It is not plausible to suggest that these results are due to certain expectations and stereotyped ideas; in the case of contraceptive pill studies this would presuppose that the women studied not only knew the precise amounts of the different hormonal substances, but also the different accompanying moods which might be expected with each hormone combination. Further confirmation of these results would of course be welcome but the few well-controlled studies available which included pill-users give clear indications of a close relationship between hormonal levels and feelings and behaviour. This has been shown not only in studies which rely on self-report, but also in investigations of observed behaviour (see for example Bardwick, 1976); on ratings of verbal content (Paige, 1971) and on measures of reactivity (see for example Baker, Kostin, Mishara, and Parker, 1979; Marinari, Leshner, and Doyle, 1976).

Finally, the animal work that is available supports the notion of biologically determined mood and behavioural changes with the cycle. For example, records have been kept of monkeys and apes showing systematic 'mood' and behavioural changes associated with the reproductive cycle (Janiger, Riffenburgh, and Kersh, 1972). One study found a relationship between aggressive behaviour and menstrual cycle stage in rhesus monkeys (Mallow, 1981). The author points out that although phase of the cycle and behaviour were clearly associated, some social influence was not ruled out. This is a general point to be remembered, even with animals; also to be noted are the dangers of generalizing from animal work to the complexities of human behaviour. Nevertheless, the fact that 'mood' and behaviour changes are observed in close association with the cycle in the higher mammals strengthens the case for such elements being inherent in the human cycle.

It is reasonable to conclude that physical, psychological, and behavioural changes are associated with the hormonal changes of the menstrual cycle. Nevertheless it is abundantly clear that although the general implications of the neuroendocrine interactions are not in doubt, many of the details of the mechanisms are poorly understood. The challenge for research is to discover the actual routes by which events are related, and the review above suggests that as regards the menstrual cycle there are many signs of progress towards that goal.

VARIABLES WHICH MAY INFLUENCE THE NEUROENDOCRINE EVENTS OF THE CYCLE

Beach (1975) notes that, in general, many hormonal-behavioural relationships are reciprocal, or linked in other ways. The complexity is considerable, with stimuli aroused by behaviour sometimes feeding back into the brain and thence to the endocrine system, where they excite or inhibit the secretion of hormones, which in turn exert additional effects on behaviour. Let us consider briefly the reverse effects of the ones just discussed. That is, the effects of some psychological and behavioural factors on the neuroendocrine processes of the menstrual cycle. Some environmental variables, which are anyway connected with behaviour, are also mentioned.

SEXUAL ACTIVITY

Although the influence of sexual activity on endocrine states has been demonstrated in some mammals, the situation is less clear for humans. Cutler, Garcia, and Krieger (1979a, 1979b, 1980) have shown a relationship between sexual activity and length of cycle and, among infertile women, a short luteal phase. These authors suggest that, whatever the direction of causality, there may be a neuroendocrine feedback loop in which sexual activity alters endocrine levels or patterns as well as the better known reverse effect. Morris and Udry (1977) investigated specifically the possibility that coitus and/or orgasm triggers ovulation. They found that this was not the case, at least in so far as marital coitus is concerned. If sexual behaviour and certain aspects of the reproductive cycle are related, the details of the mechanisms of interaction are not clear and things are further complicated by the probably considerable influence of other variables.

EMOTION AND STRESS

There is a lack of controlled studies which have specifically investigated the effect of emotional and stress factors on the menstrual cycle. One survey (Ihalainen, 1975) found no great differences on various psychological tests between a group of amenorrheic women and a group of normally menstruating women. Real-life observations during wartime do provide some evidence that sudden emotional shocks can bring about cessation of menstruation in previously normally menstruating women; what is more, a relationship has been reported between frequency of amenorrhea and the harshness of the conditions and the fear aroused in the victims. Although malnutrition played some part in the effect, the psychological factors appear to have also been important. Some peacetime studies have also indicated an association between sudden emotional upheavals and amenorrhea (Russell, 1972). In animals there is ample evidence of the effect on menstrual function of social and environmental factors which could be said to give rise to something analogous to human notions of stress. Rowell (1970) for example has shown this in baboons and the author suggests it is prolonged rather than acute stress which produces these effects. It is reasonable to suppose that emotional and stress factors may influence the neuroendocrine events of the cycle, but that these factors have to be intense and prolonged. Nevertheless, even in less obvious circumstances, as Sommer (1978) has pointed out the demonstrable presence of metabolic or hormonal pathology does not rule out contributory psychological factors. Also, less intense and less prolonged emotion and stress may of course play some part in less obvious effects on menstrual function than amenorrhea.

If, as seems likely, emotional and stress factors are able to influence the course of the menstrual cycle, how precisely does this come about? All kinds of psychological and physiological stress, including emotion, are followed by increased secretion of adrenal steroids (McEwen, 1976) which has the various associations with the menstrual cycle already discussed above. McEwen mentions the animal evidence that rhesus monkeys subjected to decisive defeat by dominant males have a dramatic decline of testosterone levels. Fortunately when the defeated males are exposed to female companions, the testosterone levels are rapidly restored to normal. It has already been noted that the autonomic nervous system may be involved in the control of ovulation and that more generally it has reciprocal interactions with various neuroendocrine processes. It could presumably be an intermediary mechanism in any effects of emotional feelings and behaviour on the reproductive cycle. It has been made clear above how direct is the involvement of various transmitters in every aspect of the cycle. These transmitters are also of course quite fundamental in emotion and stress, and there can be no doubt that they are important in mediating the effects of emotion and stress on the cycle. We can broadly conclude that the main mechanisms in the influence of emotion and stress on the cycle seem to reside predominantly in the

148

secretions of the adrenal glands, the sympathetic division of the autonomic nervous system and the neurotransmitters. The central nervous system structures underlying these interactions between emotion and reproductive processes are doubtless those which are known to serve emotion and which are target regions of the steroid hormones; that is, the hypothalamus and the structures of the limbic system, especially the hippocampus, the septum, and the amygdala.

NUTRITION

There is evidence of some control of the reproductive system by nutritional factors. In addition to wartime studies mentioned above which indicate that food deprivation was partly responsible for a markedly high incidence of amenorrhea, there are many animal studies and human clinical studies showing a similar association. There is inhibition of cyclic processes both by obesity (with a return to full functioning when normal weight is restored) and by emaciation, whether by anorexia nervosa or by enforced shortage of food. Famine can also result, in addition to amenorrhea and its effect on fertility, in a higher incidence of spontaneous abortion and lower birth weight, (see for example Cutler and Garcia, 1980).

FLYING AND ALTITUDE

There has not been much systematic investigation of the effect of flying on reproductive processes. One study (Preston, Bateman, Short and Wilkinson, 1974) found that air stewardesses had a higher than expected proportion of irregular menstrual cycles. This mainly took the form of prolonged cycles, presumably by delayed ovulation, since the post-ovulatory phase is fairly stable. This is presumed to be due to stress imposed by constant time-zone changes. It may also be partly a function of altitude.

The menstrual cycle appears to be disturbed by high altitudes, and, in both men and women, fertility is adversely affected by high altitudes (see Cutler and Garcia, 1980). It is not clear how prolonged the stay in a higher altitude must be for these effects to appear.

LIGHT

It is likely that one of the many effects of light is the photoperiodic regulation of reproductive cycles, in mammals anyway, and probably similarly in human beings. Lewey, Wehr, Goodwin, Newsome, and Markey (1980) have reported results which support this view. Further, more general, studies of the effect of light on neuroendocrine processes through the cycle would be useful. The possible influence of the moon on the cycle has often been thought to be related to available light. It has already been said, in Chapter 1, that any association between the lunar and menstrual cycles appears to exist in the absence of direct photic influences. This is therefore probably an example of entrainment of rhythms via geophysical forces rather than a direct influence of external light on reproductive processes (Cutler and Garcia, 1980).

There also seems to be a seasonal effect related to temperature, conception rates being less in warmer weather (see for example Cutler and Garcia, 1980).

LIVING CONDITIONS

Living conditions were found to be related to the incidence of ovulation, in a rather thorough survey of women from 15–39 years (Metcalf and Mackenzie, 1980). Women living in flats and hostels ovulated considerably less often than those living with families. Also, students ovulated less than non-students. The mechanisms underlying these differences are not clear.

From all that we have so far said about cause and effect there can be little doubt that there are marked, fundamental patterns of change in many processes and systems of women, including biologically relevant changes in mood and behaviour, which are directly related to the menstrual cycle. It is also clear that psychological and behavioural factors can in turn modify the events of the cycle and that the mechanisms underlying these interactions are known at least in outline.

It will also be clear that in response to these changes each individual has developed a set of learned feelings and attitudes and behaviour. In addition, environmental events will constantly influence the ways in which the changes are experienced. It is to the mechanisms of these acquired aspects of the menstrual changes that we now turn our attention.

CHAPTER 9

Cause and effect: II

THE MECHANISMS OF LEARNED INFLUENCES ON THE INDIVIDUAL'S EXPERIENCE OF THE CYCLE

There are some general points to be borne in mind when assessing the contribution of acquired psychological and social influences to the experience of menstrually related change.

The biologically determined elements of the cycle which have been discussed are better seen as trends, rather than strongly defined changes. In all women there will be a tendency to experience, for example, more positive feelings of assertiveness, self-confidence, and well-being around ovulation, and more negative feelings, fluid-retention and headaches just before menstruation. Of course these feelings and most of the physical symptoms may occur, though less markedly and less systematically, at other times of life in women, and in men. In this respect, two points are worth noting. Firstly, there are also some neuroendocrine fluctuations throughout those other times (Hutton, Jacobs, and James, 1979). Secondly, there are cyclical hormonal fluctuations in men; for instance rhythms, of much lower frequency, are known in men for FSH, LH, testosterone, and 17-ketosteroids, see Smolensky (1980). So that a neuroendocrine basis for such feelings and symptoms is not thereby discounted. Secondly, it is the pattern, the timing and the magnitude of the menstrual cycle variations which make it clear that these particular series of changes are specifically related to that cycle. The precise extent of the manifestations of these cyclical tendencies will depend on many individual and environmental factors. The tendencies are inevitable, the precise manifestations are determined by a multitude of factors over which the individual has varying degrees of control. In addition to all the differences between individuals, and at different times for one individual, there are, within the changes, certain aspects which are more strongly biologically determined than others. Breast tenderness is doubtless predominantly biologically determined, whereas the premenstrual increase in attempted suicides would seem to be much more dependent on the individual's learned approach to feelings of tension and hostility, and on various personality factors. A biological response is the detection of certain odours, seemingly unique to ovulating women, which has already been mentioned in

150

Chapter 3. A largely learned response, to be discussed more fully later, is the use of awareness of the cycle changes to perform better premenstrually on various tasks. There is good reason to assume some biological basis to the reported well-being, assertiveness, hostility, aggression, and tension, whereas anxiety may be somewhat more determined by learned responses to various aspects of menstruation. It would not be suprising if considerable learned anxiety has become centred around the actual bleeding for various personal and cultural reasons. Also, as menstruation approaches, there may often be acquired apprehensions about feelings and symptoms previously experienced, and in certain circumstances and in certain groups, there may be anxiety about the possibility of being pregnant. Clearly, in assessing the contribution to the menstrual changes of learned psychological and social influences, it has to be remembered that in addition to differences between individuals and, for any individual, differences between occasions, there will be for each of the changes varying amounts of biological and/or learned influences. Finally to be remembered is that here, as in all work on the menstrual cycle, virtually all discussion of learned elements is about negative changes, since the positive aspects have been neglected, both in research and in commentary.

The mechanisms of learned influences on the individual's experience of the cycle to be discussed here are additional to the individual characteristics which appear to have bearing on the incidence of changes associated with the cycle and which have already been discussed in Chapter 5. They are age, cycle characteristics, personality, emotional adjustment, and psychiatric illness. Also discussed were the important, but virtually unexplored, individual differences in hormonal levels and in sensitivity to changes in those levels, as well as physiological responsiveness and genetic influence. Given those individual characteristics; given the complexity of the neuroendocrine events and their modification by such factors as sexual activity, stress, nutrition, and environmental variables, all discussed in the last chapter, how in addition do learned elements help determine the ways in which an individual will experience the cycle? The various ways are doubtless not all yet known, but some of them can be suggested, with varying degrees of conjecture. Three broad areas will be considered: attitudes and beliefs; attribution and labels; variations in physiological responsiveness.

ATTITUDES AND BELIEFS

The importance of attitudes to the experience of physical, psychological, and behavioural changes in general has been increasingly recognized. As regards attitudes to the menstrual cycle, there are two different questions which in practice prove difficult to separate. These are the questions of, firstly, how attitudes and feelings affect the actual changes and, secondly, how feelings and attitudes affect the reporting of the changes. It is not yet possible to decisively unravel the effects of these two factors from each other, but we shall attempt to look separately at the studies which have related attitudes to the cycle to *experienced* change and those which more specifically have releated attitudes to the *manner of reporting* changes. (It has to be noted that not all of these studies were wholly or primarily concerned with the effect of attitudes on the changes or the reporting of them, but they nevertheless provide this sort of information whether incidentally or not).

The first group of studies essentially assumes that both the attitudes and feelings about the cycle, and the changes reported, are an accurate reflection of the experience of the person reporting. The second group of studies raises the question of whether the changes reported are perhaps not an accurate reflection of the actual state of affairs, but rather of certain attitudes and feelings about the menstrual cycle. This is far from being an unimportant quibble. It has implications not only for the interpretation of many of the findings on the menstrual cycle, since so many of the studies rely on self-report, but also for any practical plans for improved information, education, therapy, and so forth.

Attitudes and experience

Studies of the first kind, which take reports of changes at face value and relate those changes to attitudes to, or awareness of, the menstrual cycle, are few. That is, they have investigated the effects of attitudes on women's actual experience of the changes with the cycle and they assume that this experience is accurately reported by women. These few are almost exclusively concerned with negative changes. A study which compared the incidence of menstrual symptoms in Spanish students with a British group found that, in spite of greater inhibitions towards sex and menstruation in the Spanish women, the incidence of premenstrual symptoms was entirely comparable in the two groups (Theano, 1968). Another study found just a slight difference in attitudes between women complaining mainly of premenstrual, as opposed to menstrual, distress; the group with premenstrual complaints was deemed to be less traditional than the menstrual distress group (May, 1976). An early study, already mentioned, of suicide with the cycle suggests that women who report premenstrual distress, that is, who are aware of it and express it verbally, attempt suicide less than women who do not acknowledge distress (Tonks, Rack, and Rose, 1968). A cross-cultural survey found that, regardless of culture, the main premenstrual symptoms are reported, though with rather different patterns of frequency and severity (Janiger, Riffenburgh, and Kersh, 1972; see Table 5). A large cross-cultural survey by the World Health Organization (1981a) similarly found that across cultures both physical discomfort and mood changes prior to or during menstruation were widely reported, but with differing frequencies, see Table 4. Different attitudes presumably contribute at least partially to these varying patterns of symptoms in different cultures. As regards sub-cultures, one report suggests that women from different religious groups in America experience some of the menstrual changes slightly differently. It was found that religious attitudes were related to experience of menstrual distress in Catholic and Jewish women (Paige, 1973), Catholic women especially reporting more anxiety premenstrually and orthodox Jewish women more likely to have menstrual problems. It is probable that this influence of religious beliefs and attitudes is most evident with cyclical changes in anxiety which, as already mentioned, is possibly more likely to be determined by learned factors than are some other changes. Religious beliefs would also be expected to influence some cyclical fluctuations, such as sexual behaviour, more than others. A study of American student nurses suggested that high scores on an index of premenstrual tension, pain with menstruation, and with ovulation, and either absence of or excess flow, were related to an 'unwholesome' menstrual attitude and to certain psychiatric and personality problems (Levitt and Lubin, 1967). Not only would such findings have to be confirmed with more representative groups, and the validity of the measures used verified, but also the direction of the relationships would have to be clarified. Brooks-Gunn and Ruble (1980) developed a Menstrual Attitude Questionnaire in order to explore, in some detail, women's attitudes to menstruation. They found that attitudes were complex; that menstruation is sometimes seen as a positive as well as a negative event; that over 60% of women consider it as a bother though natural; most women, without denying its effects, accept it rather routinely. Two-thirds of the women in fact do not see it as debilitating. As regards the relationship between these attitudes and cycle changes, as we might expect some attitudes are more strongly associated with menstrual distress than others. Attitudes about debilitation and prediction were related to premenstrual and menstrual symptoms; this was not the case for naturalness and 'bothersomeness'. Denying the effects of menstruation (which was rare) was related to lower symptomatology in a group of Princeton University undergraduates, but not in a group of women from three New Jersey State Colleges. This last point demonstrates the importance of sampling in menstrual studies. It is unfortunate that virtually all self-report studies, and nearly all other types of study, of the menstrual cycle have been of women in higher education or closely connected with it. This will be mentioned again later on in this chapter.

Conclusions about the extent to which attitudes determine actual experience of the cycle must await more comprehensive studies. The rather hazy picture which at present emerges is that some aspects of cyclical change are probably more related to feelings about the cycle than others. Where there are indications of some relationship between attitudes and cyclical changes, it is not clear if it is a causal relationship, nor is there any way of knowing the direction of causality.

Attitudes and reporting of experience

Studies of the second kind, which examine (whether as their primary concern or not) the whole basis of the replies to menstrual questionnaires, are an important part of the attempts to achieve a more accurate view of the cycle. The issue essentially is whether self-reports of changes with the cycle largely reflect (i) socially induced attitudes about the cycle or (ii) actual personal experience of the cycle.

Several authors interpret their results as suggesting that menstrual questionnaires are filled in according to social beliefs rather than to actual events. General discussion of these interpretations will follow the review of the studies. In one investigation (Ruble, 1977) the subjects were led to believe that they were in either the premenstrual or in the intermenstrual phase of the cycle. The 'as if premenstrual' subjects had higher scores on water retention, changes in eating, sexual arousal, than the 'as if intermenstrual' group. There were no differences between the groups on negative affect, concentration, behaviour, autonomic reactions, arousal (a blanket term to include well-being, energy, activity). The author concludes that these results show that psychosocial factors can influence reports of menstrually related symptoms. In this study, categories of negative affect and behaviour, perhaps particularly relevant in connection with self-reporting methods, were not significantly different in the two conditions so that the author's conclusions about social bias do not apply to these changes. It is worth noting that, as regards water retention, a premenstrual increase has been demonstrated by various objective measurements (for example Janowsky, Berens, and Davis, 1973; Voda, 1980; see Chapter 3). Another study using the 'as if' method (Brooks, Ruble, and Clark, 1977), found that regardless of actual cycle phase the 'as if premenstrual' group expected more severe symptoms than the 'as if intermenstrual, group. These authors suggest that their findings are consistent with reports that premenstrual state may reflect stereotyped expectations, but that other explanations may be possible. They make some other important points, such as over-dependence on symptom scales which present menstruation as a negative event and which do not represent all attitudes about it. Also that a distinction has to be made between expectations about physical, and about psychological, changes with the cycle. The study also gleaned information on positive attitudes: 77% of the women saw menstruation as at least slightly positive, without denying its effects. This is a further indication that, as mentioned in Chapter 5, if women were asked to express views about positive aspects a more balanced understanding of their experience would be possible. In one investigation a group of men and a group of women were asked to answer a Menstrual Distress Questionnaire in terms of the symptoms which women experience. The men and women reported very similar patterns of symptoms and symptom changes with, if anything, the men's answers reflecting greater severity (Parlee, 1974). The author believes that these results indicate that there is no reason to suppose that

155

the answers reflect direct personal experience. A later study by the same author (Parlee, 1980) similarly concluded that self-reports may measure stereotypes. Also that daily self-report, with the subject unaware of the purpose of the study, is the best questionnaire method. The author also points to the need to take account of other cycles. Another study also found that more consistent differences between cycle phases were reported in retrospective reports than in reports of present state, and that it is only when the menstrual cycle is explicitly made salient that broad cyclical variations are found. The author concludes that these results support the view that 'salient' questionnaires may exaggerate possible cyclical variations in moods and behaviours (Englander-Golden, Whitmore, and Dienstbier, 1978). Golub and Harrington (1981) also found that in adolescents whereas there was mood impairment during menstruation when measured by the menstrual distress questionnaire there was an absence of change in mood-scales which were not menstrually related. The authors feel that stereotypic responses are one possible explanation. The other possibility is that mood complaints may be secondary to dysmenorrhea, as the result of a response generalization occurring between menstrual pain and other symptoms. In support of this, Golub cites a report by Moos (1969) of a significant correlation between the pain scale and, for example, the negative affect, concentration and behavioural change scales of the menstrual distress questionnaire. Another study which used both restropective and concurrent symptom reporting concluded that, as regards negative affect anyway, the two methods do not produce equivalent data and so may not be assessing similar aspects of experience (Abplanalp, Donnelly, and Rose, 1979). There is one report of lack of agreement between free-associative and self-report measures of emotional change with the cycle (Dan, 1980). The author emphasizes the importance of different individual patterns of mood.

Ruble and Brooks-Gunn (1979) reviewed studies on the effects on symptoms of labelling self-report questionnaires as menstrually related, as well as comparisons between retrospective and current reports. The conclusion is that beliefs about the symptoms associated with menstruation cannot be fully accounted for by physiological factors, though the authors do not deny the existence of these factors. The claimed unjustifiably strong and generalized beliefs about symptoms are explained in this report by biased processing of information about cyclicity. Chernovetz, Jones, and Hansson (1979) agree that reports are influenced by whether or not they are labelled as related to menstruation. However, in their own study, both men and women reported *less* distress when the symptoms were labelled as being menstrual. This study also found that women who were more feminine reported more severe distress, and women with high masculinity scores were less socially inhibited about menstruation. It was also found that more positive feelings were associated with greater predictability of onset of menstruation even in the case of more severe distress. One study of all phobic patients and therefore rather different from the others cited, is worth noting. Replies

156

on retrospective and concurrent questionnaires, both in women taking contraceptive pills and in those who were not, were analysed. Whereas negative mood changes were reported retrospectively, this was not the case when the purpose of the study was disguised (presumably the concurrent testing). The authors express reservations about certain methodological problems in their study, but feel that over all it gives some indication of interaction between biological and attributional processes (Vila and Beech, 1980).

Before discussing the problems of methodology and interpretation of these studies, let us consider findings which either provide evidence contrary to the social expectation view, or which indicate alternative explanations.

Markum (1976) studied two groups of women who were given a menstrual distress questionnaire; one group did not know it was about menstrual symptoms, the other did know. The knowledge about the purpose of the questionnaire did not significantly affect the symptom reports. A study of anxiety and depression found that the higher premenstrual scores could hardly be determined by stereotypic beliefs since scores on one questionnaire were unrelated to scores on another, which would not be expected if they were both being filled in on the basis of social expectation. Also the author reports that very few of the women recognized that they were being tested premenstrually, and concludes that her results cannot be explained in terms of stereotyped thinking, (Golub, 1976). Another study (Taylor, 1979) found that results on a general self-report questionnaire and a retrospective menstrual questionnaire were similar. Some studies have noted whether responses to questionnaires differ according to which phase of the cycle the woman is in when actually filling out the questionnaire. They find that the point at which the answers are given does not affect the reports (Coppen and Kessell, 1963; Moos, 1969; Rouse, 1978).

One report, in a wider context than the present one but which is relevant here, reviewed 24 prospective studies of changes in affect with the cycle (Dennerstein and Burrows, 1979). The great majority of these studies used no measures specific to the menstrual cycle, and for the most part data were collected daily. The authors conclude that the results give substantial evidence of cyclical variations with the cycle. So that in many studies using measures which presumably could not be reflecting stereotyped menstrual attitudes, significant fluctuations were found. There is some indication that personal characteristics and style may be a useful field of inquiry into the determinants of replies to questionnaires. One study found a difference between arts and science students in reporting menstrual symptoms; science students report less symptoms, as do other groups with certain cycle characteristics. The authors feel this different reporting is one of a cluster of attributes which define the form of 'self-management' adopted by the person (Sheldrake and Cormack, 1976a). Presumably, different standards for assessing quantity and quality of symptoms may be a part of the different modes of self-management. The Type A pattern is a collection of characteristic behaviours said to predispose to greater risk of coronary heart disease. Mathews and Carra (1982) report that Type A women actually ignore, and under-report, menstrual symptoms both positive and negative more than do Type B. This implies that there are significant personal factors both in attitudes to symptoms and to the answering of questionnaires.

In trying to draw firm conclusions from these studies of the various factors determining the replies women give to questionnaires about the menstrual cycle, whether obviously so or not, some problems of methodology and interpretation have to be borne in mind. Some of the scales used have poor reliability and validity and cover very restricted areas of menstrual experience. Many of the investigations studied unrepresentative samples of women. In the reports which support the role of social expectations in self-report on the cycle, for instance, the subjects were women in or closely connected with higher education. (The one exception is Parlee who in 1980 studied employees of a medical centre.) Such women are atypical in many ways, but are particularly so as regards knowledge of menstruation. The constant demonstrations of the influence of such methodological points on results often do not have much impact on the ways in which investigations are carried out. There are also flaws in the interpretation of the findings. When there is a discrepancy between results on daily self-report and retro-spective report, and/or between questionnaires obviously about menstruation and those which are not, it is usually assumed that the ones which show less fluctuations are reflecting the true position and that the others are exaggerating the real situation. This may be so, but could equally not be the case. The corollary of the assumption is that no attempt is made to wonder what factors might affect replies to the ones which show less cyclical variation; that is, usually the current reports and the ones which are not ostensibly related to menstruation. It is possible to imagine factors which might produce under-reporting of menstrual changes. For example, women responding to a questionnaire unrelated to menstruation may simply omit any changes which they have linked to the menstrual cycle, considering them irrelevant. In current daily self-report studies, there may be some positive effect which is generated by the constant stimulus of being an object of study. Those questionnaires which specifically ask women to report on how they feel at that point in time may reflect only very momentary feelings while engaged in that task, which possibly does not represent an accurate description of their general state at that time. It would at least be fitting to ask whether there are reasons for the possible under-reporting of cyclical variations.

On the basis of the evidence presented it would be premature to suppose that women are gullible enough to report, on a large scale, because of certain social expectations, symptoms and changes which they do not in fact experience. The exponents of such a view would also have to explain why, on the extremely rare occasions when women are asked about possible positive aspects of the cycle, the majority are found in general to have a positive view of it (Brooks, Ruble, and Clark, 1977; Heczey, 1980; Levitt and Lubin, 1967; May, 1976). Are these positive feelings about menstruation also a result of social beliefs? Until more is known about this and other aspects, conclusions about social influences determining women's replies to menstrual questionnaires must be incomplete.

There are further points to be noted in considering the extent to which self-report accounts reflect the real experience of the cycle. If most women often have pronounced changes (not always to the same extent; for instance some cycles are anovulatory, see Chapter 2, and the typical reproductive hormonal situation does not prevail) they will develop an idea of and feelings about those changes. There is convincing evidence and it is a matter of common observation that past experience of feelings and sensations associated with a set of events can evoke similar responses on another occasion, even in the absence of the original state of affairs. This is particularly true of the autonomic activation which is the basis of emotional response and emotional behaviour (see for example Mandler, 1975). So that a precisely similar situation may not exist in every detail each month but women, when specifically asked, will evoke their usual over-all experience of the cycle. Also to be noted as regards the premenstrual phase is the point made by Friedman, Hurt, Arnoff, and Clarkin (1980) that attitudes about this phase and the reported increase in negative affect for example may be both related to a third factor which is responsible for their association, say, personality and/or biological factors. Certainly, at least some of the attitudes which are sometimes said to be socially generated and to largely determine the self-report answers about menstruation, may be substantially based on a 'real' situation.

It would be absurd to deny the effect of social and cultural factors on the ways in which women experience the cycle and some of the mechanisms of this effect are outlined later in this chapter. Nevertheless more evidence is needed before the conclusion can be drawn that self-reports are considerably biased and exaggerated accounts which are not reflections of biological realities. One solution to the problem is to have more studies which measure cyclical change other than by self-report or methods which may be contaminated by expectations. Various 'objective' measurements of cyclical change have been mentioned in this book, often of physical changes. Objective studies of behavioural change are also possible; for example, Baker, Kostin, Mishara, and Parker (1979); Friedman and Meares (1979); Ward, Stone, and Sandman (1978) which have been included in Chapter 3. As regards changes in affect with the cycle, there are examples of studies in which there is at least reduced room for expectations to influence assessment. For example, the study by Silbergeld, Brast, and Noble (1971), already mentioned, used ratings by interviewers of verbal material produced by women (the study found cyclical variations in several aspects of affect). Another study previously mentioned, (Paige, 1971) also used interviewer ratings of verbal material and reported marked affective fluctuations with the cycle. In an early study Altman, Knowles, and Bull (1941) collected daily mood ratings by an interviewer and found increased depression, tension, and irritability premenstrually. Most of the 24 studies in the review by Dennerstein and Burrows (1979), mentioned above, included some objective measurements in their assessment of cyclical change. Increased use of objective measures of stress would be useful. Also, more systematic studies of behavioural indices such as suicide and attempted suicide. Finally, it may be that investigation of individual differences in replying to questionnaires in general and to menstrual surveys in particular would be more fruitful than the study of the more global notion of the effect of social expectations. For example, much more information is needed about women's interpretations of each question, of the context in which they answer the question, and so on.

The problem of the determinants of women's replies to questionnaires about the menstrual cycle has been discussed at some length because it is fundamental to any appraisal of the evidence on changes with the cycle. In conclusion, it seems that learned psychological and social attitudes undoubtedly influence the way in which the menstrual cycle is actually experienced. It has not been demonstrated that socially-determined beliefs significantly affect the way in which women *report* their experience of the cycle, though this may be a noteworthy factor in the reporting of certain changes in certain individuals. Nothing is known about any possible relationship between social expectations or stereotyped beliefs and reports of positive changes with the cycle.

ATTRIBUTION AND LABELS

Attribution is the process by which an individual interprets events as being caused by some event or process. Clearly there will be individual differences in the nature and the extent of attribution. The influence of attribution on experience and behaviour has been amply demonstrated. The interpretation put on the causes of events will affect the ways in which the events are perceived and dealt with. People differ in their preferred modes of attribution especially as regards the choice between external and internal (self) attribution. Some individuals will consider their internal sensations important, some will not. In general, women make more 'internal' attributions than men; also women make less diffuse attributions and attribute emotional behaviour more often to personal causation than do men. It has also been shown that the provision of a source of attribution for physiological reactions reduces the likelihood of maladaptive emotional responses to those reactions (Storms and Nisbett, 1970; Valins, 1967). In this respect, neutral and also normative (that is, the knowledge that most people have similar experience) attributions tend to be particularly effective. In addition, attribution of causes can influence expectations, and when expectations are subsequently confirmed, emotional distress is reduced, performance is improved, difficulties overcome, and so forth (Johnson, 1973; Staub and Kellett, 1972).

As regards the menstrual cycle, Koeske (1980) has defined the attributional approach as an examination of the common beliefs and explanatory principles women themselves use to understand their own and others' behaviour. Koeske (1976, 1977) investigated premenstrual emotionality and her results suggest that negative premenstrual behaviours are attributed to biological sources whereas positive ones are attributed to personality or situational factors. In addition, the results also suggest that premenstrual negative behaviour may be judged to be more unreasonable than the same behaviour in non-menstruating women and in men. Koeske's further suggestion, that the premenstrual tension notion originated with women themselves as an explanation or excuse for their own behaviour, presumably does not preclude the possibility, or indeed implies, that this was the outcome of unusually negative behaviour and feelings at that time.

Consideration of the role of attribution raises the question of the factors which determine how events will be labelled. May (1976) has suggested that inaccurate awareness may be due to anxiety about menstruation. His clinical impression is of two broad areas of anxiety; firstly menstruation may be experienced as helplessness and being controlled by bodily processes and secondly it may be perceived as dirty and dangerous. This would need confirmation, but it seems possible that anxiety affects awareness of the cycle and its effects, see for example Paige (1971). Campos and Thurow (1978) have suggested that identification is an important determinant of attribution, and that states that covary with the cycle will be more easily identified and attributed to the cycle. They also claim that women taking a contraceptive pill, which makes the onset of bleeding highly predictable and therefore easier to identify as a source of attribution, make more cycle attributions premenstrually than do non-pill-takers. The women not taking a contraceptive pill made more cycle attributions during the menstrual phase. Changes in levels of physiological arousal are known, from the work of Schachter and Singer (1962) to lead to an urge to label the source of arousal, an 'evaluative need'. As already mentioned such a source of attribution reduces maladaptive responses to the physiological reactions. Rodin (1976) showed, in a non-menstrual context, that aroused subjects who were given a pill attribution, or who were correctly warned of arousal effects, performed significantly better on various cognitive tasks than aroused subjects given no attribution. In a second study, she compared the performance of menstruating women complaining of moderate or severe symptoms with others not currently menstruating. The high-symptom menstruating group performed significantly better than the other two aroused groups. Rodin feels these results suggest that women who can clearly attribute stress to menstruation perform better. She suggests that correct expectations may benefit performance by direct stress-reducing effects, or through self-preparation and increased effort.

The work on the practical implications of attribution can be outlined. In the Chapter 4 discussion of cyclical changes in cognitive and perceptual motor performance, taking group figures only, the results (with one exception) appear to show that objective measures of competence on various skills and tasks do not vary with the cycle. There are indications, though, that if individual differences are looked at more closely women with differing approaches can be discerned and that these differences are obscured in the group figures. A small group of women report that they perform less well premenstrually (Sommer, 1973) and this is contrary to the objective test results. For this small group it appears that their negative feelings at this time incline them to the belief that they are incompetent. This is a general and frequent effect of negative mood. On the other hand there are some women who actually perform better around menstruation and Rodin, above, has indicated that those who expect menstruation to render them anxious or nervous perform better than those who do not. Women who are experiencing strong negative feelings from the demands of a task and/or the menstrual phase, and have no source of attribution, perform poorly. This also seems to apply more generally than just to performance on tasks. An awareness of the timing of the menstrual cycle and its effects provides a label, an explanation, for feelings of inadequacy, hostility, anxiety, and tension which otherwise remain inexplicable, and where the lack of explanation again increases those feelings. Knowledge of the cycle can provide a reason for feelings and behaviour which, if such a reason is not available, will tend to be attributed to shortcomings in the woman herself, or in the people around her. It has been shown that a vicious circle of self-condemnation and anxiety may result from self-attribution (Valins and Nisbett, 1971). The same effect can rather paradoxically arise in women who are aware of the biological basis of their negative moods, feelings of incompetence, physical feelings, and so forth, but who nevertheless feel personally responsible for their particular reaction to them (Koeske and Koeske, 1975). In addition, the process of non-attribution of a solid basis for positive feelings and behaviours (postulated for example by Koeske) will tend to diminish the reality and the importance of positive changes at any time during the cycle.

Conclusions about the effects of attribution on the experience of the cycle are tentative because more detail is required and because most of the information comes from university women who are atypical as regards their knowledge of the cycle. Nevertheless in general there is a substantial body of work on attribution, and its effects on feelings and behaviour cannot be doubted.

VARIATIONS IN PHYSIOLOGICAL RESPONSIVENESS

Within the context of the mechanisms of learned factors which influence the way the individual experiences the cycle, the question arises of variations in physiological responsiveness. This has already been mentioned in Chapter 5 under individual differences. In Chapter 3 a small amount of evidence was presented of a premenstrual increase in sensitivity to aversive stimulation which might make the formation of negative conditioned responses more likely. There are theoretical and empirical reasons for supposing that unexplained fluctuations in physiological arousal render people more susceptible to a process in which the heightened arousal may become attached to certain events or thoughts which happen to coincide with the increased arousal (see for example Vila and Beach, 1977). Vila and Beach (1978) are also of the view that the premenstrual increased susceptibility to conditioning and greater resistance to extinction that they have found is true of various response systems. Tedford, Warren, and Flynn (1979) report variations in sensitivity to pain, from a minimum at ovulation to a maximum through menstruation (see Chapter 3). The authors suggest that their results, and those of others, suggest that discomfort around menstruation could be partly a function of this cyclical lowering of the pain threshold. The low threshold would also presumably be a basis for the formation of conditioned respones. A premenstrual combination of increased sensitivity to stimulation, no obviously satisfactory explanation for fluctuating levels of arousal and largely negative mood suggests itself as one method by which negative responses to the menstrual cycle are acquired. A possible model of the interaction between arousal and labelling in the premenstrual phase has come from Koeske (1976, 1977). She reports findings which indicate that there is a greater physiological arousability premenstrually which could enhance both positive and negative emotional behaviours, and that situational cues will determine the nature of the experience. Koeske mentions that her results are consistent with a notion of enhanced general sensitivity to strong stimuli, though there will be wide individual differences in the expression of this responsiveness. The question of whether the basis of the heightened responsiveness is predominantly the central, or the autonomic nervous system, has still to be clarified. For example, Koeske (1980) assumes that central nervous system changes are of foremost importance in the increased arousal, whereas the present author (Asso and Braier, 1982) thinks it is more likely to be increased autonomic activation which predominates premenstrually and which, in Mandler's terms, provides the physiological background of psychologically perceived arousal (see Chapter 3). Given the importance of conditioned responses in initiating and perpetuating feelings, behaviours and symptoms, more work in this area would be welcome. There can be little doubt that physiological responsiveness is an important basis for experience and behaviour. In combination with past experience and present circumstances, individual variations in characteristic and transient physiological arousal may be expected to influence the initial and continued experience of the cycle.

In any conclusions about the possible mechanisms of learning which help determine the ways in which an individual will experience the cycle, the complexity of the variables has to be borne in mind. Many of them have been discussed in Chapter 5; they are the main individual characteristics which have some association with patterns of incidence of changes through the menstrual cycle. One other variable is worth specifying, though it appears in various forms throughout this chapter, and elsewhere in the book. It is the present state of each woman at any time. The current psychological, physiological, and physical state will be the culmination of genetic factors and personal history, combined with present circumstances.

As regards the mechanisms discussed in this chapter, it is evident that the role of attitudes in the experience of the cycle is an important one. It is not possible to estimate accurately the extent to which self-reported experience corresponds, for each woman, to reality. If the subjective evidence is considered with the considerably smaller amount of more objective measurement there are indications of some agreement between them. It is not possible, from the present studies, to conclude that women's reports are based only or largely on social expectations. The tentative conclusion from the work reviewed above has to be that while the learned attitudes are doubtless reflected in the way in which the questions are answered, the attitudes are at least partly based on experience. The questionnaire replies reflect to some extent real changes in feelings and behaviour and bodily changes which take place with the cycle. The need for more work is only too apparent. Most useful would be more representative samples, comparisons using objective measurements, closer enquiry into the meanings of replies to questionnaires which appear to be quite unrelated to menstruation, and inclusion in the studies of measurement of hormonal and other variables. Attribution seems to be an important mechanism in the ways in which the cycle and its effect will be perceived and dealt with. As regards feelings and behaviour particularly, the labelling of biologically determined changes is probably a considerable factor in the individual response to those changes. Physiological responsiveness doubtless mediates the effects of the neuroendocrine events of the cycle. More work is needed on the role of the central and autonomic nervous systems and, more specifically, on the acquisition of learned responses in different phases of the cycle.

SUMMARY

The attempt, in the last two chapters, to examine cause and effect in the changes of the menstrual cycle has perhaps raised more questions than it has answered. There is nevertheless a considerable body of work upon which further research can build. The present findings give support for the view that both physiological and psychological changes are generated by the menstrual cycle. This has been demonstrated in many different kinds of studies, and at least some of the mechanisms can be outlined though there is only sparse detail of the precise relationships. In addition there are learned influences on the menstrual cycle, and on the way in which it is experienced, but they have been less extensively investigated and more information is needed. It appears that some of the menstrual changes are more susceptible to learned influences than others.

There is already a considerable amount of data on the biological and acquired mechanisms of change with the cycle. These data still need an integrating, theoretical framework. This will be one which will certainly draw upon existing models but which will permit finer and more comprehensive description and explanation of the manifold ways in which women experience the menstrual cycle. The model will have to take account of the neuroendocrine events, the biologically determined psychological and behavioural tendencies, and the interaction of those with the many personal, social, and environmental factors which have played their part in the past and continue to do so.

The large amount of research at present being carried out may be expected to provide a more accurate account of the causal relationships between the various manifestations of the menstrual cycle. In this research, certain points have emerged which could be usefully borne in mind in future work:

1. A distinction has to be made between ovulatory and anovulatory cycles.
2. Important variables such as length of cycle and regularity have to be specified.
3. If hormones are measured, only a comprehensive approach is likely to be useful. The different oestrogen compounds, progesterone, luteinizing hormone, follicle stimulating hormone, androgens, and other hormones all contribute to the physical, psychological, and behavioural changes. It has also to be remembered that blood and urine levels of hormones are only an approximate reflection of their impact in the brain.
4. Groups who are more representative of the general population will have to be studied.
5. Individual differences need further investigation.

CHAPTER 10

Living with the cycle

UNDERSTANDING THE MENSTRUAL CYCLE

It has been the aim of this book to show how the menstrual cycle brings about continual change in physiological, physical, psychological, and behavioural functions. These menstrually related changes take place within a wider pattern of biological cycles and within specific personal and social conditions. The changes are widespread, fundamental and are not confined to any phase or phases of the cycle. Although the main neuroendocrine events have been described for the whole cycle this is not true for most of the other changes. There are nonetheless clear indications that most of the cycle provides a positive basis for feelings, behaviour, and physical well-being. In the few days around menstruation there is a high incidence of negative changes; any positive aspects of this phase have hardly been investigated though preliminary work suggests they may be a significant feature. Individual characteristics, the result of a combination of biological and of learned factors, play an important part in determining the experience of the cycle. The ending of the cycle is a gradual process which takes place when the effects of ageing are becomingly increasingly apparent. The negative changes which are specific to the menopause are few. It has repeatedly been made clear that there are large gaps in the published work. There are practical and historical reasons for the emphasis on the distressing aspects of menstruation but it is already possible to discern a view of the cycle that is very different from the present one, and which provides a framework for better adaptations.

This book does not deal with detailed practical applications. The present chapter will merely outline the background, provided by the existing findings, to those applications. This includes suggestions for the future, and as such are a set of beliefs. They do, though, have some theoretical and empirical basis and there is reason to think that they could be useful. Such a discussion cannot be in terms of the individual experience and problems of each woman. Instead it will suggest the potential which is inherent in the internal environment of women as a result of the reproductive functions which they possess. The information at present available, although not complete, opens up many practical possibilities. Even the negative changes take on quite a different perspective if seen in the context of the whole cycle. The factors which may produce turmoil in the premenstrual phase combine in other ways to produce a totally different climate at other times. There are indications that the positive changes are as real as, and much more prolonged than, the negative ones. There are suggestions from both theoretical and empirical work that correct information will influence initial responses, perception, conditioning, and coping behaviour in regard to all aspects of the menstrual cycle. In general the value of relevant and understandable prescriptions for behaviour, based on reliable information rather than on interpretation, hardly needs to be emphasized. Yet the menstrual cycle which is surrounded by misunderstanding, taboo and bias, has not been fully recognized as the pervasive and continual influence that it is. It continues to retain its clinical image as a source of distress with, now, the added status of being a focus for disputes about the suitability of women for some roles in modern society. The clinical image and the doubt about women's stability and reliability are of course closely connected and the one sustains the other. The discussion of premenstrual distress widely diffused by the media, though partially effective and doubtless well-meaning, has had in some ways a retrograde effect. Added emphasis has been given to the identification of the changes at the end of the cycle as the salient feature of the whole menstrual process. There is now a belief that people are better informed about the cycle because there is more public discussion of premenstrual difficulties. This circumscribed approach has served to highlight the short-lived negative aspects of the reproductive cycle. Even the relatively well-informed are rarely aware of the extent to which the rhythmic patterns of the whole cycle have continual and far-reaching effects on their lives. The possibility of improved adaptations lies in a wider acceptance of the facts.

The biological purpose of the reproductive cycle is irrefutable; the neuroendocrine events and their effects are increasingly understood. There are already strong indications that further investigation, by more rigorous methods, of subjective experience and of objective measures will show that there is a basis for a radical reappraisal of the cycle and of attitudes to it. The internal environment of women differs from that of men in many marked and fundamental respects. The biologically determined differences are manifest in various psychological and behavioural ways, some of which are already indicated in the published work and doubtless many more will become apparent. It is difficult to see why there should be any attempt to discredit these important differences between men and women. It is presumably partly due to the widespread lack of understanding of the true nature of the menstrual cycle. In reality the facts about the particular cycle of change which women experience are entirely acceptable. Most of the time women can function to the full extent of their potential. There is practical and experimental evidence that they can also function optimally during the few days of discomfort, given the right information and, where necessary, provided with effective measures. Certainly there is no reason to believe that there are biological reasons why women cannot be successful at anything they may undertake. Some of them have, and will have, occupations which have not been theirs in the past. They probably carry them out rather differently from the ways in which men do, which introduces a new element. Others will continue to choose the more traditional feminine life. Better adjustments to the reproductive cycle will be of benefit to all of them. There is a surprising amount of theory and practice which suggests ways of living with a cycle which gives rise to the considerable changes that have been discussed.

Let us first look again at a broad outline of the phases of the cycle, as in Chapter 1 but now bearing in mind the findings that have been presented.

From the onset of menstruation oestradiol starts a slow rise and FSH shows a small peak. There is a fall in fluid retention. The levels of premenstrual negative mood begin to decline, there is an easing of emotional tension and there are more feelings of relaxation. There is increasing sexual arousal and sexual behaviour. Pain, in abdomen and back, is the feature which is consistently reported, and this probably has repercussions in any negative mood at the beginning of bleeding. Several methods of alleviation of menstrual pain, additional to medication, now exist. These include a wide range of behavioural procedures which will be mentioned again. It appears that, if pain and fatigue can be overcome, there are no other physical symptoms specific to this phase of the cycle and that positive feelings predominate.

In the follicular phase oestrogen rises at first slowly and steadily, but then sharply about Day 7. All the follicles except one start to secrete mainly androgens rather than oestrogens. Other changes have not been much investigated but there are some indications of increasing feelings of energy, self-confidence, alertness, and assertiveness. The mood is happy and affectionate with negative emotions at a very low point. It is not difficult to see that at this time the cycle provides an ideal background for positive accomplishment and constructive action.

Around mid-cycle, the oestrogen peak occurs around Day 13 and the peak of LH, and usually of FSH, follow soon after; the level of androgens is higher than at any other time. The 17α-hydroxyprogesterone rise which started towards the end of the follicular phase also reaches a peak. Moods and behaviour are generally at their most positive, cortical arousal is high, sensory acuity is high. Levels of sexual arousal and sexual behaviour are raised. There are strong indications that optimal physical and psychological well-being is usual at this time.

In the luteal phase the levels of most hormones are low with the notable exception of progesterone, which tends to reduce central nervous system activation. Progesterone is responsible, in the luteal phase, for the preparation of the lining of the womb for pregnancy. It is therefore not surprising that the few available accounts suggest a mood that is predominantly passive, inward-turning without active negative elements. Sexual arousal is low. There is a biological basis for physiological and psychological processes being conducive to the safeguarding and consolidation of a fertilized ovum and the start of pregnancy. Pregnancy is now a rare event for most women in our society but there is every reason to take full advantage of an internal setting which has the purpose of preparation and consolidation.

In the premenstrual phase if there is no pregnancy there is a sharp decline in progesterone and oestrogen levels from about Day 24. LH remains low, FSH starts a slight rise. Levels of autonomic activation are usually high, central nervous system levels rather low. Sexual arousal and behaviour is at a peak. Physical symptoms of various kinds are frequent, the prevailing mood is negative, though there are clinical accounts, to be further investigated, of labile moods with swings from negative to positive. Even if, on finer investigation, the premenstrual days are shown to be characterized by mood swings, the fact remains that the negative tone of these few days is very real. Also, while lability of mood might give patches of relief it also produces sudden changes which are difficult to deal with, by a woman herself and by those around her. Unless the negative patches are competently dealt with, they can produce a series of events with unfortunate repercussions. This lack of control over the consequences of sudden negative feelings and behaviour may account for some of the depressed feelings which are reported. There are many ways of fostering control over mood swings and negative changes and many steps which can be taken to mitigate other effects of the premenstrual phase. These will be mentioned later in this chapter.

Obviously, there will frequently be times when the broad tendencies just outlined will be more or less obscured by events and when there will be no question of being positive and acting constructively. Nevertheless once a full knowledge of all the facts is available, and attitudes have been changed and adaptations learned, their effects will continue in less propitious circumstances, and indeed will be useful instruments for reducing stress. There is no suggestion that women should constantly plan their activities and their feelings according to the background trends of the cycle. When the whole atmosphere surrounding the cycle is improved and when the facts are fully known, better adjustments will become a matter of course. The profound accommodations that are continually made, for instance, to the extensive circadian rhythms have become a part of life which in general no-one is aware of. A minority of women will have unusually protracted and severe distress and discomfort which will require treatment. This will be mentioned again in relation to therapy. A changed view of the menstrual cycle will come about only by social and personal planning based on the known facts. The first step will be to provide reliable information about all the changes which take place and about the implications of living with this particular pattern of rhythmic variation.

THE INFORMATION EXERCISE

The message is a clear one:

The reproductive process provides a cycle of change which is specific to women. These changes are continuous, they do not start a few days before menstruation and end with the cessation of bleeding. This particular cycle, like many others, has advantages if appropriate adaptations are made to it. For most of the cycle favourable physical, neurophysiological, and psychological conditions prevail. For various biological, social, and psychological reasons women experience the effects of the cycle in different ways. With a full awareness of the constant changes of the reproductive cycle women can benefit from the advantages, and mitigate any disadvantages. The menstrual cycle is not an added burden which men do not have; it creates an internal environment which is different from that of men.

The value of factual information has been demonstrated. For example, Heczey (1980), in a dysmenorrhea treatment study, found that women in both the experimental and the control groups showed a substantial decrease in negative affect and increase in positive affect following 'communication aimed to correct misperceptions of the affect of the menstrual experience'. It is the quality of the information that is important. Needless to say it has to be relevant and understandable to each individual and has to be clear about the implications. The great advantage of realistic information is that it confers the possibility of a measure of personal control. There is a current tendency to assume that the cyclical distress (the only aspect of the cycle which receives attention) is largely imposed from without. It is suggested that the psychological and social overtones to the cycle are somehow the cause of the distress and that the 'condition' only exists because society or learned maladaptive attitudes on the part of the individual allow it to. The implication is often that the multitude of women, of all types of personality and at all levels of articulateness and intelligence, have only to 'think differently', and fight off social pressures, in order to deal with substantial changes in their bodies, their physiological processes and their feelings. This is unrealistic and reminiscent of the 'pull-yourself-together' morality. Every individual has to have the right knowledge in order to improve their lives. Fluid retention, for example, can be uncomfortable, unsightly, and depressing. It will not go away in response to a little creative thinking, but it will be easier to accept and to deal with if the cause and likely duration are known, as well as the fact that most other women have a similar experience. This is all even more true for those women who suffer unusual amounts of menstrually-related distress; they will need both a knowledge of the cycle and appropriate treatment. The correct view of the menstrual cycle could be presented to both men and women through the media and through a number of agencies who in the course of their work have the opportunity to give the information. There will be no revolution, but a consistent effort to pass on the facts and their implications would eventually reverse the worst effects of the clinical

170

image of the cycle. Clinicians will rightly wish to continue to direct their efforts mainly to the understanding and relief of premenstrual and menstrual distress. They may be helped in their efforts by a more accurate and more comprehensive view of the cycle. It would also be useful, for them and for everyone, if in their clinical contacts and in their writings, especially the more popular ones, they made it clear that severe and prolonged menstrual distress is an unusual manifestation of the cycle and that the women who suffer from it will benefit not only from specific treatment but also from a change in attitude to the cycle.

In general, many of the publications about the menstrual cycle, usually directed at the more articulate members of the population, devote a lot of space to the past, to folklore, and to blind prejudice. The implication is that nothing has changed, which is patently not so. More change will come about if we now turn to constructive plans for the future rather than brandishing images of primitive menstrual huts and the attitudes of some gynaecologists. These books, pamphlets, and articles are extremely important in the diffusion of ideas about the cycle. They are read by people who often work with women and with women's problems in various ways and who could be very effective in achieving more rational approaches. Most of the more balanced and well-informed writings, mainly in scientific and professional journals and books, have a relatively small readership. In various areas of knowledge the media have been very effective in helping scientists and professional people communicate their findings to the general population and this will doubtless eventually be true for the menstrual cycle. Many of the people who are responsible for some of the research cited in this book know about the inadequate nature of general information about the cycle, and have written with great awareness about the problems. It is to be hoped that they will pass on the message to the widest possible audience. The important role of health workers, social workers, teachers, doctors, nurses, family planning clinics, and counsellors in encouraging a new approach to the menstrual cycle is obvious. They will only be able to be effective in this if they themselves have the fullest information. As more research into the whole cycle is carried out and if the results of that research is made available to a wide circle of people, the advantages of different attitudes will become increasingly apparent.

THE BENEFITS

There is a wide range of benefits that can be expected from the information exercise. It is not within the scope of this book to examine specific measures to be taken, but some general points can be made about the advantages which would arise from an awareness of the facts:
1. The knowledge that the cycle is, for most of the time, conducive to positive feelings and behaviour gives added confidence and optimism and mitigates the effects of the negative manifestations.

2. As with many other cycles where learned adaptations become automatic, adjustments to the changes of the menstrual cycle can be made as a matter of course.

3. Clinicians and practitioners can make use of reliable information about the timing of changes in, for example alcohol metabolism, attempted suicides, glucose tolerance and tension. Also, when more is known about positive changes, the many theoretical and applied models of learning and behaviour which now exist can be used to maximize the effectiveness of procedures such as biofeedback techniques, and relaxation, and to institute new ones.

4. Awareness, on the part of women and of clinicians, of the relationship between physiological state and the formation of long-lasting conditioned responses is of potential importance. The changes in central and autonomic nervous system activity and in sensitivity to stimulation, combined with marked positive or negative feelings, provide a terrain for acquisition of conditioned responses. Just as in the premenstrual phase negative behaviour and reactions may be acquired and perpetuated, at other times conditions will be ideal for learning adaptive responses.

5. Individuals have different patterns of menstrual variation, just as they do, for instance, in the systematic variations of efficiency during the diurnal cycle. Awareness of the individual's pattern of variations could be used, rather than ignored. Moreover, awareness of the effects of, especially, the circadian cycle in combination with the menstrual cycle would be particularly valuable. Both positive and negative effects of the menstrual cycle will be different, for instance, in the mornings and the evenings, according to individual differences.

6. The knowledge provides an explanation of things which were previously unexplained. The evidence shows that if, in general, states remain unexplained there is a strong tendency to find an explanation. More specifically, with regard to the menstrual cycle some women tend to attribute the feelings of hostility, aggression, and incompetence to their own shortcomings or to those of the people around them, and this increases their negative feelings and makes the situation worse. It is common knowledge, and it has been empirically demonstrated, that physical symptoms also appear more severe and are more alarming if they are unexplained. So that knowledge about the cycle provides a source of attribution for the swings in feelings, behaviour, and bodily state which otherwise remain inexplicable and unpredictable.

7. The possession of a source of attribution for arousal and/or anxiety can lead to improved performance.

8. The realization that the cyclical changes are normal, shared by others, and not due to some abnormality or weakness is reassuring and introduces a different perspective. Normative attribution has been shown to have various positive effects.

9. More accurate information about the premenstrual phase can change the response to it. Awareness that the mood at that time tends to be volatile will provide a basis for improved control. It should also be more widely known that the negative mood that is reported is not in general of great magnitude.

10. Women who have irregular cycles may have more difficulty in obtaining the full benefit of knowledge of the cycle. Nevertheless, the cycle will turn for them, albeit less regularly, with the same opportunities for constructive behaviour.

11. Knowledge of the effects of the cycle gives women insight into the impact that they are having on the people around. Premenstrual negative behaviour may be more liable to be considered unreasonable by other people than equally negative behaviour in other contexts. Responses, by other people, which may be perceived as hurtful and worrying, at least become more comprehensible. They can be avoided if women have developed a measure of control over the behaviour in the first place.

12. A wide diffusion of accurate information would enable other people to see the cyclical changes more accurately, and in a wider perspective.

There are some special points to be made regarding the menopause. With the end of the cyclical changes, in both their positive and negative aspects, new adaptations are required, and these will be made easier by the fullest possible information. There is no reason to assume that the ending of the reproductive years is an irretrievable loss; in fact, contrary to the view of many writers, most women themselves do not see it as a disaster and report it as a time of well-being, with opportunities for new, unencumbered enjoyment in many areas of life. There is no justification for the idea of a menopausal state of mind, with various distressing psychological symptoms. The menopause has mistakenly been used as a focus for problems and reactions which occur in various forms at any time of life, and which exist in analogous form in men throughout their lives. It is inaccurate to suggest that women at this time have special problems of a different magnitude to those of men. Much has been made, for example, of the inevitable emotional impact on women of the departure of children about this time and hence the collapse of their usefulness and happiness. There is no reason to suppose that men do not also suffer from the loss of children, and they likewise have to deal with problems of ageing and declining powers. Men (as do many women) frequently have problems about the ending of their working life and finding meaningful ways of spending their time. The physical changes of the menopausal years which sometimes give rise to symptoms, either during those years or after the menopause are, without exception, amenable to some kind of treatment. Increasing knowledge of the most effective, and least harmful, methods of treatment opens up real possibilities of ensuring well-being and enjoyment throughout and after the menopause.

THE CONTRACEPTIVE PILL

The natural reproductive cycle is the subject of this book, and the effects of the contraceptive pill are not within its scope. The findings discussed are not without implications for those who use oral contraceptives and it is worth making a few brief comments about them. The number of women taking the contraceptive pill appears to be decreasing, especially over the age of 30, and the trend is for women to be advised not to take it for protracted periods. So that although in the United Kingdom, for example, about a quarter of all women between 15 and 44 are taking the contraceptive pill at any one time, most women do not take it continuously over a great number of years. If we assume then, that a majority of women who take the pill do so intermittently (though many under 30 may take it for long timespans) everything that has been said about the natural cycle will apply to them for much of the time. The adaptations which are made by any individual to the natural cycle will probably influence their experience of the contraceptive pill. While they are taking the pill the usual neuroendocrine events of the cycle will not take place. The small amount of evidence available suggests that many other cyclical fluctuations will be experienced to a lesser degree, or not at all. For women taking the pill the marked swings in many functions and processes will generally be absent. Many of the learned patterns of responses will continue, however, and any established adaptations to the cycle will be carried over into the pill regime. Informed and competent ways of dealing with positive and negative feelings, about menstruation specifically, and also in a more general context, will continue to be of great advantage. There will be individual differences in reacting to the change in atmosphere brought about by the pill. In some, the learned responses to the normal cycle will tend to continue more than in others. All will benefit from an understanding of their own rhythms and of the reaction of other people to them. A knowledge of the basic facts about hormonal levels and the other biological and learned states which are related to them will facilitate adaptation to the contraceptive pill.

DEALING WITH MENSTRUAL DISTRESS

There are reasons to believe that the provision of relevant and understandable information aimed at changing attitudes and enabling women to gain better control over their responses to the cycle will lead among other things to a diminution of the negative effects. There will nevertheless be some women who will at times suffer from menstrually-related distress. All aspects of mild and severe cyclical distress are constantly discussed in lay and professional publications and it is not the present aim to cover that ground. There is a thorough account of the neuroendocrine, physical, and psychological characteristics of the premenstrual syndrome in Reid and Yen (1981). Theories and treatment of premenstrual mood changes are discussed in

Steiner and Carrol (1977). There is a summary of treatments of premenstrual symptoms by Clare (1979). Gannon (1981) has critically reviewed the evidence of a psychological aetiology of menstrual disorders. The diagnosis of dysmenorrhea is discussed by Webster (1980) and its management by Nicassio (1980). The purpose of this section is to outline very briefly the main approaches which are available to reduce the negative effects of some of the changes discussed in this book.

Ultimately, the development of predictably effective therapy will depend on an improved understanding of the mechanisms underlying the distress. It is clear that the disappointing results found in all reviews of treatments of menstrual distress arise from insufficient knowledge of the causes. Clearly for any individual sufferer there will be one or more of a number of physiological and psychological factors. In Chapter 5, under discussion of individual differences, in addition to age, features of the cycle, personality characteristics, and physiological responsiveness, mention was made of the role of individual hormonal levels in determining other changes with the cycle. In spite of the large amount of research into premenstrual and menstrual distress very little is known about any differences between levels of hormones in sufferers and non-sufferers. Even in women with marked premenstrual syndrome, no clear relationship with any hormonal characteristics has been shown. Most of the studies, cited in the last section of Chapter 5, have investigated only one or two hormones. Until more is known about the different effects of over-all patterns of hormonal functioning the implications for hormone therapy will be uncertain. We therefore have to rely on further research before consistent statements can be made about the hormonal basis, and hence hormonal treatment, of menstrual disorders.

There are no consistent findings about the effects of other administered treatments, such as diuretics, vitamins, tranquillizers, lithium, and so on. No clear evidence of general efficaciousness of any of these, or of means of predicting which women might benefit from a particular treatment, has emerged. It seems likely, though, that some will be effective when the causes of different symptoms are known and specific physical treatments can be offered.

A group of methods, usually discussed in relation to dysmenorrhea, can be broadly subsumed under the heading of self-management. They now cover a wide range and a review of many of these methods by Nicassio (1980) has already been mentioned. That author advocates a comprehensive approach which would include a full assessment of all factors which may be maintaining or exacerbating the disorder, followed by a particular treatment based on the assessment process. The 'mode-specific' treatments of dysmenorrhea include relaxation, with and without various types of biofeedback, of uterine and abdominal muscle tissue; systematic desensitization aimed at reducing anxiety about pain and menstruation; self-regulation of tension and stressful situations; education about dysmenorrhea and about possible self-regulation of it; pain control strategies, including autohypnotic suggestion. Self-management methods would also doubtless be useful for some or all premenstrual symptoms but there appear to have been no quantified reports of this application.

Effective alleviation of distress related to the menstrual cycle will be increasingly possible as more knowledge is gained of the physiological and psychological mechanisms. More accurate delineation of symptoms and patterns of symptoms will be part of that exercise. Controlled studies of various therapeutic approaches for different types of distress with assumed specific aetiologies will then be possible. At present, the ideal approach seems to be a careful evaluation in each case of the most likely contributing factors and the use of specific therapies. In all cases the encouragement of women to acquire some control over the effects of the cycle may be expected to substantially reduce the negative effects and to improve the therapeutic outcome.

AWARENESS AND ADAPTATION

Throughout this book there are, necessarily, generalizations about women. Some of the variables which contribute to any individual's experience of the effects of the cycle have been discussed. Another factor, which is a central concern of this book, and mentioned specifically in Chapter 9, is knowledge of the cycle and its effects. There is relatively little published work on the effects that knowledge of the cycle has. It appears that two broad approaches among relatively 'aware' women can be discerned. Some will feel that, because they are being controlled by biological processes, they are helpless to remedy the situation. Others will use their knowledge to attribute adverse responses to the cycle, and will compensate for its effects. There is no indication as to whether these different attitudes in 'aware' women are entirely characteristic, habitual ways of responding, or whether the same woman sometimes takes one attitude, sometimes another. As regards the 'unaware' women, there are also two broad groups. Firstly, those who do experience and report biologically-based variations which they do not relate specifically to the menstrual cycle. Secondly, there are those, apparently a small minority, who state that they do not experience any significant changes. There is some evidence, mentioned in this book, that this group do in fact experience changes of the same magnitude as the women who do report changes. For example, there is the finding that women who report no premenstrual symptoms attempt suicide more often premenstrually than women who do report symptoms; a quite different, but relevant, finding is that women who do report premenstrual symptoms (and therefore label their state) more often take the constructive step of telephoning suicide organizations rather than attempting suicide. Another example is a study showing that, in response to the same amount of stress, there was a significantly greater (measurable) physiological reaction premenstrually than at other times in the cycle, for all women, including those who reported no change in their subjective state. There is no need to invoke hypothetical mechanisms such as 'denial' to explain this lack of awareness of important menstrual changes on the part of some women. Some of them believe that the changes are part of the general course of events and do not know that they are specific manifestations of the menstrual cycle. All women have had to incorporate and adjust to the changes as best they can, with very little information or support, and some have preferred to see them as an unremarkable matter of course rather than to appear awkward, self-important, neurotic, and so forth. We have seen, for example, that in general some individuals label their internal sensations as important and some do not. The point of interest is that profound changes take place during the cycle in all women, including those who do not report them.

There are several reasons why the time is favourable for a more adaptive approach to the menstrual cycle. There is growing interest in biological cycles in general, and in their influence on everyday life. Many people in our society are sympathetic to the new aspirations of women and wish to make the best possible adjustment to them. There are increasingly diverse channels of communication for spreading knowledge. A full awareness of all aspects of the menstrual cycle will not be the great panacea, but a better understanding can improve the whole atmosphere in which women, and the people around them, spend their lives.

References

Abplanalp, J. M., Donnelly, A. F., and Rose, R. M. (1979). Psychoendocrinology of the menstrual cycle: I. Enjoyment of daily activities and moods. *Pyschosomatic Medicine*, **41**, 587–604.

Abplanalp, J. M., Livingston, L., Rose, R. M., and Sandwisch, D. (1977). Cortisol and growth hormone responses to psychological stress during the menstrual cycle. *Psychosomatic Medicine*, **39**, 158–177.

Abraham, S. F., Beumont, P. J. V., Argall, W. J., and Haywood, P. (1981). Nutrient intake and the menstrual cycle. *Australian and New Zealand Journal of Medicine*, **11**, 210–211.

Abramovitz, M., and Dubrovsky, B. (1980). CNV characteristics throughout the normal menstrual cycle. *Progress in Brain Research*, **54**, 441–446.

Abramowitz, E. S., Baker, A. H., and Fleischer, S. F. (1982). Onset of depressive pyschiatric crises and the menstrual cycle. *American Journal of Psychiatry*, **139**, 475–478.

Adams, D. B., Gold, A. R., and Burt, A. D. (1978). Rise in female-initiated sexual activity at ovulation and its suppression by oral contraceptives. *New England Journal of Medicine*, **299**, 1145–1150.

Ahlgren, A. (1974). Biorhythms. *International Journal of Chronobiology*, **2**, 107–109.

Akerstedt T. (1979). Altered sleep/wake patterns and circadian rhythms. *Acta Physiologica Scandinavica*, **Supplement 469**.

Alington-MacKinnon, D., and Troll, L. E. (1981). The adaptive function of the menopause: a devil's advocate position. *Journal of the American Geriatrics Society*, **29**, 349–353.

Altman, M., Knowles, E., and Bull, H. D. (1941). A psychosomatic study of the sex cycle in women. *Psychosomatic Medicine*, **3**, 199–224.

Ambrus, J. L. (1976). Estrogens and clotting factors, in van Keep, P.A., Greenblatt, R. B., and Albeaux-Fernet, M. (eds.), *Consensus on menopause research*, MTP Press, Lancaster.

Amoore, J. E., Popplewell, J. R., and Whissell-Buechy, D. (1975). Sensitivity of women to musk odor. No menstrual variation. *Journal of Chemical Ecology*, **1**, 291–297.

Anders, T. F. (1982). Biological rhythms in development. *Psychosomatic Medicine*, **44**, 61–72.

Anonymous (1970). Effects of sexual activity on beard growth in man. *Nature*, **226**, 869–870.

Asso, D. (1978). Levels of arousal in the premenstrual phase. *British Journal of Social and Clinical Psychology*, **17**, 47–55.

Asso, D., and Beech, H. R. (1975). Susceptibility to the acquisition of a conditioned response in relation to the menstrual cycle. *Journal of Psychosomatic Research*, **19**, 337–344.

Asso, D., and Braier, J. R. (1982). Changes with the menstrual cycle in psychophysiological and self-report measures of activation. *Biological Psychology*, **15**, 95–107.

Awaritefe, A., Awaritefe, M., Diejomaoh, F. M. E., and Ebie, J. C. (1980). Personality and menstruation. *Psychosomatic Medicine*, **42**, 237–251.

Aylward, M. (1978). Coagulation factors in opposed and unopposed oestrogen treatment at the climacteric. *Postgraduate Medical Journal*, **54**, **Supplement 2**, 31–36.

Backstrom, T. (1976). Epileptic seizures in women related to plasma estrogen and progesterone during the menstrual cycle. *Acta Neurologica Scandinavica*, **54**, 321–347.

Backstrom, T. (1977). Estrogen and progesterone in relation to different activities in the central nervous system. *Acta Obstetricia Gynaecologica Scandinavica*. **Supplement 66**, 1–17.

Backstrom, T., and Aakvaag, A. (1981). Plasma prolactin and testosterone during the luteal phase in women with premenstrual tension syndrome. *Psychoneuroendocrinology*, **6**, 245–251.

Bain, C., Willett, W., Hennekens, C. H., Rosner, B., Belanger, C., and Speizer, F. E. (1981). Use of postmenopausal hormones and risk of myocardial infarction. *Circulation*, **64**, 42–46.

Baker, A. H., Kostin, I. W., Mishara, B. L., and Parker, L. (1979). Menstrual cycle affects kinesthetic aftereffect, an index of personality and perceptual style. *Journal of Personality and Social Psychology*, **37**, 234–236.

Baker, H. W. G., Burger, H. G., de Kretser, D. M., Hudson, B., O'Connor, S., Wang, C., Mirovics, A., Court, J., Dunlop, M., and Rennie, G. C. (1976). Changes in the pituitary-testicular system with age. *Clinical Endocrinology*, **5**, 349–372.

Ball, P., Haupt, M., and Knuppen, R. (1978). Comparative studies on the metabolism of oestradiol in the brain, the pituitary and the liver of the rat. *Acta Endrocrinologica*, **87**, 1–11.

Ballinger, C. B. (1977). Psychiatric morbidity and the menopause: survey of a gynaecological out-patient clinic. *British Journal of Psychiatry*, **131**, 83–89.

Bancroft, J. (1978). The relationship between hormones and sexual behaviour, in Hutchinson, J. B. (ed.), *Biological determinants of sexual behaviour*, John Wiley, Chichester.

Bancroft, J. (1981). Hormones and human sexual behaviour. *British Medical Bulletin*, **37**, 153–158.

Bardwick, J. M. (1976). Psychological correlates of the menstrual cycle and oral contraceptive medication, in Sachar, E. J. (ed.), *Hormones, behaviour and psychopathology*, Raven Press, New York.

Baron, M., Levitt, M., and Perlman, R. (1980). Human platelet monoamine oxidase and the menstrual cycle. *Psychiatry Research*, **3**, 323–327.

Barris, M. C., Dawson, W. W., and Theiss, C. L. (1980). The visual sensitivity of women during the menstrual cycle. *Documenta Ophthalmologia*, **42**, 293–301.

Bates, G. W. (1981). On the nature of the hot flash. *Clinical Obstetrics and Gynecology*, **24**, 221–241.

Beach, F. A. (1975). Behavioural endocrinology: an emerging discipline. *American Scientist*, **63**, 178–187.

Beard, R. J. (1976). Genital organs in the menopause, in van Keep, P. A., Greenblatt, R. B., and Albeaux-Fernet, M. (eds.), *Consensus on menopause research*, MTP Press, Lancaster.

Belfer, M. L., and Shader, R. I. (1976). Premenstrual factors as determinants of alcoholism in women, in Greenblatt, M., and Schuckit, M. A. (eds.), *Alcoholism problems in women and children*. Grune and Stratton, New York.

Bell, B., Christie, M. J., and Venables, P. H. (1975). Psychophysiology of the menstrual cycle, in Venables, P. H., and Christie, M. J. (eds.), *Research in psychophysiology*, John Wiley, Chichester.

Belmaker, R. H., Murphy, D. L., Wyatt, R. J., and Loriaux, L. (1974). Human platelet monomine oxidase changes during the menstrual cycle. *Archives of General Psychiatry*, **31**, 553–556.

Ben-David, M., and van Look, P. F. A. (1979). Hypothalamic-pituitary-ovarian relationships around the menopause, in van Keep, P. A., Serr, D. M., and Greenblatt, R. B. (eds.), *Female and male climacteric*. MTP Press, Lancaster.

Benedek, T., and Rubinstein, B. (1939). The correlation between ovarian activity and psychodynamic processes. I. The ovulative phase. *Psychosomatic Medicine*, **1**, 245–270; II. The menstrual phase. *Psychosomatic Medicine*, **1**, 461–485.

Berry, C., and McGuire, F. L. (1972). Menstrual distress and acceptance of sexual role. *American Journal of Obstetrics and Gynecology*, **114**, 83–87.

Beumont, P. J., Richards, D. H., and Gelder, M. G. (1975). A study of minor psychiatric and physical symptoms during the menstrual cycle. *British Journal of Psychiatry*, **126**, 431–434.

Birtchnell, J., and Floyd, S. (1974). Attempted suicide and the menstrual cycle—a negative conclusion. *Journal of Psychosomatic Research*, **18**, 361–369.

Bloom, L. J., Shelton, J. L., and Michaels, A. C. (1978). Dysmenorrhea and personality. *Journal of Personality Assessment*, **42**, 272–276.

Brady, J. (1979). Biological cycles. *The Institute of Biology's Studies in Biology*, Volume 104, Edward Arnold, London.

Brand, P. C., and Lehert, P. H. (1978). A new way of looking at environmental variables that may affect the age at menopause. *Maturitas*, **1**, 121–132.

British Medical Journal, Editorial. (1979). Premenstrual tension syndrome, *British Medical Journal*, **i**, 212.

Brooks, J., Ruble, D., and Clark, A. (1977). College women's attitudes and expectations concerning menstrual-related changes. *Psychosomatic Medicine*, **39**, 288–298.

Brooks-Gunn, J., and Ruble, D. N. (1980). The menstrual attitude questionnaire. *Psychosomatic Medicine*, **42**, 503–512.

Broverman, D. M., Klaiber, E. L., Kobayashi, Y., and Vogel, W. (1968). Roles of activation and inhibition in sex differences in cognitive abilities. *Psychological Review*, **75**, 23–50.

Broverman, D. M., Vogel, W., Klaiber, E. L., Majcher, D., Shea, D., and Paul, V. (1981). Changes in cognitive task performance across the menstrual cycle. *Journal of Comparative and Physiological Psychology*, **95**, 646–654.

Brown, A. D. G. (1977). Postmenopausal urinary problems, in Greenblatt, R. B., and Studd, J. (eds.), *The menopause. Clinics in Obstetrics and Gynaecology*, Volume 4, W. B. Saunders, London.

Brown, F. A. Jr. (1980). The exogenous nature of rhythms, in Scheving, L. E., and Halberg, F. (eds.), *Chronobiology: Principles and applications to shifts in schedules*. Sijthoff & Noordhoff, Alphen aan den Rijn, Netherlands.

Brown, F. A., Jr., and Park, Y. J. (1967). Synodic monthly modulation of the diurnal rhythm of hamsters. *Proceeding of the Society for Experimental Biology and Medicine*, **125**, 712–715.

Brush, M. G. (1977). The possible mechanisms causing the premenstrual tension syndrome. *Current Medical Research and Opinion*, **4**, **Supplement 4**, 9–15.

Bullough, V. L. (1981). Age at menarche: a misunderstanding. *Science*, **213**, 365–366.

Bungay, G. T., Vessey, M. P., and McPherson, C. K. (1980). Study of symptoms in middle life with special reference to the menopause. *British Medical Journal*, **ii**, 181–183.

Bunning, E. (1973). *The physiological clock*. 3rd ed. The English Universities Press Ltd., London.

Burger, H. G. (1981) Neuroendocrine control of human ovulation, *International Journal of Fertility*, **26**, 153–160.

180

Buzzelli, B., Voegelin, M. R., Procacci, O. and Bozza, G. (1968) Modificazionni della soglia del dolore cutanes durante il ciclo menstruale. *Bolletino della Societa Italiana di Biologia Sperimentale*, **44**, 235–236.

Calkins, E. (1981). Aging of cells and people. *Clinical Obstetrics and Gynecology*, **24**, 165–179.

Campbell, C. S., and Turek, F. W. (1981). Cyclic function of the mammalian ovary, in Aschoff, J. (ed.), *Handbook of Behavioural Neurobiology, Biological rhythms*, Volume 4, Plenum Press, New York.

Campbell, D. E., and Beets, J. L. (1978). Lunacy and the moon. *Psychological Bulletin*, **85**, 1123–1129.

Campbell, S. (1976). Intensive steroid and protein hormone profiles on post-menopausal women experiencing hot flushes, and a group of controls, in Campbell, S. (ed.), *The management of the menopause and post-menopausal years*, MTP Press, Lancaster.

Campbell, S., McQueen, J., Minardi, J., and Whitehead, M. I. (1978). The modifying effect of progestogen on the response of the post-menopausal endometrium to exogenous oestrogens. *Postgraduate Medical Journal*, **54, Supplement 2**, 59–64.

Campbell, S., and Whitehead, M. I. (1977). Oestrogen therapy and the menopausal syndrome, in Greenblatt, R. B., and Studd, J. (eds.), *The menopause. Clinics in Obstetrics and Gynaecology*, Volume 4, W. B. Saunders, London.

Campos, F., and Thurow, C. (1978). Attributions of moods and symptoms to the menstrual cycle. *Personality and Social Psychology Bulletin*, **4**, 272–276.

Carney, A., Bancroft, J., and Mathews, A. (1978). Combination of hormonal and psychological treatment for female sexual unresponsiveness: a comparative study. *British Journal of Psychiatry*, **133**, 339–346.

Chakravarti, S., Collins, W. P., Forecast, J. D., Newton, J. R., Oram, D. H., and Studd, J. W. W. (1976). Hormone profiles after the menopause. *British Medical Journal*, **ii**, 784–787.

Chern, M. M., Gatewood, L. C., and Anderson, V. E. (1980). The inheritance of menstrual traits, in Dan, A. J., Graham, E. A., and Beecher, C. P. (eds.), *The Menstrual Cycle*, Volume I., Springer, New York.

Chernovetz, M. E., Jones, W. H., and Hansson, R. O. (1979). Predictability, attentional focus, sex role orientation, and menstrual-related stress. *Psychosomatic Medicine*, **41**, 383–391.

Christie, M. J., and McBrearty, E. M. T. (1979). Psychophysiological investigations of post lunch state in male and female subjects. *Ergonomics*, **22**, 307–323.

Clare, A. W. (1977). Psychological profiles of women complaining of premenstrual symptoms. *Current Medical Research and Opinion*, **4, Supplement 4**, 23–28.

Clare, A. W. (1979). The treatment of premenstrual symptoms. *British Journal of Psychiatry*, **135**, 576–579.

Claridge, G. S. (1967). *Personality and arousal. A psychophysiological study of psychiatric disorder*. International Series Monographs in Experimental Psychology, Pergamon, Oxford.

Clemens, J. A., Fuller, R. W., and Owen, N. V. (1978). Some neuroendocrine aspects of aging. *Advances in Experimental Medicine and Biology*, **113**, 77–100.

Cohen, D. B. (1972). Failure to recall dream content: contentless vs. dreamless reports. *Perceptual and Motor Skills*, **34**, 1000–1002.

Cohen, D. B. (1979). *Sleep and dreaming: origins, nature and function*. Pergamon, Oxford.

Conroy, R. T. W. L., and Mills, J. N. (1970). *Human circadian rhythms*. J. A. Churchill, London.

Coppen, A. (1965). The prevalence of menstrual disorders in psychiatric patients. *British Journal of Psychiatry*, **111**, 155–167.

181

Coppen, A., and Kessell, N. (1963). Menstruation and personality. *British Journal of Psychiatry*, **109**, 711–721.
Coronary Drug Project Research Group (1973). The coronary drug project. Findings leading to discontinuation of the 2.5-mg/day estrogen group. *Journal of the American Medical Association*, **226**, 652–657.
Costoff, A., and Mahesh, V. (1975). Primordial follicles with normal oocytes in the ovaries of postmenopausal women. *Journal of the Amerian Geriatrics Society*, **23**, 193–196.
Coulam, C. B. (1981). Age, estrogens, and the psyche. *Clinical Obstetrics and Gynecology*, **24**, 219–229.
Council of Medical Women's Federation of England (1933). Investigation of menopause of 1000 women. *Lancet*, **i**, 106–108.
Creutzfeldt, O. D., Arnold, P. M., Becker, D., Langenstein, S., Tirsch, W., Wilhelm, H., and Wuttke, W. (1976). EEG changes during spontaneous and controlled menstrual cycles and their correlation with psychological performance. *Electroencephalography and Clinical Neurophysiology*, **40**, 113–131.
Crilly, R. G., Francis, R. M., and Nordin, B. E. C. (1981). Steroid hormones, ageing and bone. *Clinics in Endocrinology and Metabolism*, **10**, 115–139.
Culberg, J. (1972). Mood changes and menstrual symptoms with different gestagen-estrogen combinations. *Acta Psychiatrica Scandinavica*. **Supplement 236**, 1–86.
Cutler, W. B. (1980). Lunar and menstrual phase locking. *American Journal of Obstetrics and Gynecology*, **137**, 834–839.
Cutler, W. B., and Garcia, C. R. (1980). The psychoneuroendocrinology of the ovulatory cycle of woman: A review. *Psychoneuroendocrinology*, **5**, 89–111.
Cutler, W. B., Garcia, C. R., and Krieger, A. M. (1979a). Sexual behaviour frequency and menstrual cycle length in mature premenopausal women. *Psychoneuroendocrinology*, **4**, 297–309.
Cutler, W. B., Garcia, C. R., and Krieger, A. M. (1979b). Luteal phase defects: A possible relationship between short hyperthermic phase and sporadic sexual behaviour in women. *Hormones and Behaviour*, **13**, 214–218.
Cutler, W. B., Garcia, C. R., and Krieger, A. M. (1980). Sporadic sexual behaviour and menstrual cycle length in women. *Hormones and Behaviour*, **14**, 163–172.
Dalton, K. (1959). Menstruation and acute psychiatric illness. *British Medical Journal*, **i**, 148–149.
Dalton, K. (1960). Effect of menstruation on schoolgirls' weekly work. *British Medical Journal*, **i**, 326–328.
Dalton, K. (1961). Menstruation and crime. *British Medical Journal*, **ii**, 1752–1753.
Dalton, K. (1964a). The influence of menstruation on health and disease. *Proceedings of the Royal Society of Medicine*, **57**, 18–20.
Dalton, K. (1964b). *The premenstrual syndrome*. Charles C. Thomas, Springfield, Illinois.
Dalton, K. (1966). The influence of mother's menstruation on her child. *Proceedings of the Royal Society of Medicine*, **59**, 1014.
Dalton, K. (1968). Menstruation and examinations. *Lancet*, **ii**, 1386–1388.
Dalton, K. (1979). *Once a month: The menstrual syndrome, its causes and consequences*. Harvester Press, Hassocks, Sussex.
Dalton, K. (1980). Cyclical criminal acts in premenstrual syndrome. *Lancet*, **ii**, 1070–1071.
Dalvit, S. P. (1981). The effect of the menstrual cycle on patterns of food intake. *The American Journal of Clinical Nutrition*, **34**, 1811–1815.
Damon, A., and Bajema, C. J. (1974). Age at menarche: Accuracy of recall after thirty-nine years. *Human Biology*, **46**, 381–384.
Dan, A. J. (1980). Free-associative versus self-report measures of emotional change over the menstrual cycle, in Dan, A. J., Graham, E. A., and Beecher, C. P. (eds,), *The menstrual cycle*. Volume 1. Springer, New York.

182

Davidson, J. M. (1978). Gonadal hormones and human behaviour, in Diamond, M. D., and Korenbrot, C. G. (eds.), *Hormonal contraceptives, estrogens, and human welfare*. Academic Press, New York.

Davis, K. B. (1929). *Factors in the sex life of 2000 women*. Harper and Row, New York.

de Jong, F. H., and Sharpe, R. M. (1976). Evidence for inhibin-like activity in bovine follicular fluid. *Nature*, **263**, 71–72.

De Marchi, W. G. (1976). Psychophysiological aspects of the menstrual cycle. *Journal of Psychosomatic Research*, **20**, 279–287.

De Marchi, W. G., and Tong, J. E. (1972). Menstrual, diurnal, and activation effects on the resolution of temporally paired flashes. *Psychophysiology*, **9**, 362–367.

Dennerstein, L., and Burrows, G. D. (1979). Affect and the menstrual cycle. *Journal of Affective Disorders*. **1**, 77–92.

Dennerstein, L., Burrows, G. D., Hyman, G. J., and Sharpe, K. (1979). Hormone therapy and affect. *Maturitas*, **1**, 247–259.

Dewan, E. M., Menkin, M. F., and Rock, J. (1980). Effect of photic stimulation on the human menstrual cycle. *Photochemistry and Photobiology*, **27**, 581–585.

Diamond, M., Diamond, A. L., and Mast, M. (1972). Visual sensitivity and sexual arousal levels during the menstrual cycle. *Journal of Nervous and Mental Diseases*, **55**, 170–176.

Diamond, S. B., Rubinstein, A. A., Dunner, D. L., and Fieve, R. R. (1976). Menstrual problems in women with primary affective illness. *Comprehensive Psychiatry*, **17**, 541–548.

Diespecker, D. D., and Kolokotronis, E. (1971). Vibrotactile learning and the menstrual cycle. *Perceptual and Motor Skills*, **33**, 233–234.

Dominian, J. (1977). The role of psychiatry in the menopause, in Greenblatt, R. B., and Studd, J. (eds.), *The menopause. Clinics in Obstetrics and Gynaecology*, Volume 4, W. B. Saunders, London.

d'Orban, P. T., and Dalton, J. (1980). Violent crime and the menstrual cycle. *Psychological Medicine*, **10**, 353–359.

Doty, R. L., Ford, M. Preti, G., and Huggins, G. R. (1975). Changes in the intensity and pleasantness of human vaginal odors during the menstrual cycle. *Science*, **190**, 1316–1318.

Doty, R. L., Huggins, G. R., Snyder, P. J., and Lowry, L. D. (1981). Endocrine, cardiovascular, and psychological correlates of olfactory sensitivity changes during the human menstrual cycle. *Journal of Comparative and Physiological Psychology*, **95**, 45–60.

Doyle, J. B. (1951). Exploratory culdotomy for observation of tubovarian physiology at ovulation time. *Fertility and Sterility*, **2**, 475–484.

Dunn, J. (1972). Vicarious menstruation. *American Journal of Obstetrics and Gynecology*, **114**, 568–569.

Engel, P., and Hildebrandt, G. (1974). Rhythmic variations in reaction time, heart rate and blood pressure at different durations of the menstrual cycle, in Ferin, M., Halberg, F., Richart, R. M., and Vande Wiele, R. L. (eds.), *Biorhythms and human reproduction*. John Wiley, New York.

Englander-Golden, P., Chang, H-S., Whitmore, M. R., and Dienstbier, R. A. (1980). Female sexual arousal and the menstrual cycle. *Journal of Human Stress*, **6**, 42–48.

Englander-Golden, P., Whitmore, M. R., and Dienstbier, R. A. (1978). Menstrual cycle as a focus of study and self-report of moods and behaviours. *Motivation and Emotion*, **2**, 75–86.

Englander-Golden, P., Willis, K. A., and Dienstbier, R. A. (1977). Stability of perceived tension as a function of the menstrual cycle. *Journal of Human Stress*, **3**, 14–21.

Epstein, M. T., Hockaday, J. M., and Hockaday, T. D. R. (1975). Migraine and reproductive hormones throughout the menstrual cycle. *Lancet*, **ii**, 543–548.

Erlik, Y., Meldrum, D. R., and Judd, H. L. (1982). Estrogen levels in postmenopausal women with hot flushes. *Obstetrics and Gynecology*, **59**, 403–407.

Ernster, V. L., and Petrakis, N. L. (1981). Effect of hormonal events in earlier life and socioeconomic status on age at menopause. *American Journal of Obstetrics and Gynecology*, **140**, 471–472.

Felthous, A. R., Robinson, D. B., and Conroy, R. W. (1980). Prevention of recurrent menstrual psychosis by an oral contraceptive. *American Journal of Psychiatry*, **137**, 245–246.

Filler, W. W., and Hall, W. C. (1970). Dysmenorrhea and its therapy. *American Journal of Obstetrics and Gynecology*, **106**, 104–109.

Fishman, J., and Martucci, C. P. (1980). New concepts of estrogenic activity: the role of metabolites in the expression of hormone action, in Pasetto, N., Paoletti, R., and Ambrus, J. L. (eds.), *The menopause and postmenopause*. MTP Press, Lancaster.

Fliess, W. (1909). *Von Leben und vom Tod*. Diederichs, Jena.

Flint, M. (1976). Cross-cultural factors that affect age of menopause, in van Keep, P.A., Greenblatt, R. B., and Albeaux-Fernet, M. (eds.), *Consensus on menopause research*, MTP Press, Lancaster.

Flint, M. P. (1979). Sociology and anthropology of the menopause, in van Keep, P. A., Serr, D. M., and Greenblatt, R. B. (eds.), *Female and male climacteric*. MTP Press, Lancaster.

Freedman, S. H., Ramcharan, S., Hoag, E., and Goldfien, A. (1974). Some physiological and biochemical measurements over the menstrual cycle, in Ferin, M., Halberg, F., Richart, R. M., and Vande Wiele, R. (eds.), *Biorhythms and human reproduction*. John Wiley, New York.

Friedman, J., and Meares, R. A. (1979). The menstrual cycle and habituation. *Psychosomatic Medicine*, **41**, 369–381.

Friedman, R. C., Hurt, S. W., Arnoff, M. S., and Clarkin, J. (1980). Behaviour and the menstrual cycle. *Signs. Journal of Women in Culture and Society*, **5**, 719–738.

Frisch, R. E., Revelle, R., and Cook, S. (1973). Components of weight at menarche and the initiation of the adolescent growth spurt in girls: estimated total water, lean body weight and fat. *Human Biology*, **45**, 469–483.

Froberg, J. E. (1977). Twenty-four-hour patterns in human performance, subjective and physiological variables and differences between morning and evening active subjects. *Biological Psychology*, **5**, 119–134.

Frommer, D. J. (1964). Changing age of the menopause. *British Medical Journal*, **ii**, 349–351.

Furuhjelm, M., and Fedor-Freybergh, P. (1976). The influence of estrogens on the psyche in climacteric and post-menopausal women, in van Keep, P. A., Greenblatt, R. B., and Albeaux-Fernet, M. (eds.), *Consensus on menopause research*, MTP Press, Lancaster.

Gambrell, R. D. (1982). Clinical use of progestins in the menopausal patient. *Journal of Reproductive Medicine*, **27**, 8 (Supplement), 531–538.

Gannon, L. (1981). Evidence for a psychological etiology of menstrual disorders: A critical review. *Psychological Reports*, **48**, 287–294.

Garcia, C. R., and Rosenfeld, D. (1977). *Human fertility. The regulation of reproduction*. Davis, Philadelphia.

Garfield, P. L. (1974). Women, blood and dreams. *Sleep Research*, **3**, 106.

Garling, J., and Roberts, S. J. (1980). An investigation of cyclic distress among staff nurses, in Dan A. J., Graham, E. A., and Beecher, C. P. (eds.), *The menstrual cycle*. Volume I. Springer, New York.

Gittelson, B. (1979). *Biorhythm*. Futura Publications, London.

184

Glass, G. S., Heninger, G. R., Lansky, M., and Talan, K. (1971). Psychiatric emergency related to the menstrual cycle. *American Journal of Psychiatry*, **128**, 705–711.

Goldzieher, J. W., Moses, L. E., Averkin, E., Scheel, C., and Taber, B. A. (1971). Nervousness and depression attributed to oral contraceptives: A double-blind, placebo-controlled study. *American Journal of Obstetrics and Gynecology*, **111**, 1013–1020.

Golub, S. (1976). The magnitude of premenstrual anxiety and depression. *Psychosomatic Medicine*, **38**, 4–11.

Golub, S. (1980).Premenstrual changes in mood, personality, and cognitive function, in Dan, A. J., Graham, E. A., and Beecher, C. P. (eds.), *The menstrual cycle*, Volume 1, Springer, New York.

Golub, S., and Harrington, D. M. (1981). Premenstrual and menstrual mood changes in adolescent women. *Journal of Personality and Social Psychology*, **41**, 961–965.

Good, P. R., Geary, N. and Engen, T. (1976). The effect of estrogen on odor detection. *Chemical Senses and Flavour*, **2**, 45–50.

Goodman, A. L., Nixon, W., Johnson, D., and Hodgen, G. (1977). Regulation of folliculogenesis in the cycling rhesus monkey: selection of the dominant follicle. *Endocrinology*, **100**, 155–161.

Gordon, T., Kannel, W. B., Hjortland, M. C., and McNamara, P. M. (1978). Menopause and coronary heart disease. *Annals of Internal Medicine*, **89**, 157–161.

Gough, H. G. (1975). Personality factors related to reported severity of menstrual distress. *Journal of Abnormal Psychology*, **84**, 59–65.

Graham, C. A., and McGrew, W. C. (1980). Menstrual synchrony in female undergraduates living on a coeducational campus. *Psychoneuroendocrinology*, **5**, 245–252.

Graham, E. A. (1980). Cognition as related to menstrual cycle phase and estrogen level, in Dan, A. J., Graham, E. A., and Beecher, C. P. (eds.), *The menstrual cycle*. Volume 1. Springer, New York.

Grant, E. C. G., and Pryse-Davies, J. (1968). Effect of oral contraceptives on depressive mood changes and on endometrial MAO and phosphatases. *British Medical Journal*, iii, 777–780.

Gray, D. S., and Gorzalka, B. B. (1980). Adrenal steroid interactions in female sexual behaviour: A review. *Psychoneuroendocrinology*, **5**, 157–175.

Gray, J. A. (1972). The structure of the emotions and the limbic system, in Porter, R., and Knight, J. (eds.), *Physiology, emotion and psychosomatic illness*. Ciba Foundation Symposia 8 (New Series) Elsevier Excerpta Medica. North Holland, Amsterdam.

Gray, J. A., and Buffery, A. W. H. (1971). Sex differences in emotional and cognitive behaviour in mammals including man: adaptive and neural bases. *Acta Psychologica*, **35**, 89–111.

Green, D. J., and Gillette, R. (1982). Circadian rhythm of firing rate recorded from single cells in the rat suprachiasmatic brain slice. *Brain Research*, **245**, 198–200.

Greene, J. G., and Cooke, D. J. (1980). Life stress and symptoms at the climacterium. *British Journal of Psychiatry*, **136**, 486–491.

Gruba, G. H., and Rohrbraugh, M. (1975). MMPI correlates of menstrual distress. *Pyschosomatic medicine*, **37**, 265–273.

Haggard, M., and Gaston, J. B. (1978). Changes in auditory perception in the menstrual cycle. *British Journal of Audiology*, **12**, 105–118.

Hagnell, O. (1966). *A prospective study of the incidence of mental disorder*. Munksgaard, Copenhagen.

Hain, J. D., Linton, P. H., Eber, H. W., and Chapman, M. N. (1970). Menstrual irregularity, symptoms and personality. *Journal of Psychosomatic Research*, **14**, 81–87.

Halbreich, U., and Endicott, J. (1981). Possible involvement of endorphin withdrawal or imbalance in specific premenstrual syndromes and postpartum depression, *Medical Hypotheses*, **7**, 1045–1058.

Halbreich, U., and Kas, D. (1977). Variations in the Taylor MAS of women with pre-menstrual syndrome. *Journal of Psychosomatic Research*, **21**, 391–393.

Hallstrom, T. (1973). Mental disorder and sexuality in the climacteric, in Forssman, H. (ed.) *Reports from the Psychiatric Research Centre, St. Jorgen's Hospital, University of Goteborg, Sweden*, Scandinavian University Books, Stockholm.

Hallstrom, T. (1977). Sexuality in the climacteric, in Greenblatt, R. B., and Studd, J. (eds.), *The menopause. Clinics in Obstetrics and Gynaecology*, Volume 4, W. B. Saunders, London.

Hammond, C. B., Jelovsek, F. R., Lee, K. L., Creasman, W. T., and Parker, R. T. (1979a). Effects of long-term estrogen replacement therapy. I. Metabolic effects. *American Journal of Obstetrics and Gynecology*, **133**, 525–536.

Hammond, C. B., Jelovsek, F. R., Lee, K. L., Creasman, W. T., and Parker, R. T. (1979b). Effects of long-term estrogen replacement therapy. II. Neoplasia. *American Journal of Obstetrics and Gynecology*, **133**, 537–547.

Hanley, S. P. (1981). Asthma variation with menstruation. *British Journal of Diseases of the Chest*, **75**, 306–308.

Hart, R. D. (1960). Rhythm of libido in married women. *British Medical Journal*, **i**, 1023–1024.

Hartmann, E. (1966). Dreaming sleep (the D-state) and the menstrual cycle. *Journal of Nervous and Mental Disease*, **143**, 406–416.

Heaney, R. P. (1976). Estrogens and postmenopausal osteoporosis. *Clinical Obstetrics and Gynecology*, **19**, 791–803.

Heczey, M. D. (1980). Effects of biofeedback and autogenic training on dysmenorrhea, in Dan, A. J., Graham, E. A., and Beecher, C. P. (eds.), *The menstrual cycle*, Volume 1, Springer, New York.

Heller, R. F., and Jacobs, H. S. (1978). Coronary heart disease in relation to age, sex, and the menopause. *British Medical Journal*, **i**, 472–474.

Henderson, A., Nemes, G., Gordon, N. B., and Roos, L. (1970). The sleep of regularly menstruating women and of women taking an oral contraceptive. *Psychophysiology*, **7**, 337.

Henderson, M. (1976). Evidence for hormonally related male temperature cycle and synchrony with the female cycle. *Australian and New Zealand Journal of Medicine*, **6**, 254.

Henkin, R. I. (1974). Sensory changes during the menstrual cycle, in Ferin, M., Halberg, F., Richart, R. M., and Vande Wiele, R. (eds.), *Biorhythms and human reproduction*, John Wiley, New York.

Hertz, D. G., and Jensen, M. R. (1975). Menstrual dreams and psychodynamics: emotional conflict and manifest dream content in menstruating women. *British Journal of Medical Psychology*, **48**, 175–183.

Herzberg, B., and Coppen, A. (1970). Changes in psychological symptoms in women taking oral contraceptives. *British Journal of Psychiatry*, **116**, 161–164.

Hilgers, T. W., Daly, D., Prebil, A. M., and Hilgers, S. K. (1981). Natural family planning III. Intermenstrual symptoms and estimated time of ovulation. *Obstetrics and Gynecology*, **58**, 152–155.

Hoffman, G., and Petre-Quadens, O. (1979). Maturation of REM-patterns from childhood to maturity. *Waking and Sleeping*, **3**, 255–262.

Holloway, F. A. (1977). Overview of research in bio-behavioural rhythms. *Biological Psychology Bulletin*, **5**, 39–41.

Hoon, P. W., Bruce, K., and Kinchloe, B. (1982). Does the menstrual cycle play a role in sexual arousal? *Psychophysiology*, **19**, 21–27.

Horne, J. A., and Ostberg, O. (1977). Individual differences in human circadian rhythms. *Biological Psychology*, **5**, 179–190.

186

Houser, B. B. (1979). An investigation of the correlation between hormonal levels in males and mood, behavior and physical discomfort. *Hormones and Behaviour*, **12**, 185–197.

Hutt, S. J., Frank, G., Mychalkiw, W., and Hughes, M. (1980). Perceptual-motor performance during the menstrual cycle. *Hormones and Behaviour*, **14**, 116–125.

Hutton, J. D., Jacobs, H. S., and James, V. H. T. (1979). Steroid endocrinology after the menopause: a review. *Journal of the Royal Society of Medicine*, **72**, 835–841.

Ihalainen, P. (1975). Psychosomatic aspects of amenorrhea. *Acta Psychiatrica Scandinavica*, **(Supplement)**, **262**, 1–139.

Ivey, M. E., and Bardwick, J. M. (1968). Patterns of affective fluctuation in the menstrual cycle. *Psychosomatic Medicine*, **30**, 336–345.

Jacobs, H. S. (1979). Hormone replacement therapy. *Journal of the Royal Society of Medicine*, **72**, 797–798.

Jacobs, H. S., and Murray, M. A. F (1976). The premature menopause, in Campbell, S. (ed.), *The management of the menopause and post-menopausal years*. MTP Press, Lancaster.

Jacobs, T. E., and Charles, E. (1970). Correlation of psychiatric symptomatology and the menstrual cycle in an outpatient population. *American Journal of Psychiatry*, **126**, 1504–1508.

James, H., and Pollitt, J. (1974). Personality and premenstrual tension. *Proceedings of the Royal Society of Medicine*, **67**, 920–923.

James, W. H. (1971). The distribution of coitus within the human intermenstruum. *Journal of Biosocial Science*, **3**, 159–171.

Janiger, O., Riffenburgh, M. D., and Kersh, M. S. (1972). Cross cultural study of premenstrual symptoms. *Psychosomatics*, **13**, 226–235.

Janowsky, D. S., Berens, S. C., and Davis, J. M. (1973). Correlations between mood, weight and electrolytes during the menstrual cycle: A renin-angiotensin-aldosterone hypothesis of premenstrual tension. *Psychosomatic Medicine*, **35**, 143–154.

Janowsky, D. S., Gorney, R., and Castelnuovo-Tedesco, P. (1969). Premenstrual-menstrual increases in psychiatric hospital admission rates. *American Journal of Obstetrics and Gynecology*, **103**, 189–191.

Jaszmann, L., van Lith, N. D., and Zaat, J. C. A. (1969). The perimenopausal symptoms: The statistical analysis of a survey. *Medical Gynaecology and Sociology*, **4**, 268–277.

Jick, H., and Porter, J. (1977). Relation between smoking and age of natural menopause. *Lancet*, **i**, 1354–1355.

Johnson, J. (1973). Effects of accurate expectations about sensations on the sensory and distress components of pain. *Journal of Personality and Social Psychology*, **27**, 261–275.

Jones, B. M., and Jones, M. K. (1976). Alcohol effects in women during the menstrual cycle. *Annals of the New York Academy of Sciences*, **273**, 576–587.

Judd, H. L. (1976). Hormonal dynamics associated with the menopause. *Clinical Obstetrics and Gynecology*, **19**, 775–788.

Judd, H. L., and Yen, S. S. C. (1973). Serum androstenedione and testosterone levels during the menstrual cycle. *Journal of Clinical Endocrinology and Metabolism*, **36**, 475–481.

Kahana, E., Kiyak, A., and Liang, J. (1980). Menopause in the context of other life events, in Dan, A. J., Graham, E. A., and Beecher, C. P. (eds.), *The menstrual cycle*, volume 1. Springer, New York.

Kaiser, I. H., and Halberg, F. (1962). Circadian periodic aspects of birth. *Annals of the New York Academy of Sciences*, **98**, 1056–1058.

Karlson, P., and Luscher, M. (1959). 'Pheromones': A new term for a class of biologically active substances. *Nature*, **183**, 55–56.

Kashiwagi, T., McClure, J. N., and Wetzel, R. D. (1976). Premenstrual affective syndrome and psychiatric disorder. *Diseases of the Nervous System*, **37**, 116–119.

Katchadourian, H. (1977). *The biology of adolescence*. W. H. Freeman, San Francisco.

Kawamura, H., and Ibuka, N. (1978). The search for circadian rhythm pacemakers in the light of lesion experiments. *Chronobiologia*, **5**, 69–88.

van Keep, P. A. (1970). *The menopause. A study of the attitudes of women in Belgium, France, Great Britain, Italy and West Germany*. International Health Foundation, Geneva.

van Keep, P. A., and Haspels, A. A. (1979). Het premenstruele syndroom, een epidemilogisch onderzoek. *Journal of Drug Research*, **4**, 568.

van Keep, P. A. and Lehert, P. (1981). The premenstrual syndrome—an epidemiological and statistical exercise, in van Keep, P. A., and Utian, W. H. (eds.), *The premenstrual syndrome*. MTP Press, Lancaster.

Kessel, N., and Coppen, A. (1963). The prevalence of common menstrual symptoms. *Lancet*, **ii**, 61–64.

Kinsey, A. C., Pomeroy, W. B., Martin, C. E., and Gebhard, P. H. (1953). *Sexual behaviour in the human female*, W. B. Saunders, Philadelphia.

Kirstein, L., Rosenberg, G., and Smith, H. (1980–81). Cognitive changes during the menstrual cycle. *International Journal of Psychiatry in Medicine*, **10**, 339–346.

Klaiber, E., Broverman, D. M., Vogel, W., and Kobayashi, Y. (1974). Rhythms in plasma MAO activity, EEG, and behaviour during the menstrual cycle, in Ferin, M., Halberg, F., Richart, R. M., and Vande Wiele, R. L. (eds.), *Biorhythms and human reproduction*. John Wiley, New York.

Koelega, H. S., and Koster, E. P. (1974). Some experiments on sex differences in odor perception. *Annals of the New York Academy of Sciences*, **237**, 234–246.

Koeske, R. K. D. (1976). Premenstrual emotionality: Is biology destiny? *Women and Health*, **1**, 11–14.

Koeske, R. K. D. (1977). *The interaction of social-cognitive and physiological factors in premenstrual emotionality*, Unpublished doctoral dissertation, Carnegie-Mellon University.

Koeske, R. K. D. (1980). Theoretical perspectives on menstrual cycle research: The relevance of attributional approaches for the perception and explanation of premenstrual emotionality, in Dan, A. J., Graham, E. A., and Beecher, C. P. (eds.), *The menstrual cycle*. Volume 1, Springer, New York.

Koeske, R. K., and Koeske, G. F. (1975). An attributional approach to moods and the menstrual cycle. *Journal of Personality and Social Psychology*, **31**, 473–478.

Kolodny, R. C., and Bauman, J. E. (1979). Female sexual activity (letters to the editor). *New England Journal of Medicine*, **300**, 626.

Kopell, B. S., Lunde, D. T., Clayton, R. B., and Moos, R. H. (1969). Variations in some measures of arousal during the menstrual cycle. *Journal of Nervous and Mental Diseases*, **148**, 180–187.

Kopera, H. (1979). Effects, side-effects and dosage schemes of various sex hormones in the peri- and post-menopause, in van Keep, P. A., Serr, D. M., and Greenblatt, R. B., (eds.), *Female and male climacteric*. MTP Press, Lancaster.

Kraemer, H. C., Becker, H. B., Brodie, H. K. H., Doering, C. H., Moos, R. H., and Hamburg, D. A. (1976). Orgasmic frequency and plasma testosterone levels in normal human males. *Archives of Sexual Behaviour*, **5**, 125–132.

Kramp, J. L. (1968). Studies on the premenstrual syndrome in relation to psychiatry. *Acta Psychiatrica Scandinavica*, **Supplement 203**, 261–267.

Kripke, D. F., Yelverton, H., and Kripke, Z. D. (1979). 'Biorhythm' is Bio-Nonsense. *The American Biology Teacher*, **41**, 108–109; 128.

188

Kutner, S. J., and Brown, W. I. (1972). Types of oral contraceptives, depression and premenstrual symptoms. *Journal of Nervous and Mental Disease*, **155**, 153–162.

Lacey, J. I. (1967). Somatic response patterning and stress: Some revisions of activation theory, in Appley, M. H., and Trumbull, R. (eds.), *Psychological Stress*, Appleton-Century-Crofts, New York.

Ladisch, W. (1977). Influence of progesterone on serotonin metabolism: A possible causal factor for mood changes. *Psychoneuroendocrinology*, **2**, 275–266.

Lahmeyer, H., Miller, M., and DeLeon-Jones, F. (1982). Anxiety and mood fluctuation during the normal menstrual cycle. *Psychosomatic Medicine*, **44**, 183–194.

Laidlaw, J. (1956). Catamenial epilepsy. *Lancet*, **ii**, 1235–1237.

Lamb, W. M., Ulett, G. A., Master, W. H., and Robinson, D. W. (1953). Premenstrual tension: EEG, hormonal and psychiatric evaluation. *American Journal of Psychiatry*, **109**, 840–848.

Lederer, J. (1963). Kleptomanie prémenstruelle dans un cas d'hyperfolliculinie liée à une hypothyroidie. *Annales d'Endocrinologie*, **24**, 460–465.

Le Magnen, J. (1952). Les phenomenes olfacto-sexuels chez l'homme. *Archives des Sciences Physiologiques*, **6**, 125–160.

Levitt, E. E., and Lubin, B. (1967). Some personality factors associated with menstrual complaints and menstrual attitudes. *Journal of Psychosomatic Research*, **11**, 267–270.

Lewey, A. J., Wehr, T. A., Goodwin, F. K., Newsome, D. A., and Markey, S. P. (1980). Light suppresses melatonin secretion in humans. *Science*, **210**, 1267–1269.

Lewis, S. A., and Burns, M. (1975). Manifest dream content: changes with the menstrual cycle. *British Journal of Medical Psychology*, **48**, 375–377.

Lindquist, O. (1979). Menopausal age in relation to smoking. *Acta Medica Scandinavica*, **205**, 73–77.

Lindsay, R., Hart, D. M., Maclean, A., Garwood, J., Aitken, J. M., Clark, A. C., and Coutts, J. R. T. (1978). Pathogenesis and prevention of post-menopausal osteoporosis, in Cooke, I. D. (ed.), *The role of estrogen/progestogen in the management of the menopause*, MTP Press, Lancaster.

Lindsay, R., Hart, D. M., Purdie, D., Ferguson, M., Clark, A., and Kraszewski, A. (1978). Comparative effects of estrogen and a progestogen on bone loss in postmenopausal women. *Clinical Science and Molecular Medicine*, **54**, 193–195.

Lindsay, R., MacLean, A., Kraszewski, A., Hart, D. M., Clark, A. C., and Garwood, J. (1978). Bone response to termination of oestrogen treatment. *Lancet*, **i**, 1325–1327.

Little, B. C., and Zahn, T. P. (1974). Changes in mood and autonomic functioning during the menstrual cycle. *Psychophysiology*, **11**, 579–590.

Lobo, R. A., and Gibbons, W. E. (1982). The role of progestin therapy in breast disease and central nervous system function, *Journal of Reproductive Medicine*, **27**, 8 (Supplement), 515–521.

Logue, P. E., Linnoila, M., Wallman, L., and Erwin, C. W. (1981). Effects of ethanol and psychomotor tests on state anxiety: interaction with menstrual cycle in women. *Perceptual and Motor Skills*, **52**, 643–648.

McAdoo, B. C., Doering, C. H., Kraemer, H. C., Dessert, N., Brodie, H.K.H., and Hamburg, D. A. (1978). A study of the effects of gonadotropin-releasing hormone on human mood and behaviour. *Psychosomatic Medicine*, **40**, 199–209.

McClintock, M. K. (1971). Menstrual synchrony and suppression. *Nature*, **229**, 244–245.

McConnell, J. V. (1978). Biorhythms: A report and analysis. *Journal of Biological Psychology*, **20**, 13–24.

McEwen, B. S. (1976). Interactions between hormones and nerve tissue. *Scientific American*, **235**, 48–67.

189

McGeer, P. L., and McGeer, E. G. (1978). Aging and neurotransmitter systems. *Advances in Experimental Medicine and Biology*, **113**, 41–57.

McGeer, P. L., and McGeer, E. G. (1980). Chemistry of mood and emotion. *Annual Review of Psychology*, **31**, 273–307.

McKinlay, S., and Jefferys, M. (1974). The menopausal syndrome. *British Journal of Preventive and Social Medicine*, **28**, 108–115.

McKinlay, S., Jefferys, M., and Thompson, B. (1972). An investigation of the age at menopause. *Journal of Biosocial Science*, **4**, 161–173.

MacKinnon, I. L., MacKinnon, P. C. B., and Thomson, A. D. (1959). Lethal hazards of the luteal phase of the menstrual cycle. *British Medical Journal*, **i**, 1015–1017.

Mair, R. G., Bouffard, J. A., Engen, T., and Morton, T. H. (1978). Olfactory sensitivity during the menstrual cycle. *Sensory Processes*, **2**, 90–98.

Malek, J., Gleich, J., and Maly, V. (1962). Characteristics of the daily rhythm of menstruation and labor. *Annals of the New York Academy of Sciences*, **98**, 1042–1055.

Mallow, G. K. (1981). The relationship between aggressive behaviour and menstrual cycle stage in female rhesus monkeys (macaca mulatta). *Hormones and Behaviour*, **15**, 259–269.

Mandel, F. P., Davidson, B. J., Erlik, Y., Judd, H. L., and Meldrum, D. R. (1982). Effects of progestins on bone metabolism in postmenopausal women. *Journal of Reproductive Medicine*, **27**, 8 (Supplement), 511–514.

Mandell, A. J., and Mandell, M. P. (1967). Suicide and the menstrual cycle. *Journal of the American Medical Association*, **200**, 792–793.

Mandler, G. (1975). *Mind and Emotion*, John Wiley, New York.

Marinari, K. T., Leshner, A. I., and Doyle, M. P. (1976). Menstrual cycle status and adrenocortical reactivity to psychological stress. *Psychoneuroendocrinology*, **1**, 213–218.

Marks, R., and Shahrad, P. (1977). Skin changes at the time of the climacteric, in Greenblatt, R. B., and Studd, J. (eds.), *The menopause. Clinics in Obstetrics and Gynaecology*, Volume 4, W. B. Saunders, London.

Markum, R. A. (1976). Assessment of the reliability of and the effect of neutral instructions on the symptom ratings on the Moos Menstrual Distress Questionnaire. *Psychosomatic Medicine*, **38**, 163–172.

Martin, I. (1973). Somatic reactivity: Interpretation, in Eysenck, H. J. (ed.), *Handbook of Abnormal Psychology*, Pitman, London.

Masters, W. H., and Johnson, V. E. (1966). *Human sexual response*, Little, Brown, Boston.

Mathews, K. A., and Carra, J. (1982). Suppression of menstrual distress symptoms: A study of Type A behaviour. *Personality and Social Psychology Bulletin*, **8**, 146–151.

May, R. R. (1976). Mood shifts and the menstrual cycle. *Journal of Psychosomatic Research*, **20**, 125–130.

Meema, H. E., Bunker, M. L., and Meema, S. (1965). Loss of compact bone due to menopause. *Obstetrics and Gynecology*, **26**, 333–343.

Meema, S., and Meema, H. E. (1976). Menopausal bone loss and estrogen replacement. *Israel Journal of Medical Science*, **12**, 601–606.

Meldrum, D. R., Shamonki, I. M., Frumar, A. M., Tataryn, I. V., Chang, R. J., and Judd, H. L. (1979). Elevations in skin temperature of the finger as an objective index of postmenopausal hot flushes: Standardization of the technique. *American Journal of Obstetrics and Gynecology*, **135**, 713–717.

Menaker, W., and Menaker, A. (1959). Lunar periodicity in human reproduction: A likely unit of biological time. *American Journal of Obstetrics and Gynecology*, **77**, 905–914.

Metcalf, M. G., and Mackenzie, J. A. (1980). Incidence of ovulation in young women. *Journal of Biosocial Science*, **12**, 345–352.

Metral, G. (1981). The action of natural selection on the human menstrual cycle: A simulation study. *Journal of Biosocial Science*, **13**, 337–343.

Michael, R. P., Zumpe, D., Keverne, E. B., and Bonsall, R. W. (1972). Neuroendocrine factors in the control of primate behaviour. *Recent Progress in Hormone Research*, **23**, 665–706.

Miles, L. E. M., Raynal, D. M., and Wilson, M. A. (1977). Blind man living in normal society has circadian rhythm of 24.9 hours. *Science*, **198**, 421–423.

Minors, D. S., and Waterhouse, J. M. (1981). *Circadian rhythms and the human*. Wright, Bristol.

Minorsky, N. (1962). *Nonlinear oscillations*. Van Nostrand, New York.

Moghissi, K. S., Syner, F. N., and Evans, T. N. (1972). A composite picture of the menstrual cycle. *American Journal of Obstetrics and Gynecology*, **114**, 405–416.

Montgomery, J. D. (1979). Variations in perception of short time intervals during menstrual cycle. *Perceptual and Motor Skills*, **49**, 940–942.

Moos, R. H. (1968). The development of a menstrual distress questionnaire. *Psychosomatic Medicine*, **30**, 853–867.

Moos, R. H. (1969). *Menstrual Distress Questionnaire*. Preliminary Manual. Stanford University, Stanford, California.

Moos, R. H. (1977). *Menstrual Distress Questionnaire Manual*. Department of Psychiatry and Behavioural Sciences, Stanford University, Stanford.

Moos, R. H., Kopell, B. S., Melges, F. T., Yalom, I. D., Lunde, D. T., Clayton, R. B., and Hamburg, D. A. (1969). Fluctuations in symptoms and moods during the menstrual cycle. *Journal of Psychosomatic Research*, **13**, 37–44.

Moos, R. H., and Leiderman, D. B. (1978). Towards a menstrual cycle symptom typology. *Journal of Psychosomatic Research*, **22**, 31–40.

Morrell, F. (1959). The role of oestrogens in catamenial exacerbation of epilepsy. *Neurology*, **9**, 352–360.

Morris, D. (1967). *The Naked Ape*. Corgi Books, London.

Morris, N. M., and Udry, J. R. (1977). Study of the relationship between coitus and LH surge. *Fertility and Sterility*, **28**, 440–442.

Morton, J. H., Additon, H., Addison, R. G., Hunt, L., and Sullivan, J. J. (1953). A clinical study of premenstrual tension. *American Journal of Obstetrics and Gynecology*, **65**, 1182–1191.

Nachtigall, L. E., Nachtigall, R. H., Nachtigall, R. D., and Beckman, E. M. (1979). Estrogen replacement therapy I: A 10-year prospective study in the relationship to osteoporosis. *Obstetrics and Gynecology*, **53**, 277–281.

Natrajan, P. K., Muldoon, T. G., Greenblatt, R. B., and Mahesh, V. B. (1981). Estradiol and progesterone receptors in estrogen-primed endometrium. *American Journal of Obstetrics and Gynecology*, **140**, 387–392.

Nattero, G. (1982). Menstrual headache. *Advances in Neurology*, **33**, 215–226.

Neugarten, B. L., and Kraines, R. J. (1965). Menopausal symptoms in women of various ages. *Psychosomatic Medicine*, **3**, 266–273.

Nicassio, P. M. (1980). Behaviour management of dysmenorrhea, in Dan, A. J., Graham, E. A., and Beecher, C. P. (eds.), *The menstrual cycle*. Volume 1. Springer, New York.

Nieschlag, E. (1979). The male climacteric, in van Keep, P. A., Serr, D. M., and Greenblatt, R. B. (eds.), *Female and male climacteric*. MTP Press, Lancaster.

Nisker, J. A., and Siiteri, P. K. (1981). Estrogens and breast cancer. *Clinical Obstetrics and Gynecology*, **24**, 302–322.

Notelovitz, M. (1977). Coagulation, oestrogen, and the menopause, in Greenblatt, R. B., and Studd, J. (eds.), *The menopause. Clinics in Obstetrics and Gynaecology*, Volume 4, W. B. Saunders, London.

191

Notelovitz, M. (1979). Clotting factors and oestrogen replacement therapy, in van Keep, P. A., Serr, D. M., and Greenblatt, R. B. (eds.), *Female and male climateric.* MTP Press, Lancaster.

Oatley, K., and Goodwin, B. C. (1971). The explanation and investigation of biological rhythms, in Colquhoun, W. P. (ed.), *Biological rhythms and human performance*, Academic Press, London.

O'Connor, J. F., Shelley, E. M., and Stern, L. O. (1974). Behavioural rhythms related to the menstrual cycle, in Ferin, M., Halberg, F., Richart, R. M., and Vande Wiele, R. (eds.), *Biorhythms and human reproduction*, John Wiley, New York.

Ojeda, S. R., and McCann, S. M. (1973). Evidence for participation of a catecholaminergic mechanism in the post-castration rise in plasma gonadotropins. *Neuroendocrinology*, **12**, 295–315.

Oliver, M. F. (1976). The menopause and coronary heart disease, in Campbell, S. (ed.), *The management of the menopause and post-menopausal years*. MTP Press, Lancaster.

O'Malley, B. W., and Schrader, W. T. (1976). The receptors of steroid hormones. *Scientific American*, **235**, 32–43.

Osborne, J. L. (1976). Post-menopausal changes in micturition habits and in urine flow and urethral pressure studies, in Campbell, S., (ed.), *The management of the menopause and post-menopausal years.* MTP Press, Lancaster.

Paige, K. E. (1971). Effects of oral contraceptives on affective fluctuations associated with the menstrual cycle. *Psychosomatic Medicine*, **33**, 515–537.

Paige, K. E. (1973). Women learn to sing the menstrual blues. *Psychology Today*, **September 1973**, 41–46.

Parlee, M. B. (1974). Stereotypic beliefs about menstruation: A methodological note on the Moos Menstrual Distress Questionnaire and some new data. *Psychosomatic Medicine*, **36**, 229–240.

Parlee, M. B. (1980). Changes in moods and activation levels during the menstrual cycle in experimentally naive subjects, in Dan, A. J., Graham, E. A., and Beecher, C. P. (eds.), *The menstrual cycle*, Volume 1, Springer, New York.

Parvathi, D. S., and Venkoba, R. A. (1972). The premenstrual phase and suicide attempts. *Indian Journal of Psychiatry*, **14**, 375–379.

Patkai, P. (1971a). The diurnal rhythms of adrenaline secretions in subjects with different working habits. *Acta Physiologica Scandinavica*, **81**, 30–34.

Patkai, P. (1971b). Interindividual differences in diurnal variations in alertness, performance and adrenaline excretion. *Acta Physiologica Scandinavica*, **81**, 35–46.

Patkai, P., Johannson, G., and Post, B. (1974). Mood, alertness, and sympathetic-adrenal medullary activity during the menstrual cycle. *Psychosomatic Medicine*, **36**, 503–512.

Persky, H., Charney, N., Lief, H. I., O'Brien, C. P., Miller, W. R., and Strauss, D. (1978). The relationship of plasma estradiol level to sexual behaviour in young women. *Psychosomatic Medicine*, **40**, 523–535.

Persky, H., O'Brien, C. P., and Khan, M. A. (1976). Reproductive hormone levels, sexual activity and moods during the menstrual cycle. *Psychosomatic Medicine*, **38**, 62.

Persky, H., O'Brien, C. P., Lief, H. I., Strauss, D., and Miller, W. R. (1979). Female sexual activity at ovulation (letters to the editor). *New England Journal of Medicine*, **300**, 626.

Peters, H. (1979). The ageing ovary, in van Keep, P. A., Serr, D. M., and Greenblatt, R. B. (eds.), *Female and male climacteric*, MTP Press, Lancaster.

Petre-Quadens, O., and De Lee, C. (1974). Sleep-cycle alterations during pregnancy, postpartum, and the menstrual cycle, in Ferin, M., Halberg, F., Richart, R. M., and Vande Wiele, R. L. (eds.), *Biorhythms and human reproduction*, John Wiley, New York.

Pfeiffer, E., and Davis, G. C. (1972). Determinants of sexual behaviour in middle and old age. *Journal of the American Geriatrics Society*, **20**, 151–158.

Pfeiffer, E., Verwoerdt, A., and Davis, G. C. (1972). Sexual behaviour in middle life. *American Journal of Psychiatry*, **128**, 1262–1267.

Pfetter, R. I., Whipple, G. H., Jurosaki, T. T., and Chapman, J. M. (1978). Coronary risk and estrogen use in postmenopausal women. *American Journal of Epidemiology*, **107**, 479–487.

Presser, H. B. (1974). Temporal data relating to the human menstrual cycle, in Ferin, M., Halberg, F., Richart, R. M., and Vande Wiele, R. (eds.), *Biorhythms and human reproduction*, John Wiley, New York.

Preston, F. S., Bateman, S. C., Short, R. V., and Wilkinson, R. T. (1974). The effects of flying and of time changes on menstrual cycle length and on performance in airline stewardesses, in Ferin, M., Halberg, F., Richart, R. M., and Vande Wiele, R. (eds.), *Biorhythms and human reproduction*, John Wiley, New York.

Quadagno, D. M., Shubeita, H. E., Deck, J., and Francoeur, D. (1981). Influence of male social contacts, exercise and all-female living conditions on the menstrual cycle. *Psychoneuroendocrinology*, **6**, 239–244.

Rauramo, L., and Kopera, H. (1976). Non-genital target tissues of estrogens, in van Keep, P. A., Greenblatt, R. B., and Albeaux-Fernet, M. (eds.), *Consensus on menopause research*, MTP Press, Lancaster.

Recker, R. R., Saville, P. D., and Heaney, R. P. (1977). Effect of estrogens and calcium carbonate on bone loss in post-menopausal women. *Annals of Internal Medicine*, **87**, 649–655.

Redgrove, J. A. (1971). Menstrual cycles, in Colquhoun, W. P. (ed.), *Biological rhythms and human performance*, Academic Press, London.

Reeves, B. D., Garvin, J. E., and McElin, T. W. (1971). Premenstrual tension: symptoms and weight changes related to potassium therapy. *American Journal of Obstetrics and Gynecology*, **109**, 1036–1041.

Reid, R. L., and Yen, S. S. C. (1981). Premenstrual syndrome. *American Journal of Obstetrics and Gynecology*, **139**, 85–104.

Reinke, U., Ansah, B., and Voigt, K. D. (1972). Effect of the menstrual cycle on carbohydrate and lipid metabolism in normal females. *Acta Endocrinologica*, **69**, 762–768.

Ribeiro, A. L. (1962). Menstruation and crime. *British Medical Journal*, i, 640.

Richter, C. P. (1968). Periodic phenomena in man and animals: their relation to neuroendocrine mechanisms (a monthly or nearly monthly cycle), in Michael, R. P. (ed.), *Endocrinology and human behaviour*, Oxford University Press, Oxford.

Rigg, L. A., Hermann, H., and Yen, S. S. C. (1978). Absorption of estrogens from vaginal creams. *New England Journal of Medicine*, **298**, 195–197.

Robinson, J. E., and Short, R. V. (1979). Changes in breast sensitivity at puberty, during the menstrual cycle, and at parturition. *British Medical Journal*, i, 1188–1191.

Rodin, J. (1976). Menstruation, reattribution and competence. *Journal of Personality and Social Psychology*, **33**, 345–353.

Rodriguez, G., Faundes-Latham, A., and Atkinson, L. E. (1976). An approach to the analysis of menstrual patterns in the critical evaluation of contraceptives. *Studies in Family Planning*, **7**, 42–51.

Rogel, M. J. (1978). A critical evaluation of the possibility of higher primate reproductive and sexual pheromones. *Psychological Bulletin*, **85**, 810–830.

Rogel, M. J. (1980). Analysis of data from menstrual cycles of unknown or unequal length, in Dan, A. J., Graham, E. A., and Beecher, C. P. (eds.), *The menstrual cycle*, Volume 1. Springer, New York.

Romero, J. A. (1978). Biologic rhythms and sympathetic neural control of pineal metabolism. *Advances in Experimental Medicine and Biology*, **108**, 235–249.

Rosciszewska, D. (1980). Analysis of seizure dispersion during menstrual cycle in women with epilepsy. *Monographs in Neural Sciences*, **5**, 280–284.

Rosenberg, L., Slone, D., Shapiro, S., Kaufman, D., Stolley, P. D., and Miettinen, O. S. (1980). Non-contraceptive estrogens and myocardial infarction in young women. *Journal of the American Medical Association*, **244**, 339–342.

Rosenfeld, D. L., and Garcia, C. R. (1976). A comparison of endometrial histology with simultaneous plasma progesterone determinations in infertile women. *Fertility and Sterility*, **27**, 1256–1266.

Rossi, A. S., and Rossi, P. E. (1977). Body time and social time: Mood patterns by menstrual cycle phase and day of the week. *Social Science Research*, **6**, 273–308.

Rouse, P. (1978). Premenstrual tension: A study using the Moos Menstrual Questionnaire. *Journal of Psychosomatic Research*, **22**, 215–222.

Rowell, T. E. (1970). Baboon menstrual cycle affected by social environment. *Journal of Reproduction and Fertility*, **21**, 133–141.

Ruble, D. N. (1977). Premenstrual symptoms: A reinterpretation. *Science*, **197**, 291–292.

Ruble, D. N., and Brooks-Gunn, J. (1979). Menstrual symptoms: A social cognition analysis. *Journal of Behavioural Medicine*, **2**, 171–194.

Russell, G. F. M. (1972). Psychological and nutritional factors in disturbances of menstrual function and ovulation. *Postgraduate Medical Journal*, **48**, 10–13.

Russell, M. J., Switz, G. M., and Thompson, K. (1980). Olfactory influences on the human menstrual cycle. *Pharmacology Biochemistry and Behaviour*, **13**, 737–738.

Ryan, K. J. (1976). Estrogens and atherosclerosis. *Clinical Obstetrics and Gynecology*, **19**, 805–815.

Sampson, G. A. (1979). Premenstrual syndrome: a double-blind controlled trial of progesterone and placebo. *British Journal of Psychiatry*, **135**, 209–215.

Sanders, D. and J. Bancroft. (1982). Hormones and the sexuality of women and the menstrual cycle. Clinics in Endocrinology and Metabolism, 11, 639–659

Satinder, K. P., and Mastronardi, L. M. (1974). Sex differences in figural after-effects as a function of the phase of the menstrual cycle. *Psychologia*, **17**, 1–5.

Saunders, D. T. (1977). *An introduction to biological rhythms*. Blackie, Glasgow.

Schachter, S., and Singer, J. E. (1962). Cognitive, social, and physiological determinants of emotional state. *Psychological Review*, **69**, 379–399.

Schiff, I. (1982). The effects of progestins on vasomotor flushes. *Journal of Reproductive Medicine*, **27**, 8 (Supplement), 498–502.

Schreiner-Engel, P., Schiavi, R. C., Smith, H., and White, D. (1981). Sexual arousability and the menstrual cycle. *Psychosomatic Medicine*, **43**, 199–214.

Schuckit, M. A., Daly, V., Herrman, G., and Hineman, S. (1975). Premenstrual symptoms and depression in a university population. *Diseases of the Nervous System*, **36**, 516–517.

Schultz, D. P. (1969). The human subject in psychological research. *Psychological Bulletin*, **72**, 214–228.

Schultz, K. J., and Koulack, D. (1980). Dream affect and the menstrual cycle. *Journal of Nervous and Mental Disease*, **168**, 436–438.

Schwartz, N. B., and Channing, C. P. (1977). Evidence for ovarian 'inhibin': Suppression of the secondary rise in serum follicle stimulating hormone levels in proestrous rats by injection of porcine follicular fluid. *Proceedings of the National Academy of Science* (Washington), **74**, 5721–5724.

Schwarz, B. E. (1981). Does estrogen cause adenocarcinoma of the endometrium? *Clinical Obstetrics and Gynecology*, **24**, 243–251.

Shaffer, J. W., Schmidt, C. W., Zlotowitz, H. I., and Fisher, R. S. (1978). Biorhythms and highway crashes: Are they related? *Archives of General Psychiatry*, **35**, 41–46.

Shahrad, P., and Marks, R. (1976). The effect of estrogens on the skin, in Campbell, S. (ed.), *The management of the menopause and post-menopausal years*, MTP Press, Lancaster.

Shaw, R. (1978). Neuroendocrinology of the menstrual cycle in humans. *Clinics in Endocrinology and Metabolism*, **7**, 531–559.

Sheldrake, P., and Cormack, M. (1974). Dream recall and the menstrual cycle. *Journal of Psychosomatic Research*, **18**, 347–350.

Sheldrake, P., and Cormack, M. (1976a). Variations in menstrual cycle symptom reporting. *Journal of Psychosomatic Research*, **20**, 169–177.

Sheldrake, P., and Cormack, M. (1976b). Dream recall and the contraceptive pill. *Journal of Nervous and Mental Disease*, **163**, 59–60.

Sherman, B. M., and Korenman, S. G. (1975). Hormonal characteristics of the human menstrual cycle throughout reproductive life. *Journal of Clinical Investigation*, **55**, 699–706.

Sherman, B. M., West, J. H., and Korenman, S. G. (1976). The menopausal transition: analysis of LH, FSH, estradiol and progesterone concentrations during menstrual cycles of older women. *Journal of Clinical Endocrinology and Metabolism,* **42**, 629–636.

Silbergeld, S., Brast, N., and Noble, E. P. (1971). The menstrual cycle: a double-blind study of symptoms, mood and behaviour, and biochemical variables using Enovid and placebo. *Psychosomatic Medicine*, **33**, 411–428.

Silverman, E. M., Zimmer, C. H., and Silverman, F. H. (1974). Variability of stutterers' speech disfluency: The menstrual cycle. *Perceptual and Motor Skills*, **38**, 1037–1038.

Slade, P., and Jenner, F. A. (1979). Autonomic activity in subjects reporting changes in affect in the menstrual cycle. *British Journal of Social and Clinical Psychology*, **18**, 135–136.

Smith, S. L. (1975). Mood and the menstrual cycle, in Sachar, E. J., (ed.), *Topics in Psychoneuroendocrinology*, Grune and Stratton, New York.

Smith, S. L., and Sauder, C. (1969). Food cravings, depression and premenstrual problems. *Psychosomatic Medicine*, **31**, 281–287.

Smolensky, M. H. (1980). Chronobiologic considerations in the investigation and interpretation of circamensual rhythms in women, in Dan, A. J., Graham, E. A., and Beecher, C. P., (eds.), *The menstrual cycle*, Volume 1, Springer, New York.

Smolensky, M. H., Halberg, F., and Sargent, F. (1972). Chronobiology of the life sequence, in Ito, S., Ogata, K., and Yoshimura, H. (eds.), *Advances in climatic physiology*, Igaku Shoin, Tokyo.

Smolensky, M. H., Reinberg, A., Lee, R. E., and McGovern, J. P. (1974). Secondary rhythms related to hormonal changes in the menstrual cycle: special reference to allergology, in Ferin, M., Halberg, F., Richart, R. M., and Vande Wiele, R. L. (eds.), *Biorhythms and human reproduction*, John Wiley, New York.

Sommer, B. (1972). Menstrual cycle changes and intellectual performance. *Psychosomatic Medicine*, **34**, 263–269.

Sommer, B. (1973). The effect of menstruation on cognitive and perceptual-motor behaviour: A review. *Psychosomatic Medicine*, **35**, 515–534.

Sommer, B. (1978). Stress and menstrual distress. *Journal of Human Stress*, **4**, 5–10; 41–47.

Southam, A., and Gonzaga, F. P. (1965). Systemic changes during the menstrual cycle. *American Journal of Obstetrics and Gynecology*, **91**, 142–165.

Speroff, L. (1977). Hormonal events and disorders of the menstrual cycle, in Givens, J. R. (ed.), *Gynecologic Endocrinology*, Year Book Medical Publishers, Inc., Chicago.

Spicer, C. C., Hare, E. H., and Slater, E. (1973). Neurotic and psychotic forms of depressive illness: evidence from age-incidence in a national sample. *British Journal of Psychiatry*, **123**, 535–541.

Staub, E., and Kellett, D. S. (1972). Increasing pain tolerance by information about aversive stimuli. *Journal of Personality and Social Psychology*, **21**, 198–203.

Steiner, M., and Carroll, B. J. (1977). The psychobiology of premenstrual dysphoria: review of theories and treatments. *Psychoneuroendocrinology*, **2**, 321–325.

Storms, M. D., and Nisbett, R. E. (1970). Insomnia and the attribution process. *Journal of Personality and Social Psychology*, **16**, 319–328.

Strauss, B., Schultheiss, M., and Cohen, R. (1983). Autonomic reactivity in the premenstrual phase. *British Journal of Clinical Psychology*, **22**, 1–9.

Studd, J. W. W., Chakravarti, S., and Oram, D. (1977). The climacteric, in Greenblatt, R. B., and Studd, J. (eds.), *The menopause. Clinics in Obstetrics and Gynecology*, Volume 4, W. B. Saunders, London.

Studd, J. W. W., Dubiel, M., Kakkar, V. V., Thom, M. H., and White, P. J. (1978). The effect of hormone replacement therapy on glucose tolerance, clotting factors, fibrinolysis and platelet behaviour in post-menopausal women, in Cooke, I. D., (ed.), *The role of estrogen/progestogen in the management of the menopause*, MTP Press, Lancaster.

Studd, J. W. W., and Thom, M. H. (1981). Ovarian failure and ageing. *Clinics in Endocrinology and Metabolism*, **10**, 89–113.

Sturdee, D. W., Wilson, K. A., Pipili, E., and Crocker, A. D. (1978). Physiological aspects of menopausal hot flush. *British Medical Journal*. **ii**, 79–80.

Sundaraj, N., Chem, M., Gatewood, L., Hickman, L., and McHugh, R. (1978). Seasonal behaviour of human menstrual cycles: a biometric investigation. *Human Biology*, **50**, 15–31.

Sutherland, H., and Stewart, I. (1965). A critical analysis of the premenstrual syndrome. *Lancet*, **i**, 1180–1183.

Swanson, E. M., and Foulkes, S. D. (1967). Dream content and the menstrual cycle. *Journal of Nervous and Mental Disease*, **145**, 358–363.

Swerdloff, R. S., and Rubin, T. (1978). Psychological and endocrinological changes in puberty, in Brambilla, F., Bridges, P. K., Endroczi, E., and Heuser, G. (eds.), *Perspectives in endocrine psychobiology*, John Wiley, Chichester.

Taylor, J. W. (1979). The timing of menstruation-related symptoms assessed by a daily symptom rating scale. *Acta Psychiatrica Scandinavica*, **60**, 87–105.

Tedford, W. H., Warren, D. E., and Flynn, W. E. (1977). Alteration of shock aversion thresholds during the menstrual cycle. *Perception and Psychophysics*, **21**, 193–196.

Terman, L. M. (1938). *Psychological factors in marital happiness*, McGraw Hill, New York.

Tersman, I. (1979). Female sexual activity at ovulation (letters to the editor). *New England Journal of Medicine*, **300**, 626.

Thayer, R. E. (1970). Activation states as assessed by verbal report and four psychophysiological variables. *Psychophysiology*, **7**, 86–94.

Thayer, R. E. (1978). Toward a psychological theory of multidimensional activation (arousal). *Motivation and Emotion*, **2**, 1–34.

Theano, G. (1968). The prevalence of menstrual symptoms in Spanish students. *British Journal of Psychiatry*, **114**, 771–773.

Thin, R. N. T. (1968). Premenstrual symptoms in women who attempt suicide. *Journal of the Royal Army Medical Corps*, **114**, 136–139.

Thom, M. H., White, P. J., Williams, R. M., Sturdee, D. W., Paterson, M. E. L., Wade-Evans, T., and Studd, J. W. W. (1979). Prevention and treatment of endometrial disease in climacteric women receiving oestrogen therapy. *Lancet*, **ii**, 455–457.

Thommen, G. (1973). *Is this your day?* Crown Publishers, New York.

196

Thompson, B., Hart, S. A., and Durno, D. (1973). Menopausal age and symptomatology in a general practice. *Journal of Biosocial Science*, **5**, 71–82.

Thorneycroft, I. H., Sribyatta, B., Tom, W. K., Nakamura, R. M., and Mishell, D. R. (1974). Measurement of serum LH, FSH, progesterone, 17-hydroxyprogesterone and estradiol-17 levels at four hour intervals during the periovulatory phase of the menstrual cycle. *Journal of Clinical Endocrinology and Metabolism*, **39**, 754–758.

Timonen, S., and Procopé, B. J. (1973). The premenstrual syndrome; frequency and association of symptoms. *Annals Chirurgiae et Gynaecologiae Fenniae*, **62**, 108–116.

Tonks, C. M., Rack, P.H., and Rose, M. J. (1968). Attempted suicide and the menstrual cycle. *Journal of Psychosomatic Research*, **11**, 319–323.

Trinder, J., Van de Castle, R., Bourne, R., and Frisbie, D. (1973). Dream recall as a function of menstrual cycle. *Sleep Research*, **2**, 114.

Tuch, R. H. (1975). The relationship between a mother's menstrual status and her response to illness in her child. *Psychosomatic Medicine*, **37**, 388–394.

Udry, J. R., and Morris, N. M. (1968). Distribution of coitus in the menstrual cycle. *Nature*, **220**, 593–596.

Udry, J. R., and Morris, N. M. (1972). Effect of contraceptive pills on the distribution of sexual activity in the menstrual cycle. *Nature*, **227**, 502–503.

Utian, W. H. (1980). *Menopause in modern perspective. A guide to clinical practice*, Appleton-Century-Crofts, New York.

Utian, W. H., and Gordan, G. S. (1979). Metabolic changes due to menopause and their response to oestrogen, in van Keep, P. A., Serr, D. M., and Greenblatt, R. B. (eds.), *Female and male climacteric*, MTP Press, Lancaster.

Valins, S. (1967). Emotionality and information concerning internal reactions. *Journal of Personality and Social Psychology*, **6**, 458–463.

Valins, S., and Nisbett, R. E. (1971). *Attribution processes in the development and treatment of emotional disorder*, General Learning Corporation, Morristown, N. J.

Vande-Wiele, R. L., Bogumil, J., Dyrenfurth, I., Ferin, M., Jewelewicz, R., Warren, M., Rizkallah, T., and Mikhail, G. (1970). Mechanisms regulating the menstrual cycle in women. *Recent Progress in Hormone Research*, **26**, 63–95.

Vaughn, T. C., and Hammond, C. B. (1981). Estrogen replacement therapy. *Clinical Obstetrics and Gynecology*, **24**, 253–283.

Vermeulen, A. (1976). The hormonal activity of the postmenopausal ovary. *Journal of Clinical Endocrinology and Metabolism*, **42**, 247–253.

Vermeulen, A., Rubens, R., and Verdonck, L. (1972). Testosterone secretion and metabolism in male senescence. *Journal of Clinical Endocrinology and Metabolism*, **34**, 730–735.

Vila, J., and Beech, H. R. (1977). Vulnerability and conditioning in relation to the menstrual cycle. *British Journal of Social and Clinical Psychology*, **16**, 69–75.

Vila, J., and Beech, H. R. (1978). Vulnerability and defensive reactions in relation to the human menstrual cycle. *British Journal of Social and Clinical Psychology*, **17**, 93–100.

Vila, J., and Beech, H. R. (1980). Premenstrual symptomatology: An interaction hypothesis. *British Journal of Social and Clinical Psychology*, **19**, 73–80.

Voda, A. (1980). Pattern of progesterone and aldosterone in ovulating women during the menstrual cycle, in Dan, A. J., Graham, E. A., and Beecher, C. P. (eds.), *The menstrual cycle*, Volume 1, Springer, New York.

Vogel, W., Broverman, D. M., and Klaiber, E. L. (1971). EEG responses in regularly menstruating women and in amenorrheic women treated with ovarian hormones. *Science*, **172**, 388–391.

Vollman, R. F. (1974). Some conceptual and methodological problems in longitudinal studies on human reproduction, in Ferin, M., Halberg, F., Richart, R. M., and

Vande Wiele, R. (eds.), *Biorhythms and human reproduction*, John Wiley, New York.

Vollman, R. F. (1977). The menstrual cycle, in Friedman, E. A. (ed.), *Major Problems in Obstetrics and Gynecology*, Volume 7, W. B. Saunders, Philadelphia.

Wald, A., Van Thiel, D. H., Hoechstetter, L., Gavaler, J. S., Egler, K. M., Verm, R., Scott, L., and Lester, R. (1981). Gastrointestinal transit: the effect of the menstrual cycle. *Gastroenterology*, **80**, 1497–1500.

Ward, M. M., Stone, S. C., and Sandman, C. A. (1978). Visual perception in women during the menstrual cycle. *Physiology and Behaviour*, **20**, 239–243.

Ward, R. R. (1972). *The living clocks*. Collins, London.

Warren, D. E., Tedford, W. H., and Flynn, W. E. (1979). Behavioural effects of cyclic changes in serotonin during the human menstrual cycle. *Medical Hypotheses*, **5**, 359–364.

Webster, S. K. (1980). Problems for diagnosis of spasmodic and congestive dysmenorrhea, in Dan, A. J., Graham, E. A., and Beecher, C. P. (eds.), *The menstrual cycle*, Volume 1, Springer, New York.

Weismann, M. M. (1979). The myth of involutional melancholia. *Journal of the American Medical Association*, **242**, 742–744.

Weissman, M. M., and Slaby, A. E. (1973). Oral contraceptives and psychiatric disturbance: Evidence from research. *British Journal of Psychiatry*, **123**, 513–518.

Weizenbaum, F., Benson, B., Solomon, L., and Brehony, K. (1980). Relationship among reproductive variables, sucrose, taste reactivity and feeding behaviour in humans. *Physiology and Behaviour*, **24**, 1053–1056.

Wetzel, R. D., and McClure, J. N. (1972). Suicide and the menstrual cycle: A review. *Comprehensive Psychiatry*, **13**, 369–374.

Wetzel, R. D., McClure, J. N., and Reich, T. (1971). Premenstrual symptoms in self-referrals to a suicide prevention service. *British Journal of Psychiatry*, **119**, 525–526.

Wetzel, R. D., Reich, T., McClure, J. N., and Wald, J. A. (1975). Premenstrual affective syndrome and affective disorder. *British Journal of Psychiatry*, **127**, 219–221.

Wever, R. A. (1974). ELF-effects on human circadian rhythms, in Persinger, M. A. (ed.), *ELF and VLF electromagnetic field effects*, Plenum Press, New York-London.

Wever, R. A. (1979). *The circadian system of man*, Springer-Verlag, Berlin.

Whitehead, M. I., McQueen, J., Minardi, J., and Campbell, S. (1978). Clinical considerations in the management of the menopause: the endometrium. *Postgraduate Medical Journal*, **54. Supplement 2**, 69–73.

Whitehead, M. I., Townsend, P. T., Pryse-Davies, J., Ryder, T., Lane, G., Siddle, N. C., and King, R. J. B. (1982). Effects of various types and dosages of progestogens on the postmenopausal endometrium. *Journal of Reproductive Medicine*, **27**, 8 (Supplement), 539–548.

Whitehead, R. E. (1934). Women pilots. *Journal of Aviation Medicine*, **5**, 47–49.

Widholm, O. W., and Kantero, R. L. (1971). A statistical analysis of the menstrual patterns of 8000 Finnish girls and their mothers. *Acta Obstetricia and Gynecologica Scandinavica*, **50, Supplement 14**.

Wiener, J., and Elmadjian, F. (1962). Excretion of epinephrine and norepinephrine in premenstrual tension. *Federation Proceedings*, **21**, 184.

Wilcoxon, L. A., Schreider, S. L., and Sherif, C. W. (1976). Daily self-reports on activities, life events, moods, and somatic changes during the menstrual cycle. *Psychosomatic Medicine*, **38**, 399–417.

Williams, C. I., Levine, H., Teslow, T. N., and Halberg, F. (1980). Rhythms revealed by automatically recorded and self-measured human blood pressure during three menstrual cycles, in Dan, A. J., Graham, E. A., and Beecher, C. P. (eds.), *The menstrual cycle*, Volume 1, Springer, New York.

Wilson, E. O. (1975). *Sociobiology: the new synthesis*, Harvard University Press, Cambridge, Mass.

Wineman, E. W. (1971). Autonomic balance changes during the human menstrual cycle. *Psychophysiology*, **8**, 1–6.

Wolcott, J. H., McMeekin, R. R., Burgin, R. E., and Yanowitch, R. E. (1977). Correlation of general aviation accidents with biorhythm theory. *Human Factors*, **19**, 283–293.

Wong, S., and Tong, J. E. (1974). Menstrual cycle and contraceptive hormonal effects on temporal discrimination. *Perceptual and Motor Skills*, **39**, 103–108.

Wood, C. (1979). Menopausal myths. *Medical Journal of Australia*, **1**, 496–499.

Wood, C., Larsen, L., and Williams, R. (1979a). Menstrual characteristics of 2,343 women attending the Shepherd Foundation. *Australian and New Zealand Journal of Obstetrics and Gynaecology*, **19**, 107–110.

Wood, C., Larsen, L., and Williams, R. (1979b). Social and psychological factors in relation to premenstrual tension and menstrual pain. *Australian and New Zealand Journal of Obstetrics and Gynaecology*, **19**, 111–115.

Wood, L. A., Krider, D. W., and Fezer, K. D. (1979). Emergency room data on 700 accidents do not support biorhythm theory. *Journal of Safety Research*, **11**, 172–175.

World Health Organization (1981a). A cross-cultural study of menstruation: Implications for contraceptive development and use. *Studies in Family Planning*, **12**, 3–16.

World Health Organization (1981b). Women's bleeding patterns: ability to recall and predict menstrual events. *Studies in Family Planning*, **12**, 17–27.

Worley, R. J. (1981a). The menopause. *Clinical Obstetrics and Gynecology*, **24**, 163–164.

Worley, R. J. (1981b). Age, estrogen and bone density. *Clinical Obstetrics and Gynecology*, **24**, 203–218.

Wuttke, W., Arnold, P., Becker, D., Creutzfeldt, O., Langenstein, S., and Tirsch, W. (1975). Circulating hormones, EEG and performance in psychological tests of women with and without oral contraceptives. *Psychoneuroendocrinology*, **1**, 141–152.

Wynn, V. T. (1972). Measurements of small variations in absolute pitch. *Journal of Physiology*, **220**, 627–637.

Yen, S. S.C., and Jaffe, R. B. (1978). *Reproductive endocrinology*. W. B. Saunders, Philadelphia.

Yen, S. S. C., and Lein, A. (1976). The apparent paradox of the negative and positive feedback control system on gonadotropin secretion. *American Journal of Obstetrics and Gynecology*, **126**, 942–954.

Zimmerman, E., and Parlee, M. B. (1973). Behavioural changes associated with the menstrual cycle: An experimental investigation. *Journal of Applied Social Psychology*, **3**, 335–344.

Zola, P., Meyerson, A. R., Reznikoff, M., Thornton, J. C., and Concool, B. M. (1979). Menstrual symptomatology and psychiatric admission. *Journal of Psychosomatic Research*, **23**, 241–245.

Author Index

Page numbers in italic indicate pages where reference appears in full.

200

202

206

207

Theano, G., 152, *195*
Theiss, C. L., 32, 33, 76, *178*
Thin, R. N. T., 67, *195*
Thom, M. H., 131, *195*
Thom, V. V., 120, 132, 133, *195*
Thommen, G., 1, *195*
Thompson, B., 19, 20, 99–102, 123,
 189; 123, 127, *196*
Thompson, K., 7, 8, *193*
Thomson, A. D., 45, 68, *189*
Thorneycroft, I. H., 26, *196*
Thornton, J. C., 67, *198*
Thurow, C., 160, *180*
Timonen, S., 82, 89, *196*
Tirsch, W., 47, *181*; 71, 72, *198*
Tom, W. K., 26, *196*
Tong, J. E., 32, 33, 47, 49, *198*; 47, *182*
Tonks, C. M., 67, 68, 89, 152, *196*
Townsend, P. T., 131, *197*
Trinder, J., 53, *196*
Troll, L. E., 114, *177*
Tuch, R. H., 43, 44, *196*
Turek, F. W., 8, *180*

Udry, J. R., 57, 58, *196*; 146, *190*
Ulett, G. A., 92, *188*
Utian, W. H., 20, 106, 132, *196*

Valins, S., 159, 161, *196*
Van de Castle, R., 53, *196*
Vande-Wiele, R. L., 24, *196*
van Keep, P. A., 82, 89, 90, 113, 116,
 126, *187*
van Lith, N. D., 117, 127, *186*
van Look, P. F. A., 16, 104, 107, 108,
 179
Van Thiel, D. H., 38, *197*
Vaughn, T. C., 103, 105, 106, 117, 118,
 129, 130, *196*
Venables, P. H., 36, 38, 49–51, 61, *178*
Venkoba, R. A., 67, 68, *191*
Verdonck, L., 110, *196*
Verm, R., 38, *197*
Vermeulen, A., 103, 110, *196*
Verwoerdt, A., 119, 120, 127, *192*
Vessey, M. P., 116, 117, 120, 121, 123,
 179
Vila, J., 49, 51, 156, 162, *196*
Voda, A., 16, 35, 36, 38, 61, 63, 95,
 140, 154, *196*
Voegelin, M. R., 33, *179*
Vogel, W., 16, 71, 73, 139, *179*; 47, 70,
 187; 138, *196*
Voigt, K. D., 37, *192*

Vollmann, R. F., 4, 9, 15–17, 42, *197*;
 16, *196*

Wade-Evans, T., 131, *195*
Wald, A., 38, *197*
Wald, J. A., 82, 93, *197*
Wallman, L., 38, *188*
Wang, C., 109, 110, 121, *178*
Ward, M. M., 33, 158, *197*
Ward, R. R., 1, *197*
Warren, D. E., 29, 142, *197*; 33, 51, 52,
 76, 142, 162, *195*
Warren, M., 24, *196*
Waterhouse, J. M., 1, 4, 12, *190*
Webster, S. K., 40, 41, 95, 174, *197*
Wehr, T. A., 142, 148, *188*
Weismann, M. M., 64, 123, *197*
Weizenbaum, F., 37, *197*
West, J. H., 16, 104, *194*
Wetzel, R. D., 67, 68, 82, 93, *197*; 93,
 187
Wever, R. A., 2, 3, *197*
Whipple, G. H., 118, *192*
Whissell-Buechy, D., 32, *177*
White, D., 24, 56, 95, *193*
White, P. J., 131–133, *195*
Whitehead, M. I., 115, 117, 119–122,
 125, 130, 131, *180*; 128, 131, *197*
Whitehead, R. E., 43, *197*
Whitmore, M. R., 55, 58, 62, 64, 76,
 155, *182*
Widholm, O. W., 95, *197*
Wiener, J., 142, *197*
Wilcoxon, L. A., 35, 40, 45, 62, 65, 76,
 197
Wilhelm, H., 47, *181*
Wilkinson, R. T., 17, 148, *192*
Willett, W., 132, *178*
Williams, C. I., 50, *197*
Williams, R., 17, 82, 93, 112, 113, *198*
Williams, R. M., 131, *195*
Willis, K. A., 61, 64, 76, *182*
Wilson, E. O., 7, *198*
Wilson, K. A., 114, 115, *195*
Wilson, M. A., 2, *190*
Wineman, E. W., 49, *198*
Wolcott, J. H., 1, *198*
Wong, S., 32, 33, 47, 49, *198*
Wood, C., 17, 82, 93, 112, 113, 116,
 117, 119, 123, 124, 126, *198*
Wood, L. A., 1, *198*
World Health Organization, 18, 19, 59,
 91, 152, *198*
Worley, R. J., 101, 106, 117, 129, *198*

Subject Index

214

Schizophrenia, 66
Seasonal effects, 17, 149
Self-confidence, 150
Self-management, 156, 174
Self-reports, 154–158
Sensation, 144
Sensory acuity, 81
Sensory changes, 32–35
Sensory responses, 75
Serotonin, 29, 141, 142
Sex differences, 12
Sex hormones, 71
Sexual abstinence, 59
Sexual activity, 10, 11, 56, 59, 119, 127, 135, 138, 139, 146
Sexual arousal, 55, 56, 58, 59, 167, 168
Sexual behaviour, 56–60, 75, 119–122, 127–128, 138, 146, 167, 168
Sexual desire, 58, 63
Sexual feeling, 55–56, 75, 119–122
Sexual intercourse, 119, 121, 122
Sexual interest, 122, 127–128, 134
Shock sensitivity, 78
Skin changes, 105
Skin eruptions, 39
Skin responses, 51
Sleeping, 52–54, 78, 119
Smoking, 101, 118
Sociability, 91
Social attitudes, 121
Social behaviour, 69
Social factors, 35, 46, 52, 59, 98, 122, 136, 145, 147, 150, 151, 158
Social interaction, 7
Socio-cultural differences, 18, 86
Socio-economic class, 102
Sodium levels, 38–39
Somatic symptoms, 127
State-Trait Anxiety Scale State, 64
Steroids, 99, 108, 137–138
Stomach ache, 91
Stress factors, 147
Stress level, 45
Stress reactivity, 44
Suicide, 45, 46, 67–68, 75, 89, 150, 175

Suprachiasmatic nucleus, 4
Sweating, 127, 129
Sympathetic nervous system, 143
Synchronization mechanisms, 7, 14

Tactile sensitivity, 33
Taylor Manifest Anxiety Scale, 93
Temperature curve, 9
Temperature cycle, 3, 9
Temperature effects, 149
Temporal characteristics, 15–20
Temporal Disorganization Scale, 72
Tension, 59, 61, 69, 91, 93, 112, 150, 151, 159, 161
Test performance, 70–73
Testicular function, 100, 110, 111
Testicular volume, 109, 110
Testosterone, 10, 24, 25, 109, 110, 139, 150
Testosterone binding globulin, 110
Thrombosis, 132, 133
Time of day, 6
Timing mechanisms, 5
Tolerance, 91
Triglyceride, 117, 118
Tryptophan, 142

Urinary symptoms, 116, 130
Urogenital tissues, 116
Urogenital tract, 104

Vasomotor symptoms, 115–116, 119, 135
Vasomotor systems, 129
Violence, 69
Visual acuity, 78
Visual sensitivity, 33
Vitamin B6, 142

Weight and menopausal age, 101
Weight gain, 5, 36, 78
Well being, 81, 84, 91, 150, 151, 172
World Health Organization, 18, 19, 59, 91

QP
263
. A 77
1983